"I've read plenty of books on finance  ular perspectives, but I've yet to enco biblical wisdom with down-to-earth Jim Newheiser's *Money* does. I wish it had been available to me in my early 20s, as a newly married university graduate, but even now it has helped me reassess my stewardship of the monetary resources that God has provided for my family. Whatever your current financial situation and stage of life, you'll benefit from reading this book. You can take that to the bank!"

> —**James N. Anderson**, Carl W. McMurray Professor of Theology and Philosophy, Reformed Theological Seminary, Charlotte

"I am very grateful to Jim Newheiser for this work. Jim clearly lays out from the Scriptures that we are managers and not owners of the resources that the Lord has given us. This resource will help you understand how to be a good steward not only in your giving, but also in your work, spending, and savings. I highly recommend this book, and I will refer to it often."

> —**Tony Anderson**, Pastor of Counseling/Executive Pastor, Christian Family Chapel, Jacksonville, Florida

"The combination of Dr. Newheiser's background in business, ministry, and counseling makes him well qualified to discuss difficult financial issues. He deals with broad topics, such as the blessings and dangers of wealth, the importance of work, and preparing for the future, including retirement. He also discusses very practical issues, such as laziness, creating a budget, avoiding debt (or getting out of it), and different kinds of investments. Many scriptural principles are woven through the book, and when Scripture is not entirely clear on a matter, that is also pointed out. No matter what your current financial situation is, you will benefit from this book. If you know people with financial troubles, they will certainly be helped by the practical wisdom in these pages."

> —**Richard P. Belcher Jr.**, John D. and Frances M. Gwin Professor of Old Testament, Reformed Theological Seminary; Academic Dean, Reformed Theological Seminary (Charlotte and Atlanta)

"I love reading books, but I shout out loud when I'm reading a book by a seasoned author whose wisdom has been forged in the trenches of real life, sitting across from people in desperate need of godly counsel. The book in your hands is that kind of book. Pastoring and counseling for over thirty years now has afforded me the privilege and pain of seeing the fallout from foolish financial decisions that often haunt people for decades. Jim brings practical and biblical clarity to the financial land mines that people keep stepping on as he addresses credit cards, debt, insurance, student loans, cosigning, investment strategies, the temptation of wealth, and more. You'll love this book and likely find yourself saying, 'I wish I'd read this years ago.' Read it, live it, recommend it to others."

—**Brad Bigney,** Lead Pastor, Grace Fellowship Church (Evangelical Free Church of America), Independence, Kentucky; counselor, Association of Certified Biblical Counselors (ACBC); author, *Gospel Treason*

"Jim Newheiser believes in the sufficiency of Scripture. I have known Jim for nearly twenty-five years, and I have learned much from him. He is a trusted guide. Everything Jim writes is deeply biblical and wonderfully practical, and this book is no exception. In my opinion, this is now the go-to book for biblical wisdom on finances. It is God-centered. It is biblical. It is wise. It is comprehensive. It is arranged so that you can go straight to a topic. But it is also designed so that it could be used in small groups or Sunday school classes. Jim writes so that God's people would glorify God in their work and their finances. May God be pleased to use this book to help sanctify the church by disabusing us of society's money myths and by renewing our minds by the Word of God."

—**Brian Borgman**, Founding Pastor, Grace Community Church, Minden, Nevada; author, *Feelings and Faith*

"Any Christian book on the subject of money faces a challenge: it must deal with both timeless principles and contemporary applications—issues that transcend time and context and those that are inexorably bound to a particular time and a particular context. Jim Newheiser's *Money, Debt, and Finances: Critical Questions and Answers* strikes just the right balance. It carefully distinguishes between what the Bible says to all people in all times and what it says to a certain people at a certain time. For that reason and many more, I am glad to recommend it."

—**Tim Challies**, Author, blogger, and book reviewer, www.challies.com

"Jim Newheiser has done an excellent job in writing *Money, Debt, and Finances: Critical Questions and Answers* to address the challenging issues that face most of us on our sanctifying journey as believers. Jim has devoted a lifetime to collecting information on these topics, not only from Scripture but from his experience as a pastor, a businessman, and a biblical counselor. I heartily recommend this book to anyone seeking God's answers to these critical and common financial questions."

—**Howard Dayton,** Founder, Compass—Finances God's Way

"Who knew that a seasoned pastor, seminary teacher, and biblical counselor had so much to say on the topic of money! By answering forty-one practical questions, Jim Newheiser explores the astounding relevance of scriptural principles on spending, budgets, poverty, work, debt, gambling, giving, vocation, wealth, and the intriguing-but-overlooked connection between our heart and our finances. It's difficult to imagine any reader's having unanswered questions after reading this comprehensive guide!"

—**Dave Harvey**, President, Great Commission Collective; author, *When Sinners Say I Do* and *I Still Do*

"It is always a pleasure to read a book by Jim Newheiser, and *Money, Debt, and Finances: Critical Questions and Answers* does not disappoint. As a physician, I am painfully aware that doctors are well known for playing golf badly and doing a worse job of managing our money. This book is on the list that I wish I had read when I was starting out. It offers a wide variety of biblical principles by which to govern our use of money in forty-one concise chapters. I found this book helpful in ordering my own finances. I highly recommend it for those who are looking for guidance on how to honor God with the resources he gives us."

—**Charles Hodges,** Medical Doctor; Fellow, Association of Certified Biblical Counselors (ACBC); author, *Good Mood, Bad Mood*

"Newheiser provides a comprehensive, biblically driven resource—strewn with practical suggestions—on how to view money and how to gain and spend it, when to borrow or lend it, and how to save and invest it, always with a consistent, explicit aim to honor God, who owns all our possessions. My new starter guide about money both for me and for those I disciple and counsel."

—**Robert D. Jones**, Associate Professor of Biblical Counseling, The Southern Baptist Theological Seminary; author, *Pursuing Peace* and *Uprooting Anger*

"Many books, programs, and financial gurus will tell you what to do with your money, but God's Word is the ultimate source of financial wisdom. First and foremost, it gives us our goal as Christians—not to be debt-free or to get rich, but to glorify God in all things. All other financial principles in Scripture flow out of this high calling. In an accessible Q&A format, biblical counselor and former financial consultant Jim Newheiser presents financial wisdom that is grounded in faithful biblical exegesis and rooted in sound theology. What are common misunderstandings about money? How can you create and balance a budget? How can you get out of debt? What insurance do you need? He answers these questions and more, providing a go-to resource for laypeople and those who counsel them."

—**Robert W. Kellemen**, Academic Dean, Dean of Students, Professor, Faith Bible Seminary; Founder and CEO, RPM Ministries

"I always knew that the Bible spoke a lot about money, but I never realized how much until I read this wonderful new book by Jim Newheiser.

With a commitment to the sufficiency of Scripture, and with remarkable depth and wisdom, Newheiser shows us that the Bible provides essential guidance on a wide range of financial questions. I highly recommend *Money, Debt, and Finances: Critical Questions and Answers.*"
    —**Michael J. Kruger**, President, Professor of New Testament, Reformed Theological Seminary, Charlotte

"Jim Newheiser's book on money is a must-read. You need this book to know what money is, how to think about it, what the Bible says about it, and how to honor God with it. On every page I found myself educated and edified. I am praying that this book finds its way into many hands!"
    —**Heath Lambert**, Senior Pastor, First Baptist Church, Jacksonville, Florida

"This will be my go-to book when counseling Christians about finances. It is excellent, based on biblical principles, and highly practical. It should be very helpful for young and older Christians. It will be useful for counseling people who are irresponsible in money matters. And it would be a great textbook for teaching a class. I will recommend it often. It covers a plethora of important money matters."
    —**Wayne Mack**, Elder, Lynnwood Baptist Church, Pretoria, South Africa; Director, ACBC Africa

"Books on money and personal finance are, ironically, a dime a dozen. This one by Jim Newheiser is worth its weight in gold. Not only does Jim get into the practical nuts and bolts of how to acquire, spend, save, and invest money (as well as manage debt), he also addresses the ways that finances reveal the idols of our hearts and how the gospel can wean us off such cheap God-substitutes. Jim shows us that stewarding our financial resources wisely is not just good for us; it constitutes a significant aspect of a life of worship, lived in grateful obedience to our Savior. *Money, Debt, and Finances: Critical Questions and Answers* provides hope for those who have already met financial ruin, as well as further wisdom for those who are already making good choices.

Jim's book will become the first resource I pass out to those who need mentoring in this crucial area."

—**Phillip S. Marshall**, Pastor, Adult Education & Discipleship, Founders Baptist Church, Spring, Texas; Assistant Professor, Department of Classics and Biblical Languages, School of Christian Thought, Houston Baptist University

"*Money, Debt, and Finances: Critical Questions and Answers* is an amazing book combining biblical principles and very practical advice. It will answer all your questions about money and God's perspective. I like this book a lot and plan to give it to all our children and adult grandchildren. I wish my husband and I had had it when we were young."

—**Martha Peace**, Certified biblical counselor; author, *The Excellent Wife*

"Jim Newheiser masterfully applies biblical principles and values to the dozens of important money decisions that Christians must make today. His book is one of the few that connect the big question of how to glorify God with the myriad money questions faced in daily life. The result is a veritable 'Wikipedia' of godly money guidance. *Money, Debt, and Finances: Critical Questions and Answers* charts a course around the many financial minefields for youth, college students, young couples, middle-agers, those in business, those approaching retirement, the struggling, and the wealthy. This is the most thorough money guide for Christians in print today."

—**James C. Petty**, Author, *Step by Step: Divine Guidance for Ordinary Christians* and *Act of Grace: The Power of Generosity to Change Your Life, the Church, and the World*

"Without doubt, one of the significant challenges that many people face is financial pressure, and Christians are certainly not immune. To add to this challenge, many questions are regularly raised about the use (and misuse) of money. This subject is heightened even further when you consider that Jesus himself said that 'where your treasure is, there your heart will be also' (Matt. 6:21). Given this critical truth from our

Lord, Jim Newheiser has applied his considerable skill in answering forty-one different questions related to this incredibly important topic. If you, like me, have struggled to carefully understand and practically apply what the Bible teaches about money, this is just the book for which you've been waiting."

—**Lance Quinn**, Senior Pastor, Bethany Bible Church,
Thousand Oaks, California

"People need discernment—biblical discernment. This is expressly true when it comes to money. What Dr. Jim Newheiser does here is to provide the church with an exceptional resource for developing biblical discernment about money. His book is useful to disciples of Jesus Christ who want to glorify God through their understanding and use of money. Built on faithful exegesis, Jim's volume provides biblically sufficient, practical guidance for the people of God to think rightly about money and use it wisely for the glory of God."

—**Andrew Rogers**, Pastor, Kindred Community Church,
Anaheim Hills, California; Executive Director, Overseas
Instruction in Counseling

"In his wonderful book *Money, Debt, and Finances: Critical Questions and Answers*, author Jim Newheiser shares both biblical and practical wisdom about virtually all areas of finances. In a world in which even many Christians struggle with financial bondage, stress, and pressures, this book offers solid principles that, when applied, can lead to true financial freedom. Given that money conflicts in marriage are one of the leading causes of divorce, *Money* will serve as a valuable resource for the Christian counselor who wants to know how to counsel—through the lens of biblical stewardship. I highly recommend this book to every Christian counselor and to everyone else who wants to learn biblical and practical principles that lead to wise stewardship and financial freedom."

—**Jeff Rogers**, Founder, Chairman of Stewardship Advisory
Group and Stewardship Legacy Coaching; ForbesBooks
featured author, *Create a Thriving Family Legacy: How to
Share Your Wisdom and Wealth with Your Children and
Grandchildren*; coauthor, *Investing & Faith*

"A guide full of important information for those who want to apply God's Word to their financial life. It not only discusses the many financial roadblocks that we face today, but leaves readers with answers that they can begin to reflect on. It equips them to go deeper than just getting out of debt: it encourages them to become financial disciples. I look forward to using this book as a reference to answer the many questions that we receive."

—**Julia Sizemore**, Financial Coach; Founder, Connect Financial Ministries

"Stewardship of money and resources is a frequently recurring subject for most experienced counselors because it is a persistent problem among Christians. Mark Twain sarcastically remarked, 'The lack of money is the root of all evil,' because everyone knew that it was not true. As Scripture says, it's the *love* of money that is the root of all kinds of evils (1 Tim. 6:10)! Jim Newheiser's book *Money, Debt, and Finances: Critical Questions and Answers* is a carefully written analysis of how a Christian should handle the financial resources that God has provided. The amount of money one possesses is not nearly as important as its stewardship. This book is packed full of very practical counsel, using God's Word as the standard and guide for some of the most important and difficult financial decisions that you will face in life. The biblical backdrop for handling money must be understood if you plan to bring glory to God, and this book very effectively unveils that backdrop. I believe it will benefit Christians around the world for a long time to come!"

—**John D. Street**, Graduate Professor, The Master's University & Seminary; President of the Board of Trustees, Association of Certified Biblical Counselors (ACBC)

"This book is a wonderful blend of solid biblical principles and practical application to the way we handle the money that God has entrusted to us. Jim Newheiser is a seasoned pastor, professor, and biblical counselor, and he is also a trusted friend. Readers will learn solid truths that will guide their use of money, but more importantly will be drawn into a more fulfilling relationship with Jesus as they find him to be their greatest treasure."

—**Steve Viars**, Pastor, Faith Church, Lafayette, Indiana

"I didn't want to read this book. Money can get me too nervous. Then, once I stepped in, I enjoyed its biblical clarity and reach, even extending to questions about college majors, school loans, and investments. The book helped me, it will help my adult children, and it prepared me for important conversations with friends."

—**Ed Welch**, Counselor and faculty member, Christian
    Counseling & Educational Foundation (CCEF)

"In all my years of studying, teaching, counseling, and training others to do the same with the biblical principles of handling God's money and possessions, I have always wanted a reference book like this one. A plethora of books have been written by godly businessmen who have studied God's Word and have written about God's ownership and our stewardship as well as practical subjects on budgeting, getting out of debt, giving, and operating a business. But very few books so thoroughly deal with dozens of the most common financial problems that show up in the counseling room (and in all our lives as believers) in such a thorough theological and scriptural manner. I plan to use this book heavily in my future teaching and counseling activities."

—**Tom Wells**, Certified biblical counselor, Association of
    Certified Biblical Counselors (ACBC); former seminar
    instructor and budget coach trainer for Larry Burkett and
    Howard Dayton, Crown Financial Ministries

MONEY
DEBT AND
FINANCES

MONEY
DEBT AND
FINANCES

CRITICAL QUESTIONS
AND ANSWERS

JIM NEWHEISER

P&R
PUBLISHING
P.O. BOX 817 • PHILLIPSBURG • NEW JERSEY 08865-0817

ISBN: 978-1-62995-437-0 (pbk)
ISBN: 978-1-62995-438-7 (ePub)
ISBN: 978-1-62995-439-4 (Mobi)

Library of Congress Cataloging-in-Publication Data

Names: Newheiser, Jim, author.
Title: Money, debt, and finances : critical questions and answers / Jim
   Newheiser.
Description: Phillipsburg, New Jersey : P&R Publishing, [2021] | Includes
   bibliographical references and indexes. | Summary: "Trying to budget?
   Struggling with debt? Deciding on insurance? Biblical counselor and
   former financial consultant Jim Newheiser gives guidance from Scripture
   as he answers major questions on diverse financial topics"-- Provided by
   publisher.
Identifiers: LCCN 2020038709 | ISBN 9781629954370 (paperback) | ISBN
   9781629954387 (epub) | ISBN 9781629954394 (mobi)
Subjects: LCSH: Finance, Personal--Religious aspects--Christianity. |
   Money--Religious aspects--Christianity.
Classification: LCC HG179 .N4485 2021 | DDC 332.024--dc23
LC record available at https://lccn.loc.gov/2020038709

DEDICATION

For over thirty years, I have had the privilege of working in full-time vocational ministry, which means that I get to spend my days studying the Bible, reading edifying books, and teaching and counseling God's people. So I dedicate this book to my Christian brothers and sisters who have successfully worked hard and worked smart in their vocations and have given generously to the Lord's work so that this ox could be unmuzzled. I particularly thank God for the faithful members of Grace Bible Church in Escondido, California, for the generous donors to Reformed Theological Seminary (including S. T.), and for those who have supported other Christian ministries that have generously provided our income over the past three decades. Thank you all for your faithful example of godly stewardship.

CONTENTS

Foreword by Ligon Duncan   xi

Acknowledgments   xiii

Preface   xv

PART 1: GENERAL PRINCIPLES

1. How Can the Bible Speak to Our Modern Complex Financial Issues?   3
2. What Is the Cause of Our Financial Problems?   9
3. What Are Common Misunderstandings about Money?   17
4. What Is Money?   20
5. What Are the Potential Blessings and Dangers of Wealth?   27
6. How Does God Use Financial Trials for Our Good?   35

PART 2: ACQUIRING MONEY

7. What Are Some Common Misunderstandings about Acquiring Money?   43
8. Why Is Our Work So Important?   51
9. What Are the Keys to Success in Your Vocation?   59
10. What Distinguishes the Wise Worker from the Sluggard?   65
11. What Are Illegitimate Ways of Making Money?   74
12. May Christians Gamble?   80
13. Should Christians Participate in Multilevel-Marketing Organizations?   87

14. What Practical Wisdom Can Be Offered to Those Who Need More Income?   94

PART 3: SPENDING MONEY

15. What Are Some Common Misunderstandings about Spending Money?   105
16. How Much of Your Money Belongs to God?   109
17. How Much Should You Give?   113
18. What Steps Can Be Taken to Successfully Create a Budget?   121
19. What Steps Can Be Taken to Balance Your Budget?   128
20. What Can Be Done to Help People Who Are Failing to Follow Their Budget?   133
21. What Else Can Be Done in Practical Terms to Avoid Overspending?   139

PART 4: DEBT

22. What Are Common Misunderstandings about Debt?   147
23. What Does the Bible Teach about Debt?   151
24. Is There a Wise Way to Use Credit Cards?   157
25. Is It Wise to Incur Debt to Finance Your Education?   162
26. Is It Wise, or Even Necessary, to Use Debt to Buy a Vehicle?   169
27. Is Home Ownership Always a Great Investment?   173
28. What Should We Think about the Use of Debt in Businesses and Government?   185
29. Why Is It Unwise to Lend, Borrow, or Cosign among Family and Close Friends?   193
30. How Can You Get out of Debt?   201

PART 5: PREPARING FOR THE FUTURE

31. What Are Some Common Misunderstandings about Preparing for Your Financial Future?   211

Contents

32. Why Do Christians Need to Save?   215
33. In Practical Terms, How Should Savings Be Accumulated? 222
34. What Are Wise General Principles for Investing?   227
35. What Are the Biggest Mistakes People Make When
    Investing?   234
36. What Kinds of Investments Are Available, and What Are
    the Risks? (Banks, Bonds, and Stocks)   243
37. What Other Investments Are Available, and What Are the
    Risks? (Rental Properties, Precious Metals, Etc.)   253
38. How Can You Wisely Prepare for Retirement?   260
39. What Insurance Do You Need?   267
40. How Can You Prepare for the End of Your Life? (Making
    a Will and Leaving a Legacy)   278
41. How Does Money Point Us to the Gospel?   284

Appendix A: Budgets   287
Appendix B: Balance Sheets   299
Appendix C: Randy Alcorn's Treasure Principles   305
Recommended Resources   307
Index of Scripture   311
Index of Subjects and Names   317

FOREWORD

The Bible is filled with instructions about the believer's attitude toward and use of money and material possessions. The very first page of the Bible makes it clear that God made all the material things in this world and that "it was very good" (Gen. 1:31). This reminds us of the divine blessedness of the creation and God's complacency (delight) in his creation. It directly assaults the view that matter is sinful or inherently incapable of proximity to God. He made it and delights in it! This means, among other things, that possessions and things aren't inherently bad, though our use of and preoccupation with them can be. In other words, material things—money and possessions—aren't the problem, but our love for them can be. Part of the beauty of God's material creation is that it is a gift of the Giver, and the Giver himself is greater than the gift. This is one key to the Christian attitude toward wealth. It is why Paul warned against "the love of money" (1 Tim. 6:10) and why Jesus declared that "you cannot serve God and wealth" (Matt. 6:24; Luke 16:13)—not because money, things, stuff, and material resources are bad, but because of our heart's propensity to turn even the gifts of God into idols and to treasure God's gifts more than the Giver himself.

This whole area is probably the matter in which more Christians have been conformed to the spirit of the age than any other single issue in our time and culture. And it means that we need biblical instruction, pastoral wisdom, good counsel, and deliberate discipleship on this topic in the church. That is one of the reasons I'm so thankful for Jim Newheiser's book *Money, Debt, and Finances*. Many pastors today consider themselves deficiently informed and experienced in these matters, and numerous specific issues are beset by complication and controversy. So how are we going to helpfully shepherd our people in this area? Thankfully, we have wise, experienced, and balanced pastor-teachers such as Jim to help us.

I've been helped by reading this book, and I think you will be, too. It will serve the pastor and counselor in helping Christians to think through these matters, as well as directly aid believers who wish to thoroughly work through these issues for themselves.

Ligon Duncan
Chancellor and CEO
John E. Richards Professor of Systematic and Historical Theology
Reformed Theological Seminary

ACKNOWLEDGMENTS

I am thankful to God for many people who were a tremendous help and blessing as I wrote this book. My buddy Tom Wells offered a wealth of experience and knowledge about biblical financial principles that I believe greatly enhanced this book's usefulness and accuracy (and during crunch time pulled an all-nighter for the first time since college). My TA, Taylor Wright, did an amazing job of helping me to complete and format the manuscript, while making numerous helpful suggestions about content. I am grateful to God for our friend Pat Kuhl, who did her usual careful and precise job of proofreading my manuscript. I am most thankful for my wife, Caroline, who has been a frugal and wise steward of the resources that God has entrusted to us over these past forty-plus years (Prov. 31:11–12). I am also thankful for the support and wisdom of John Hughes, Karen Magnuson, and Amanda Martin with P&R Publishing. I am blessed and humbled that they would want to publish my books, and I am thankful for how they improve what I have written, thus making it more useful for God's people. *Soli Deo Gloria.*

PREFACE

Why would a seminary professor/pastor/counselor write a book about money? I have always been a financial junkie. When I was a small child, I was eager to make money in any way I could by helping out around the house. I was a saver; by the time I was eight, I had about fifty dollars, which I invested, with my dad's advice, in the stock market. Not long after that, I started mowing neighbors' grass, and by the time I was twelve I had two paper routes and made even more money selling subscriptions door to door. When I went to college, while I yearned to go into full-time ministry, I chose to major in business so that I would have a marketable skill, remembering that Paul sometimes supported himself by making tents (Acts 18:3). I was also influenced by the fact that Jesus hadn't begun his public ministry until he was about thirty and that elders are typically older men. I wanted to be in a position to provide for my family if full-time support in ministry was not possible. After I completed college, I went to work as a financial consultant for the company that is now called Accenture, where I worked among driven, successful people in an extremely high-pressure, competitive environment. Then the Lord took my family to Saudi Arabia, where I worked for a former client, Exxon Mobil, while also serving as a tent-making pastor. The time in Saudi was richly rewarding both spiritually in the underground church and financially, since we were very well paid. As we worked and lived among people who were making more money than they had ever imagined, we watched how some foolishly wasted that bounty, while others acted more wisely. At a very young age we had to learn how to manage our newfound wealth, facing challenging choices of how much to spend, how much to save, and how much to give away. We also learned a lot about investing through both the wise and the unwise choices we made.

After we were kicked out of Saudi Arabia on religious grounds, I attended seminary, where we were with students who were struggling financially as they tried to take care of their families, engage in ministry, and pay for school. Since completing seminary, I have been engaged in local-church pastoral ministry, biblical counseling, and leadership training. In addition to counseling people about their financial problems, I have discovered that many people with other presenting problems also have major financial challenges. We have watched others make disastrous financial mistakes, often involving family and friends. We have worked with people to make budgets, get out of debt, and save for the future.

I have continued to be a bit of a financial junkie. I read the *Wall Street Journal* every day, and I devour books that deal with financial issues. My hope in writing this book is to combine my background in finance with my theological training and my practical counseling experience in order to be a blessing to Christ's church.

This book, like my *Marriage, Divorce, and Remarriage*[1] volume, is arranged around questions and answers. Some people might choose to read straight through the book. Others might find it useful as a reference by which they can seek wise biblical answers for particular issues as they come up.

I want to acknowledge that I have learned much from others who have written on the topic of finances, including Randy Alcorn, Larry Burkett, Ron Blue, Howard Dayton, and Dave Ramsey. I have sought to give credit where credit is due, but am sure that many of my ideas are among those gleaned from many sources over the past forty years. Given that God's Word is the ultimate source of financial wisdom, it

---

1. Jim Newheiser, *Marriage, Divorce, and Remarriage: Critical Questions and Answers* (Phillipsburg, NJ: P&R Publishing, 2017).

should not be surprising that many of us have some similar things to say. My hope is that my perspective will be a useful addition for the glory of God.

Why do we need another book about finances? I have three primary aims that I hope will make this book stand out:

1. Our goal is not to be debt-free or to be wealthy. Our goal is to glorify God in all things, including our finances.
2. Our objective is to present financial wisdom that is grounded in faithful biblical exegesis and rooted in sound theology.
3. This book is meant to be a reference for individuals and counselors to discover the Bible's answers and apply them to the most common financial problems and questions that people face today.

PART 1

GENERAL PRINCIPLES

1

HOW CAN THE BIBLE SPEAK TO OUR MODERN COMPLEX FINANCIAL ISSUES?

You picked up this book because you need wisdom about your finances. Perhaps you are having a difficult time making your mortgage payment. Or you are in a dead-end job with little opportunity for advancement in responsibility or salary. Or you feel that you are buried in debt from student loans and credit cards. You might wonder what the Bible, which was written thousands of years ago, can have to say about your problems. In biblical times, people didn't have credit cards, time-share payments, and student loans. Most people were farmers and didn't have the array of vocational options that we have today. There were no multinational corporations. Nor did Internet shopping and banking exist.

Second Timothy 3:16–17 tells us, "All Scripture is inspired by God and profitable for teaching, for reproof, for correction, for training in righteousness, so that the man of God may be adequate, equipped for every good work." Isaiah 40:8 proclaims, "The grass withers, the flower fades, but the word of our God stands forever." Jesus often taught about financial matters. Randy Alcorn calculates that 15 percent of everything that Jesus teaches relates to the topic of wealth.[1] God, who

---

1. Randy Alcorn, *The Treasure Principle: Discovering the Secret of Joyful Giving* (Colorado Springs: Multnomah, 2001), 9.

inspired the human authors to write his inerrant Word, knew what the future would hold and has given us not merely sufficient truth, but timeless glorious wisdom. He is the ultimate designer of human labor and commerce. His Word not only helps us to understand financial matters, but also equips us to live wisely as we seek to glorify him in all things.

While technology changes, human nature and basic economic principles remain the same throughout history. Niall Ferguson, in his book *The Ascent of Money*, points out, "Sooner or later every bubble bursts."[2] He and others liken the modern collapses in banking, stocks, and real estate to various economic crises and collapses in history, including the famous tulip bubble in seventeenth-century Holland.[3] Though our government leaders claim to have created sophisticated economic and banking systems run by highly trained experts, bubbles and financial crises still happen and will continue to happen. Many financial problems, for individuals, corporations, and nations, are caused by violating basic principles of biblical wisdom.

Scripture teaches many principles, which will be developed at greater length in subsequent chapters:

1. Private-property rights are affirmed. The Ten Commandments forbid not only stealing your neighbor's property, but even coveting what doesn't belong to you (Ex. 20:15, 17). The story of King Ahab's trying to take Naboth's vineyard (1 Kings 21) illustrates the reality that even a ruler does not have the right to take away a man's property.
2. Vocational and financial success comes through hard work and skill (Prov. 6:6–11; 10:4; 22:29). God has designed the economics of the world in such a way that you will be rewarded according to your effort and your ability. The way to get ahead is to acquire valuable skills and to work hard in your vocation.

---

2. Niall Ferguson, *The Ascent of Money: A Financial History of the World* (New York: Penguin Books, 2008), 9.
3. Ferguson, *Ascent of Money*, 137.

3. Get-rich-quick schemes are foolish and lead to poverty (Prov. 13:11; 28:19–20, 22). In every age, there are people who try to circumvent God's way of achieving financial success by going after schemes that promise prosperity without hard work and skill. Such unwise and greedy schemes will sooner or later fail, thus increasing one's financial woes.

4. Wages and prices are to be equitable (Jer. 22:13; James 5:1–7). The concern for fair wages for laborers is not merely a modern phenomenon. God's Word opposes the unjust oppression of the weak by those who possess economic power and requires that we treat others with fairness that goes beyond mere impersonal forces of supply and demand.

5. An extravagant lifestyle will make you poor (Prov. 21:17). People will always be attracted to pursue possessions and experiences that are beyond their economic means. The enjoyment of these luxuries might be pleasant in the short term, but they will lead to severe financial difficulties in the long run.

6. Going into debt (or cosigning for the debt of others) is foolish and can be financially ruinous (Prov. 6:1–5; 15:6; 17:18; 22:7, 26–27). Debt can be tantalizing. It can temporarily enable you to enjoy a standard of living far beyond your income. Corporations anticipate that they can increase their profits by financing their expansion through debt rather than equity. Governments have realized that spending on various programs is popular but that taxation is not, so they create massive amounts of debt. Debt greatly increases the risk of financial disaster for families, corporations, and governments. Sooner or later, the bills must be paid.

7. Saving for the future is wise (Gen. 41:33–36; Prov. 6:8). Those who are wise know that times of prosperity (for nations, corporations, and families) are often followed by financial downturns; thus, they exercise self-control in spending so that they can have reserves to ride out economic storms. They also put money aside for anticipated future expenses, such as major purchases (house and car), education, and retirement.

5

8. We should honor God from our wealth, which includes having compassion on the poor (Prov. 3:9; 19:17; Luke 12:21). We are stewards of the resources that God gives us. We are to give to the work of his kingdom by faith and in proportion to how he has blessed us. We are also to be concerned for the deserving poor among us, especially our earthly and spiritual families.

9. Taxation is a reality of life (Neh. 5:4; Luke 20:22; Rom. 13:6–7). As long as human government has been in existence, there have been taxes. These are not always fair. Nor do governments always spend our money wisely and justly. But we pay taxes, ultimately for the Lord's sake.

10. Wisdom thinks long term and is willing to postpone gratification (Matt. 6:19–21). This general principle of wisdom applies to many areas of life, including our finances. Living frugally and saving will produce blessing in this life. Forgoing earthly pleasures and possessions for the sake of God's kingdom will result in great blessing in the life to come.

Ferguson writes concerning modern financial crises: "Indeed, I believe that today's crisis is in some measure to be explained by ignorance of financial history—and not only among ordinary people. The 'masters of the universe' also paid far too little heed to the lessons of the past, preferring to pin their hopes on elaborate mathematical models that proved to be false gods."[4] From a biblical perspective, we would say that God has revealed financial wisdom in Scripture and that history proves that people who think they are smarter than God wind up creating financial problems not only for themselves, but also for others affected by their folly: "Do you see a man wise in his own eyes? There is more hope for a fool than for him" (Prov. 26:12).

---

4. Ferguson, *Ascent of Money*, 14.

OUR APPROACH

This book will survey what the Bible teaches about finances—general principles, earning money, spending money, borrowing money, and saving for the future. We will seek to refute some of the unwise money myths of our day while offering biblical wisdom in their place. In addition, we will seek to provide practical steps you can take to make needed changes to your financial life so that you can live more wisely. We will also use case studies in order to make these principles more understandable.

SOME QUALIFICATIONS

It is important to distinguish between biblical commands, the violation of which is sinful; principles of wisdom, the violation of which is folly; and particular ways in which one may choose to apply biblical commands and principles of wisdom.

1. For example, it is sinful to steal, to take bribes, or to refuse to pay your taxes or your other obligations. A professing Christian could be subject to church discipline for various forms of theft (1 Cor. 5:11).
2. On the other hand, taking on debt or cosigning to take on the debt of others is risky and often unwise and could result in financial problems, but such actions are not necessarily sinful. The person who chooses to cosign for the debt of a family member might be advised by church leaders not to do so, but he would not be disciplined if he made this choice.
3. There are often multiple valid ways to obey a biblical command or to follow a principle of wisdom. We need to be careful not to legalistically treat our way of doing things as the only righteous or wise way to act. For example, it is wise to make a spending plan or budget (Prov. 21:5). One could choose to do this by using an electronic app, a chart on paper, or the envelope system advocated by some financial advisers. Another

example is that Christians are obligated to pay off their debts (Ps. 37:21), but Scripture does not compel everyone to use Dave Ramsey's debt snowball (paying off the smallest debt first) as opposed to another debt-reduction technique (such as paying off high-interest debts first).

OUR GOAL

The primary goal of this book, in contrast to other financial books, is not to help you become prosperous or even debt-free. Our chief goal is to encourage you to work, spend, give, save, think, and live to the glory of God (1 Cor. 10:31; 2 Cor. 5:9).

— QUESTIONS FOR REFLECTION —

1. How can the Bible, which was written centuries ago, speak usefully to our financial issues today?
2. What are some timeless financial truths taught in Scripture?
3. Why do people, including politicians and economic experts, continue to ignore the lessons of Scripture and of history?
4. In what ways do individuals, corporations, and governments today often violate biblical principles of finance?
5. What is the difference between a biblical command and a principle of biblical wisdom?
6. What should our chief financial goal be?

2

WHAT IS THE CAUSE OF OUR FINANCIAL PROBLEMS?

There are many different kinds of financial problems. Entire nations are enduring poverty and unemployment because of failed government policies or local droughts and famines. Even in prosperous nations, many citizens can't earn enough money and are on the verge of homelessness. Families and individuals are buried under a mountain of debt from medical expenses, the cost of education, or foolish choices from the past. Some have had their retirement savings wiped out by a bad investment, a market crash, or an unscrupulous business partner. Many people are tempted to worry and fret about money.[1]

ALL FINANCIAL PROBLEMS ARE CAUSED BY SIN

In a word, financial suffering is caused by sin. God created the earth to be incredibly productive, and he entrusted humankind with stewardship over it (Gen. 2:15–16). There were to be no food or resource shortages in the unfallen world. But when man sinned, God brought consequences, including scarcity, on humankind and our world. The creation itself was decisively changed for the worse. In Adam's struggle

---

1. For a resource addressing the heart issues behind our approach to finances, see Jim Newheiser, *Money: Seeking God's Wisdom*, 31-Day Devotionals for Life's Problems (Phillipsburg, NJ: P&R Publishing, 2019).

to feed his family, the ground would yield thorns and thistles (3:17–18). There would be competition over scarce resources (13:6–7; 26:18–22). In addition, human nature was deeply infected by sin, so people would inflict suffering, including economic hardship, on one another.

MUCH FINANCIAL SUFFERING OCCURS BECAUSE CREATION IS FALLEN

What we call *natural disasters,* such as hurricanes, earthquakes, floods, droughts, blights, epidemics, and wildfires, cause immense financial damage. Homes and personal property are destroyed. Businesses are ruined. While these calamities occur in "nature," there is a sense in which they are not natural. The world was not originally designed to be such an unsafe place. Catastrophic events take place because humankind's fall has adversely affected the creation. Knowing this, we can do various things to try to avoid certain calamities (e.g., not building a house on a floodplain or an active geological fault). Or we can seek to mitigate the effects of natural disasters by purchasing insurance[2] or preparing for anticipated events, or by constructing seawalls and houses on sturdy stilts along the Gulf Coast (Prov. 21:5). In Matthew 7:24–27, the wise man anticipates storms and floods by building his house on the rock. But because we live in a dangerous fallen world, we are unable to eliminate risk. The effect of sin on our bodies could also lead to financial suffering. Many lose their life savings and then go into debt while fighting disease or treating injuries. Some become physically disabled and are unable to work to earn income, which leads to poverty.

SOME FINANCIAL SUFFERING OCCURS BECAUSE OF THE SINS OF OTHERS

Human governments have caused an immense amount of financial suffering throughout history and in modern times. Some rulers have

2. Ironically, insurance companies often call natural disasters *acts of God.*

deliberately enslaved, starved, or withheld the essentials of life from a disfavored people group or region. Others have created economic instability through corruption, confiscating private property, creating an economic climate hostile to productivity, debasing their currency through inflation and debt,[3] and other bad policies. Still others have foolishly led their nations into needless wars that sap the nation's wealth and destroy the means of production. Honest, hardworking people in such nations struggle to survive.

Our finances can also be adversely affected by the sins of other individuals. Some steal through overt acts of theft (Ex. 20:15). Burglars rob our houses (Matt. 6:19), and thugs commit armed robbery (Luke 10:30). An unscrupulous business partner might cheat you out of your fair share of the business. Or you invest or lend your money to someone who foolishly or wickedly wastes your resources. An employer might fail to pay you a fair and timely wage (Deut. 24:14–15; 1 Tim. 5:18). When we were working overseas in the Middle East, some employees from developing nations were not paid at all by employers' flagrantly violating their contracts (James 2:6; 5:1–6). Others might steal from you in less direct ways by misleading you about the quality or quantity of goods or services that they are selling to you (Prov. 20:23). The product breaks because of shoddy workmanship, and the seller won't stand behind what was sold to you.

SOMETIMES WE SUFFER FINANCIALLY BECAUSE OF OUR OWN SIN

You might be reading this book because you are in financial distress of your own making. You have failed to follow the wise principles of God's Word, and you are suffering the consequences. You have covetously lived beyond your means and have debt that you cannot repay. Your income is low because you have failed to work hard to acquire

3. Some would argue that inflation itself is theft, since it steals value from those who own the national currency by debasing its value. In the old days, less gold or silver might be put into the coin. Now governments deliberately debase their currencies through inflationary economic policies.

marketable skills to provide for your family. You have failed to be a good steward who is wise and generous with what God has given you. Yet if you are a child of God, there is hope. Your distress might be God's loving hand of chastisement on you. The Lord disciplines those whom he loves (Prov. 3:11–12). Turn to God, confess your sins, and call out to him for mercy (Isa. 55:6–7). Pray that God will use your current financial trials to transform you into Christlikeness, that he will help you to live wisely for his glory, and that he will deliver you from your current distress. He is gracious and merciful to those who call on him.

SOME FINANCIAL SUFFERING IS THE DIRECT JUDGMENT OF GOD ON SIN

Under the old covenant, Israel's faithfulness would result in economic prosperity, but disobedience to God's commands would result in judgments on the nation through drought, famine, plague, death of livestock, debilitating debt to foreign nations, and so on (Deut. 28:15–68; Joel 1–2). These judgments are carried out many times throughout Israel's history as it is recorded in the historical books and the Prophets (1 Kings 17:1; Hab. 3:17; Hag. 1:6). God sometimes judged wicked pagan nations in similar ways, especially when rulers arrogantly sought to bestow divine status on themselves (Isa. 10:5–6; 15:6–7; 19:5–10; Dan. 4–5; Hab. 2:6–8).

God also brings financial judgment on individuals, sometimes by allowing them to experience the consequences of their sin and foolishness: "God is not mocked; for whatever a man sows, this he will also reap" (Gal. 6:7; also see Ps. 37:12–15; Prov. 6:9–11; 28:19). In other cases, the Lord might see fit to humble the wicked in spite of all their financial precautions (Luke 12:13–21).

While there is no theocracy (chosen earthly nation) like Old Testament Israel in this age, God is still concerned about economic justice. He hears the cries of the oppressed (James 5:4), and his justice will be satisfied. While we cannot prophetically proclaim that specific economic disasters that fall on certain evil nations or individuals are

God's particular judgment on them, we do know that their sins will find them out (Num. 32:23).[4]

GOD SOMETIMES ALLOWS FINANCIAL SUFFERING FOR OUR GOOD AND HIS GLORY

Not all financial suffering is direct judgment on personal sin. The Lord allowed the devil to take away Job's great wealth (and much more) not because of Job's own sin, but simply for the glory of God. Sometimes he allows us to suffer loss for our sanctification so that we will grow to be more like Christ (James 1:2–4). Believers who flourish spiritually even after suffering great loss can have a wonderful testimony to God's faithfulness.

ONE DAY OUR FINANCIAL PROBLEMS WILL BE OVER

The story of Scripture ends the way it begins—in paradise. When Christ returns, the abundance of Eden will be restored (Rev. 22:2), and God will again dwell among his people. There will be no more hunger (7:16), sickness, death, or suffering (21:3–4). Until that day, we, along with the rest of creation, groan in eager anticipation (Rom. 8:18–25). In the meantime, God offers us wisdom about how we, as citizens of the world to come, should live in this fallen world.

GOD OFFERS HELP TO HIS PEOPLE IN THE MIDST OF FINANCIAL TROUBLES IN A FALLEN WORLD

God helps his people through his common-grace provision of human government. Civil authorities are called to serve God by restraining evil: punishing those who do wrong and protecting those

---

4. As I was writing this, I read about victims of wildfires in California whose large marijuana farms suffered great financial loss because they couldn't carry insurance on their valuable crop under federal law.

who do right—including their property (Rom. 13:1–7; 1 Peter 2:14). Even flawed civil governments can be a blessing as they, to some extent, enforce order and justice.[5]

God has also given us the timeless wisdom of his Word, which offers valuable principles about financial issues, including how to be successful in our vocation; the dangers of debt, cosigning, and get-rich-quick schemes; the blessings of generosity; the folly of extravagant spending; and the value of saving and planning. The Bible also offers us the opportunity to store up heavenly treasures that are secure and everlasting (Matt. 6:20). These principles will be expounded in the remaining chapters of this book.

Sometimes, even when the world at large is under judgment, the Lord provides special help to his people (Ps. 37:25). He cared for Elijah and the widow during a time of judgmental drought (1 Kings 17), and he provided for the churches undergoing famine in Judea through the Gentile churches in other parts of the world (Rom. 15:22–33; 1 Cor. 16; 2 Cor. 8–9).

MEMBERSHIP IN GOD'S COVENANT COMMUNITY LESSENS THE FALL'S EFFECTS

Beginning with Israel in the old covenant, God has established a special covenant community of his chosen people who already belong to his everlasting kingdom, but are not yet enjoying all its blessings. God's covenant community is to be separate from the world and functions as a type or picture of his glorious everlasting kingdom. We also enjoy special blessings from him on earth as we await the heavenly fulfillment.

Under the old covenant, Israel was promised earthly prosperity that would resemble that of the heavenly kingdom if the people faithfully kept God's law (Deut. 28:1–14). The Lord promised that "there will

5. My family spent six years in Saudi Arabia. Although the Islamic government there has many faults, it does a good job of making the kingdom a safe and orderly place in which there is very little crime.

14

be no poor among you, since the LORD will surely bless you in the land which the LORD your God is giving you as an inheritance to possess, if only you listen obediently to the voice of the LORD your God, to observe carefully all this commandment which I am commanding you today" (15:4–5). The law made specific provisions for the care of widows and the poor (10:18; 24:19–21). There were protections for laborers to receive a just wage in a timely fashion (24:14–15), for rest (Ex. 20:8–11), and for debts to be forgiven (Lev. 25:13). Private property, especially the rights of each family's inheritance in the land, was protected so that even a king could not justly take away a common man's inheritance (Lev. 25:23–28; 1 Kings 21). Sadly, Israel failed to follow these good and just laws, and God's judgment fell on the nation.

The church is God's new covenant community. In this age, even though there is no theocratic state like Israel under the Mosaic law (John 18:36), similar principles exist and blessings accrue to God's people. The New Testament places great emphasis on the church's care of widows, orphans, and other needy people within the covenant community (Acts 2:44–45; 6:1; Gal. 2:10; James 1:27). The apostle Paul refers to God's provision for all his people under the old covenant as an example of how he provides for believers through mutual generosity (including among churches in different regions) in the new covenant (2 Cor. 8:12–15), so that there should be no poor among God's people (Deut. 24:14–15; also see Ex. 16:17–18).

THE GOSPEL CHANGES EVERYTHING

The gospel transforms labor relations so that a believing worker is called to see his or her vocation as kingdom work for the Lord (Eph. 6:5–8), and bosses are called on to treat their employees with Christlike fairness and kindness (v. 9; Col. 4:1). The gospel empowers people to let go of earthly treasures that they used to idolize (Luke 19:8–9; Acts 19:19). The gospel transforms sluggards and thieves into workers and givers (Eph. 4:28). The gospel transforms us from people who live for earthly wealth to those who yearn instead for the heavenly inheritance that can never be taken away (1 Peter 1:4).

SUMMARY

God made the world productive and safe, but humankind plunged the creation into ruin through the fall. Both human nature and the creation have been corrupted. All financial problems ultimately stem from the fall, whether it be through calamities in creation, the sins of others, or our own personal sin. Thankfully, God offers us hope. He has brought us into covenant relationship with himself so that we now belong to a kingdom that is greater and better than this world. He has given us wisdom for how to live as his people in a fallen world. And best of all, he has given us a promise that one day both we and the creation will be renewed and perfected. In that day, all the effects of the fall will be removed, and we will live as God originally intended—in close fellowship with him, without sin, and lacking no good thing.

— QUESTIONS FOR REFLECTION —

1. What is the ultimate cause of financial distress?
2. In what particular ways are financial problems caused by the fallen creation, our fallen neighbors, and our sinful selves?
3. What are the causes of any financial distress that you are currently experiencing?
4. What help does God give us to deal with financial distress in a fallen world? How can you apply this help to your particular situation?
5. How does our knowledge of eschatology (God's plan for his everlasting kingdom) help us to deal with our current financial distress?
6. How does God use the covenant community to care for his people in a fallen world?
7. How might God use our financial hardship for our good and his glory?

3

WHAT ARE COMMON MISUNDERSTANDINGS ABOUT MONEY?

As we consider God's wisdom about money, we will also be addressing some common money myths that could potentially lead people astray.

IS MONEY THE SECRET TO HAPPINESS IN THIS LIFE?

The most common money myth among non-Christians is that money is the key to earthly happiness. This is what is reflected in the "American dream," which says that one must own a nice house, own two late-model cars, and vacation every summer at Disney World in order to be happy and fulfilled. Many devote their lives to acquiring wealth, often sacrificing their families, their spiritual lives, and their health to get ahead. Scripture warns, "He who loves money will not be satisfied with money, nor he who loves abundance with its income. This too is vanity" (Eccl. 5:10). Studies have actually been done to suggest that those with great wealth are no happier than those of more ordinary means[1] and that even the very rich still believe that they need much more wealth in order to be truly secure.[2]

1. www.psychologytoday.com/us/blog/ritual-and-the-brain/201802/the-million-dollar-link-between-wealth-and-happiness.
2. www.theatlantic.com/family/archive/2018/12/rich-people-happy-money/577231/.

This money myth has been co-opted by some so-called Christian leaders who teach a false prosperity gospel, which claims that God will bless his people with great earthly wealth if they just have enough faith. Such leaders show off their lavish lifestyles with private jets and giant mansions and promise that their followers/donors will enjoy similar blessings. Paul warns against false teachers "of depraved mind and deprived of the truth, who suppose that godliness is a means of gain" (1 Tim. 6:5), and adds that "those who want to get rich fall into temptation and a snare and many foolish and harmful desires which plunge men into ruin and destruction" (v. 9).

IS MONEY THE ROOT OF ALL EVIL?

The verse from which this myth is derived is often misquoted. Money itself is not the root of all evil; rather, Paul warns, "For the love of money is a root of all sorts of evil, and some by longing for it have wandered away from the faith and pierced themselves with many griefs" (1 Tim. 6:10). Money, like other things that God has created (sex and fire come to mind), can be good and helpful when properly used, but dangerous and destructive when idolized and misused. Money can be a good servant, but a bad master.

Money itself, like fire, is neutral and powerful. It can do great good or cause great harm. Money enables us to fulfill our God-given responsibilities to provide for ourselves and our families (1 Tim. 5:8). Wealth can be used to do good by helping the poor and furthering the Lord's work, such as by building facilities in which Christian churches meet, sending missionaries to places where the lost need to hear the gospel, and the printing of this very book that you are reading. Similarly, money can be used for evil, such as to traffic a young girl into slavery, to purchase the weapons and ammunition for a man to kill innocent schoolchildren, or to simply fund a meaningless distraction of entertainment at a time when a man should be paying attention to an urgent family need. The difference is the heart motive of those spending the money. Are they using it to glorify God, or to indulge evil or selfish motives, or even just to acquire more money for the sake of having more?

WILL CERTAIN FORMS OF WEALTH NEVER LOSE THEIR VALUE?

During times of financial crisis, one often sees many advertisements for precious metals such as gold and silver, claiming that these assets will hold their value in hard financial times. As a child, I had a relative who told me to purchase land, offering the perspective that a limited amount of real estate was available and that no more would be made. Others put their hope in blue-chip stocks or government bonds for the security they crave. Historically, there have been crashes in the value of virtually every asset category. Jesus teaches that no earthly asset will provide absolute security: "Do not store up for yourselves treasures on earth, where moth and rust destroy and where thieves break in and steal. But store up for yourselves treasures in heaven, where neither moth nor rust destroys, and where thieves do not break in or steal" (Matt. 6:19–20).

— QUESTIONS FOR REFLECTION —

1. Why is money limited in its ability to make people happy?
2. How are some professing Christians buying in to the world's lies about money?
3. Why is it wrong to say that money is evil?
4. What are good ways in which money can be used?
5. Why is no form of earthly wealth completely secure?

4

WHAT IS MONEY?

HOW DOES MONEY FUNCTION?

One thing that sets us humans apart from the animals is that we can store value. While it is true that a squirrel might store a few nuts, humans are uniquely able to store significant value in forms that are convenient and useful. Money (cash or currency) functions as a medium that allows people to exchange goods and services without having to resort to bartering. For example, Jane bakes cookies, Bill repairs toilets, Pete mows grass, and Sally builds bird feeders. If Jane wants a toilet repaired, Pete wants some cookies, Bill wants his grass mowed, and Pete wants a bird feeder, money provides a way for each to get what he or she wants. Without money, the process of exchange would be convoluted. Pete exchanges a lawn-mowing service with Bill's promise to repair Jane's toilet if Jane promises to give Pete some cookies. But how many cookies would be enough to be a fair exchange for the mowing service and the toilet repair? Perhaps far more cookies than Pete could eat. Money simplifies the process. Without money as a means of convenient exchange, national and worldwide economies would grind to a halt. As Randy Alcorn writes, "Money is a tool which simplifies trade."[1] Wayne Grudem adds, "Money is fundamentally good because it is a human invention which sets us apart from

1. Randy Alcorn, *Money, Possessions, and Eternity*, 2nd ed. (Wheaton, IL: Tyndale House, 2003), 16.

the animal kingdom and enables us to subdue the earth by producing . . . goods and services that bring benefit to others."[2]

While money is the most convenient and portable means of exchange, there are other valuable assets by which people can store wealth. These include stocks, bonds, real estate, commodities, precious metals, and collectible art. Nonmonetary assets typically have a value placed on them in money (e.g., dollars, euros, yen).

WHAT MAKES MONEY WORK?

In order for money to work as a means of exchange, there must be a limited quantity, and it must be portable. Throughout much of history, coins made of precious metals served as money; thus, the market value of the metal in a coin represented its value as a means of exchange. The relative rarity of silver and gold made these metals convenient forms of money because a large amount of value could be stored in a relatively small quantity of coins. In contrast, using common metals (or rocks) wouldn't work. For example, as of this writing, to purchase a $20,000 car would take approximately one pound of gold or ten thousand pounds of copper. It would be very inconvenient to show up at the dealership with five tons of old pennies.

Later in history, governments issued paper currency, which was even more portable than precious metals and could be exchanged for gold or silver.[3] In more recent times, governments stopped offering to exchange their currency for precious metals and relied on what is called *fiat currency*.[4] Most money is now stored electronically in banks. This

---

2. Wayne A. Grudem, *Business for the Glory of God: The Bible's Teaching on the Moral Goodness of Business* (Wheaton, IL: Crossway, 2003), 47.

3. The United States abandoned the gold standard (which allowed the exchange of paper dollars for a given amount of gold) in the early1930s for U.S. citizens and in 1971 for international transactions. For many years, U.S. paper money was called *silver certificates*, which could be exchanged for an equivalent amount of silver. This practice ended in the mid-1960s.

4. Paper money has no inherent value. I own a bag of shredded U.S. currency that was sold by the U.S. Mint. Before the money was shredded, it might have been worth thousands of dollars. Now it has virtually no value other than as an inexpensive

fiat system relies on governments to limit the supply of money so that the existing currency does not lose its value.

THE VALUE OF MONEY CAN FLUCTUATE, AND IT OFTEN DECLINES BECAUSE OF INFLATION

Some have supposed that taking all your cash and putting it into a locked safe or stuffing it in your mattress would be the safest thing to do in order to preserve your savings. The problem is that the value of your cash can shrink even as it sits in your mattress. All my life I have collected coins and currency. My collection includes an impressive-looking one-hundred-trillion-dollar bill from Zimbabwe. What is not impressive is the actual value of this note. Because the government of Zimbabwe continued to create/print more and more money, the value of its currency rapidly declined through inflation.[5] Finally, Zimbabwean currency became useless as a means of exchange, and the citizens had to resort to bartering or using other currencies (e.g., U.S. dollars and euros) instead. Such runaway inflation has taken place in many other countries (including the German Weimar Republic in 1923)[6] whose governments have printed (or by other means created) money, thus devaluing their currency.[7]

While the United States hasn't experienced high inflation in recent

---

novelty. On the other hand, I also purchased a silver dollar from the mint. Even if I were to melt it down, it would still be worth the value of an ounce of silver out of which the coin is made.

5. Inflation occurs when there is an increase in prices and a correlated decrease in the purchasing power of money. More simply, inflation happens when too much money chases too few goods. Similarly, deflation occurs when prices fall and purchasing power increases.

6. In the famous example of the Weimar Republic in Germany, before World War II its currency became worthless through hyperinflation. This led to economic and political instability, which many believe contributed to the rise of the dictatorship of Hitler.

7. This temptation for governments to inflate currencies goes far back in history. For example, many governments used to cut the corners off their silver coins to debase them. See https://www.businessinsider.com/worst-hyperinflation-episodes-in-history-2013-9 for examples of inflated currency.

years, the value of our fiat money is still gradually declining. For example, when I was a boy growing up in the 1960s, a McDonald's plain hamburger was 15 cents. As of this writing, the same burger is over a dollar. Governments are tempted to create more fiat money because spending is popular and taxation is not. Many believe that when the creation of new money devalues the existing money supply, the government is essentially stealing value from its citizens who have saved their fiat money. The economist John Maynard Keynes observes, "By a continuing process of inflation, governments can confiscate, secretly and unobserved, an important part of the wealth of their citizens."[8]

In the United States, the Federal Reserve Bank regulates the supply of dollars. Currently, it operates under a dual mandate of maximum employment and price stability. As of this writing, the bank's price-stability target for inflation is 2 percent. It desperately wants to stay away from monetary deflation, but wants the inflation to be so small that the citizens won't notice it.

MONEY (AND ANY OTHER ASSET) IS WORTH ONLY WHAT SOMEONE ELSE IS WILLING TO GIVE YOU FOR IT

The value of any asset can fluctuate in value as a result of numerous influences, such as supply and demand, economic pressures, natural disasters, currency inflation, and the increase or decrease in government regulations. Some, recognizing that inflation lowers the value of money, insist that investing in precious metals or real estate is a better way to preserve value. But all assets fluctuate in value because of numerous influences. For example, the price of gold reached almost $700 an ounce in 1980 and dropped under $300 an ounce in 1999. If a huge quantity of gold were to be discovered in Antarctica and it could be inexpensively extracted, the price of gold would greatly drop.

8. www.goodreads.com/quotes/813942-lenin-is-said-to-have-declared-that-the -best-way.

This actually happened to the value of oil as fracking and the discovery of shale oil greatly increased the available supply of oil, which brought the price down significantly. A decrease in demand for oil because of economic recession or use of other energy sources would also bring the price down. No asset, including money/currency, has inherent price stability. Everything is worth only what a buyer or seller is willing to pay or give for it. A biblical example demonstrating supply and demand can be found in 2 Kings 6–7. During the siege of Samaria by the Arameans, there was a terrible famine, and even the least desirable food sources sold for an extremely high price in silver (2 Kings 6:25). When the Lord caused the Arameans to flee, leaving all their food supplies behind, high-quality food suddenly became very inexpensive (7:16).

THE THEOLOGY OF WEALTH:
A BROAD BIBLICAL PERSPECTIVE ON ECONOMICS

1. God Is the Owner and Source of All Wealth (Deut. 8:18; 1 Chron. 29:11–12; Pss. 24:1; 50:10; Hag. 2:8)

The psalmist declares that the earth is the Lord's and all it contains (Ps. 24:1) and that God owns the cattle on a thousand hills (50:10; also see Hag. 2:8). In Deuteronomy, God's people are reminded: "You shall remember the LORD your God, for it is He who is giving you power to make wealth" (Deut. 8:18). When proud individuals, corporations, and governments take credit for what they have earned or possess, they rob God of the glory that he alone deserves for their success.

2. The Fall of Humankind Has Made Resources Scarce and Labor Hard (Gen. 3:17–19)

God made the world good and very productive. Before the fall, there was no lack of resources or opportunities. God made the world good. Immediately after the fall, Adam was told that there would be struggles, thorns, and thistles as he engaged in his vocational activity. Since then, humanity has had to struggle with difficulties in labor, limitations of resources, and injustice in the world.

3. We Are Managers (Stewards) of God's Wealth (Matt. 25:14–29; Luke 16:10–11; 1 Cor. 4:2)

A steward is someone who manages the assets that belong to someone else. Adam was originally put in the garden to be a steward of God's perfect creation (Gen. 2:15). Jesus illustrates how we are called to play that role with God's wealth in the parable of the talents (Matt. 25:14–29). Paul further reminds us that the primary responsibility of a steward is to be faithful (1 Cor. 4:2). As we continually acknowledge that God is the owner and we are the managers (stewards), it motivates us to evaluate what we do with our abilities and assets by the test of bringing glory and honor to God (1 Cor. 10:31; 2 Cor. 5:9). Jesus teaches that faithful stewards will be rewarded: "He who is faithful in a very little thing is faithful also in much; and he who is unrighteous in a very little thing is unrighteous also in much. Therefore if you have not been faithful in the use of unrighteous wealth, who will entrust the true riches to you?" (Luke 16:10–11).

4. Your Use of Wealth Reveals Your Character (Luke 16:11)

If you want to know a person's character, you study how that person spends his or her time and money. That shows you where the heart is. Those who seek to glorify God and love others with their resources demonstrate their spiritual maturity. Those who spend selfishly demonstrate their lack of faith and love toward God. Jesus says, "If you have not been faithful in the use of unrighteous wealth, who will entrust the true riches to you?" (Luke 16:11).

SUMMARY

Money and other forms of wealth are useful as a store of economic value. Money can also have spiritual value as we learn to honor and trust God. Scripture offers extensive wisdom about how to be good stewards of our resources. In our view of wealth, we must balance the lifelong task of maintaining the righteous desire to obtain and spend money to fulfill our God-given responsibilities while avoiding the temptations that the love of wealth can bring and that can lead to ruin.

— QUESTIONS FOR REFLECTION —

1. What is money?
2. Why is money useful? What forces in the world can change the value of money?
3. In what ways do I acknowledge that God is the owner of all the wealth I possess?
4. In what ways do I still act as though I were the owner of my wealth?

5

WHAT ARE THE POTENTIAL BLESSINGS AND DANGERS OF WEALTH?

As we mentioned earlier, money, like fire, can be very useful or very dangerous. Some wealthy people are extraordinarily selfish, while others are exceptionally generous. Likewise, some poor people are generous and content, while others can be covetous and envious.

WE MUST MAINTAIN A BALANCED PERSPECTIVE ON MONEY

One of my favorite Scripture passages about money is Proverbs 30:8–9: "Give me neither poverty nor riches; feed me with the food that is my portion, that I not be full and deny You and say, 'Who is the LORD?' or that I not be in want and steal, and profane the name of my God." We are warned that too much or too little wealth can be dangerous. Those who are poor can be tempted to sin in order to meet their needs. Those who are rich can be tempted to trust in their riches and not in God. Most of us have prayed against poverty. Have you ever prayed, "Lord, please don't make me too wealthy"? To suddenly become extremely rich is one of the worst things that could happen to many people. So there is a careful tightrope walk between needing money to fulfill responsibilities and having money as an idol that draws our affections away from God.

IT IS HARD TO BE POOR

Those who are poor lack the nice things that money can buy and can be tempted to covetousness, envy, and theft.

Before I attended seminary, my family lived in Saudi Arabia, where our colleagues were earning very high salaries and had a lot of disposable income. They were constantly talking about money and spending large sums on various possessions and experiences. We were reminded of the descriptions in Ecclesiastes of the vanity of trying to find satisfaction through wealth.

Poor people can be as tempted to be covetous as the rich. J. C. Ryle warns of greed: "It may be found in a cottage as well as in a palace."[1] During seminary, we had a set of friends whose financial circumstances were the opposite of those of our friends in Saudi Arabia, since the seminarians were making sacrifices to get through school. Yet to our surprise, some of them seemed to be more obsessed with finances than our wealthy friends living in the Middle East. They were under financial pressure as they struggled to make ends meet. They also suffered under significant time pressure because they had difficulty giving adequate time to studies, family, and part-time jobs. Some were tempted to look covetously at their college friends and siblings who were already getting established in their careers, buying houses, eating out often, driving late-model cars, and taking fancy vacations. On the other hand, the seminary students were living in tiny apartments in a less desirable part of town, eating ramen noodles to save money, driving beater cars, and not able to pay for decent vacations. The temptation to envy can be even greater when we look on ourselves as being more righteous than those who are wealthy (Ps. 73:3). Why is God blessing them and not us?

Scripture brings out other difficulties of being poor: "Wealth adds many friends, but a poor man is separated from his friend. . . . All the brothers of a poor man hate him; how much more do his friends

---

1. J. C. Ryle, *Practical Religion: Being Plain Papers on the Daily Duties, Experience, Dangers, and Privileges of Professing Christians*, ed. J. I. Packer (Cambridge: James Clarke & Co., 1977), 218.

abandon him! He pursues them with words, but they are gone" (Prov. 19:4, 7). Poor people are often unpopular. The proverb does not say that this is good or right. It simply observes a reality of life. Perhaps the poor man's friends and relatives avoid him because they fear that he will try to persuade them to give or lend him money. Or maybe they feel guilty being around him.

Those without financial resources are more vulnerable to calamity—high medical bills, natural disasters, economic downturns, and the like: "The rich man's wealth is his fortress, the ruin of the poor is their poverty" (Prov. 10:15). The poor person is also vulnerable to being oppressed by those with money and power: "The rich rules over the poor, and the borrower becomes the lender's slave" (22:7; also see James 2:6–7; 5:4).

POVERTY CAN BRING SPIRITUAL DANGER

As we saw in Proverbs 30:9, those who are poor might be tempted to acquire through sinful means that which they covet. We had a counseling case in which a pastor's wife who loved fashionable clothes was caught shoplifting at a high-end retailer. Another woman of limited means even stole from the church cash offerings. Many who are under financial pressure are tempted to steal by failing to pay their taxes (Mark 12:17; Rom. 13:6). Proverbs 30:9 reminds us that the worst aspect of believers' stealing is that they profane God's name by their sin. Poor people are also tempted to overcome their poverty through the foolish pursuit of easy money. For example, it is reported that the lottery's best customers are poor people, whose poverty is exacerbated through their losses.[2]

GOD OFFERS HOPE TO THOSE WHO ARE POOR

There is hope, however, for the poor person who turns to our God, who cares for those who are destitute: "For the needy will not

2. www.wsj.com/articles/powerbull-the-lottery-loves-poverty-1503868287.

always be forgotten, nor the hope of the afflicted perish forever" (Ps. 9:18). As we will see in chapter 17, God particularly cares for the poor believer through the community of his faithful people. "One who is gracious to a poor man lends to the LORD, and He will repay him for his good deed" (Prov. 19:17). "But there will be no poor among you" (Deut. 15:4). "He has given freely to the poor, His righteousness endures forever; His horn will be exalted in honor" (Ps. 112:9). God also offers to the poor valuable wisdom to help lift them out of their poverty.

THERE ARE BENEFITS TO BEING RICH

God sometimes sees fit to bless those whom he favors with prosperity: "The crown of the wise is their riches" (Prov. 14:24). "It is the blessing of the LORD that makes rich" (10:22). Abraham, David, Job, and Solomon were blessed by God with wealth. Many enjoy economic success as a result of following God's principles of wisdom (working hard and working smart, avoiding debt, being generous, living with godly integrity, saving, and so on). These passages must be understood, however, not as unconditional promises, but as maxims—principles of wisdom about how God's world works. For example, Proverbs 10:4 wisely declares, "Poor is he who works with a negligent hand, but the hand of the diligent makes rich." It is generally true that people who work harder are better off than lazy people. But sluggards sometimes inherit their parents' money or occasionally win the lottery. Of course, they usually squander their suddenly acquired riches: "Wealth obtained by fraud dwindles" (13:11). "An inheritance gained hurriedly at the beginning will not be blessed in the end" (20:21).

Having money can be good because it enables us to fulfill our responsibilities. The apostle Paul writes, "But if anyone does not provide for his own, and especially for those of his household, he has denied the faith and is worse than an unbeliever" (1 Tim. 5:8). We should be motivated to earn money in order to provide food, clothing, medical care, and shelter for our families. Paul also encourages believers to follow his example of working hard to provide for ourselves and not to expect charity from the church if we refuse to work (2 Thess. 3:7–12).

Money can also protect against life's calamities: "The rich man's wealth is his fortress" (Prov. 10:15). Just as a walled city would have offered protection against invading enemies, financial assets can protect from financial disaster. Those with savings can ride out financial downturns and recessions so that they can thrive when the economy rebounds. When their children are sick, they can afford the best medical care. When their car needs a major repair, they can pay for it without going into debt. If their home or business is damaged or destroyed through some kind of crime or disaster, they can afford to rebuild.

In contrast to the poor person who might be unpopular, "the rich has many friends" (Prov. 14:20 ESV). Again, the proverb is saying not that this is how things ought to be, but how things are in the real world. When a formerly poor person wins the lottery or becomes a sports star, he might suddenly find himself surrounded by people who want to be his friends. Of course, some who lose their wealth learn that they didn't have many true friends after all.

Those who are rich will also be able to enjoy more of the good things that the Lord has put into the world for our enjoyment (Eccl. 5:18; 1 Tim. 4:3–4; 6:17). They can eat finer food, live in nicer homes, take better vacations, and so forth. It is not wrong to enjoy these as gifts from God, so long as we are thankful to him.

Wealth also gives a person a greater opportunity to invest in the Lord's work and to love others. Paul exhorts the rich "to do good, to be rich in good works, to be generous and ready to share, storing up for themselves the treasure of a good foundation for the future, so that they may take hold of that which is life indeed" (1 Tim. 6:18–19). Notice that Paul does not rebuke them for being rich. Nor does he insist that they impoverish themselves as a condition of following Christ. Those who are well off will often live with a constant tension between their burden to invest in the Lord's work and help the poor versus their freedom to enjoy the material blessings that God has supplied.

31

WEALTH CAN BE VERY DANGEROUS

Randy Alcorn suggests that Christians fail the test of prosperity more often than they fail the test of persecution.[3] Scripture contains many warnings about how the rich can make wealth their idol and look to it for security and satisfaction rather than to God. Paul regards greed/covetousness as idolatrous (Col. 3:5). Proverbs 30:9 warns that when we have plenty, we may be tempted to be proudly independent from God, not looking to him as the source of our daily bread. Jesus tells parables of the rich fool, who trusted in his riches rather than in God (Luke 12:13–21), and of the rich man who died and was in torment, in contrast to lowly Lazarus, who was in the bosom of Abraham (16:19–31). Ryle observes of the rich man, "With all his purple and fine linen he had no garment of righteousness."[4] Conversely, Lazarus was not poor but rich: "He was a child of God. He was an heir of glory."[5] Christ also encounters the rich young ruler, who was tragically unwilling to abandon his riches to follow Jesus (18:18–30). Scripture warns us not to make the pursuit of wealth our chief goal in life: "He who trusts in his riches will fall" (Prov. 11:28). "Do not weary yourself to gain wealth, cease from your consideration of it. When you set your eyes on it, it is gone. For wealth certainly makes itself wings like an eagle that flies toward the heavens" (23:4–5). In the day of judgment, all the material treasure we acquire on earth will be useless: "Riches do not profit in the day of wrath, but righteousness delivers from death" (11:4).

WISDOM IS BETTER THAN WEALTH

The book of Proverbs repeatedly exhorts us to value God's wisdom above earthly riches: "How much better it is to get wisdom than gold! And to get understanding is to be chosen above silver" (Prov. 16:16).

3. Randy Alcorn, *Money, Possessions, and Eternity*, 2nd ed. (Wheaton, IL: Tyndale House, 2003), 46.
4. Ryle, *Practical Religion*, 207.
5. Ryle, *Practical Religion*, 207.

Proverbs teaches that it is better to be godly and live a simple lifestyle than to be rich and wicked: "Better is a little with righteousness than great income with injustice" (v. 8). Many other things are to be valued above wealth, including a good reputation (22:1) and a loving home: "Better is a little with the fear of the LORD than great treasure and turmoil with it. Better is a dish of vegetables where love is than a fattened ox served with hatred" (15:16–17). Many who are successful in finance experience total failure in their families. Riches are deceitful in that they promise satisfaction and happiness, but they fail to deliver.

MONEY-LOVE LEADS TO ALL KINDS OF EVIL

When people make money their god, they are willing to do almost anything to gain more wealth. Paul warns: "Those who want to get rich fall into temptation and a snare and many foolish and harmful desires which plunge men into ruin and destruction. For the love of money is a root of all sorts of evil, and some by longing for it have wandered away from the faith and pierced themselves with many griefs" (1 Tim. 6:9–10). In addition to worshiping wealth as an idol or a god, thus breaking the first three of the Ten Commandments, people have broken all the other commandments for the love of money. People motivated by money-love have dishonored God's name, neglected worship, divided families, hated and killed, engaged in sexual immorality, lied, and stolen. Only a recognition that God is more worthy of our love will set us free from financial idolatry.

SUMMARY

God sovereignly chooses the amount of wealth that he entrusts to us: "The LORD makes poor and rich" (1 Sam. 2:7; also see 1 Chron. 29:12). Poverty can be very hard. Wealth can be a blessing. Extremes of poverty or wealth can bring greater temptations. Moderation is generally the safest course. Seeking God and his wisdom first will keep us safe (Matt. 6:33). "The LORD will not allow the righteous to hunger, but He will reject the craving of the wicked" (Prov. 10:3). "The righteous has enough to satisfy his appetite, but the stomach of the wicked is in need" (13:25).

Many books about finances talk about setting goals. I, too, will promote goals, such as living by a budget and being debt-free. But our chief goal should be to glorify God in all things (Mark 12:28–30; 1 Cor. 10:31; 2 Cor. 5:9), including our working, our spending, our saving, and our giving. Alongside that, we should have the goal of using our financial resources to fulfill the second great commandment: to love others (Mark 12:31). Our thoughts and attitudes toward money along with our actions will be governed by these goals.

— QUESTIONS FOR REFLECTION —

1. What, according to Scripture, are some of the difficulties encountered by the poor?
2. What hope does God offer to those who are struggling with poverty?
3. What, according to Scripture, are some of the potential blessings of wealth?
4. What particular temptations do rich people face?
5. What is a biblically balanced attitude toward wealth?

6

HOW DOES GOD USE FINANCIAL TRIALS FOR OUR GOOD?

When my family lived in Southern California, we observed that the weather there tends to fluctuate between extremes. Some years, the rain would be plentiful; then there would be years of drought. There's a lake near where we lived, which during years of abundant rain swelled to the top of its banks and flowed under the freeway. During years of drought, the water level receded so much that the lake no longer made it to the freeway. When the lake was high, it looked beautiful. When the water receded, the lakebed was exposed, along with trash and debris that had accumulated there—not a pretty sight.

In a similar way, a circumstantial drought, such as a financial loss, can cause the lake of our contentment to recede so that our idols, which had been hidden under the waters of our prosperity, are exposed for all to see—like a junky car that had been previously hidden in the lakebed.

As we have already seen, financial matters such as unemployment, debt, and poverty are often the occasion of various temptations and trials. Our sinfully faithless response can compound our problems, but God can also use financial trouble to help us to grow spiritually.

MOST OF OUR MONEY PROBLEMS ARE SPIRITUAL

We in the West live in some of the wealthiest nations in the history of the world and enjoy luxuries that Solomon could have never

35

imagined. We have an abundant variety of food. We dwell in climate-controlled houses. We have incredible technology available at our fingertips that provides entertainment, information, and connection. Yet we remain dissatisfied. How can this be? It is because we are seeking satisfaction in the wrong places. The Lord speaks to us through Isaiah:

> Ho! Every one who thirsts, come to the waters;
> And you who have no money come, buy and eat.
> Come, buy wine and milk
> Without money and without cost.
> Why do you spend money for what is not bread,
> And your wages for what does not satisfy?
> Listen carefully to Me, and eat what is good,
> And delight yourself in abundance. (Isa. 55:1–2)

Many of us are dissatisfied with our finances, not because we don't have enough, but because we have believed the world's lie that more material wealth and possessions will make us happy.[1] Through Isaiah, God makes it clear that our problem is that we are putting our hope in these fleeting earthly things rather than finding our ultimate satisfaction in God. Jesus uses similar imagery as he declares that he is the Bread of Life and that he offers living water to satisfy humankind's spiritual hunger and thirst (John 4:14; 6:48). We need to learn to feed on the spiritual bounty that God offers if we are to be truly happy: "O taste and see that the LORD is good" (Ps. 34:8).

GOD USES FINANCIAL TRIALS TO SANCTIFY US

Thankfully, God cares enough about us to take steps to teach us to find our greatest pleasure and satisfaction in him. He typically does so through trials.

---

1. Randy Alcorn quotes John D. Rockefeller as saying that all his millions brought him no happiness. Randy Alcorn, *Money, Possessions, and Eternity*, 2nd ed. (Wheaton, IL: Tyndale House, 2003), 47.

James encourages us: "Consider it all joy, my brethren, when you encounter various trials, knowing that the testing of your faith produces endurance. And let endurance have its perfect result, so that you may be perfect and complete, lacking in nothing" (James 1:2–4).

While we are tempted to make our comfort our primary concern, God's primary goal for us is our holiness (sanctification). James states that God designs our trials to make us "perfect and complete," which means that God uses our particular trials for the purpose of helping us to grow in those areas in which we are lacking. Hebrews 12:5–11 similarly reminds us that God our Father might lovingly bring trouble into our lives for the purpose of disciplining us—that is, to correct our sinful patterns of thought and action. When financial trials come, such as the loss of a job, unexpected expenses, or major economic reversals, rather than being angry or anxious, we should ask what God might be seeking to teach us through these troubles. In addition to praying for relief from our trials, we should pray for spiritual growth through our trials.

FINANCIAL TRIALS PROVIDE AN OPPORTUNITY FOR US TO LEARN TO TRUST GOD

Jesus taught us to pray, "Give us this day our daily bread" (Matt. 6:11) as an expression of our ongoing dependence on God to meet our material needs. For rich people, this prayer can seem a bit superfluous because they have bread stored up for many years to come. The Lord might see fit to take away some of our earthly security for the purpose of teaching us our need of him. Many of us have experienced times when we didn't know how we would pay the rent or how we would put gas in our car or where we would get our next job. Trouble brings us to the end of ourselves and drives us to our knees in prayer. We are blessed and our faith is strengthened when God answers our prayers. As we go through life, we can reflect back on many occasions when the Lord delivered us from financial troubles. These memories also strengthen our faith as we face future trials and seek to encourage other believers. As the psalmist declares, "I have been young and now

I am old, yet I have not seen the righteous forsaken or his descendants begging bread" (Ps. 37:25).

GOD TEACHES US THE SECRET OF CONTENTMENT

One aspect of our consumeristic culture is that whatever we have never seems to be enough. People are constantly seeking the fancier car, the newer phone, and the bigger house. In contrast, Paul declares:

> I have learned to be content in whatever circumstances I am. I know how to get along with humble means, and I also know how to live in prosperity; in any and every circumstance I have learned the secret of being fulfilled and going hungry, both of having abundance and suffering need. I can do all things through Him who strengthens me. (Phil. 4:11–13)

It is important to understand the meaning of Paul's expression, "I can do all things through Him who strengthens me." This does not refer to some quest for human achievement (e.g., sports), but is in the context of being content while living the constrained frugal life as a prisoner. How could Paul find contentment and even joy in such circumstances? In his letter to the Philippians, Paul speaks of joy or rejoicing over a dozen times. How could he be joyful in prison? It is because his joy was in the Lord (Phil. 2:17–18; 3:1; 4:4) and in the work that God was doing among his people through the gospel of Jesus Christ (1:4, 18, 25; 4:1). Paul's joy was not based on earthly circumstances or wealth. He was thankful for what God gave him (4:15–18). Paul also understood that God was in control of his circumstances, even trials and persecution, and that he was using these for good (1:29). The apostle trusted that God would supply his needs and those of the saints in Philippi: "And my God will supply all your needs according to His riches in glory in Christ Jesus" (4:19). Paul also had a confident expectation of a glorious future with Christ: "For our citizenship is in heaven, from which also we eagerly wait for a Savior, the Lord Jesus Christ; who will transform the body of our humble state into conformity with the body of His glory, by the exertion of the power that He has even to subject all things to Himself" (3:20–21). This enabled him to endure hardship and deprivation, which one day would seem light and momentary compared to the everlasting bliss offered in Christ (Rom. 8:18). This same God-focused, joyful eternal perspective enabled the Philippians to be generous with their limited earthly wealth (Phil. 4:10, 14–17; also see 2 Cor. 8:1–5).

During times of economic drought, we can learn to be content by following the apostle Paul's example. As we have a joyful, Godward eternal focus, we, too, can learn to be content with whatever level of material prosperity God chooses to give us. "Godliness with contentment is great gain, for we brought nothing into the world, and we cannot take anything out of the world. But if we have food and clothing, with these we will be content" (1 Tim. 6:6–8 ESV). Jeremiah Burroughs in his book *The Rare Jewel of Christian Contentment* writes that contentment comes "not by adding more to his condition; but rather by subtracting from his desires, so as to make his desires and his circumstances even and equal."[2] Bishop Ryle adds that "one great secret of happiness in this life is to be of a patient, contented spirit."[3] Ryle wisely adds, "Money, in truth, is one of the most unsatisfying of possessions. It takes away some cares, no doubt; but it brings with it quite as many cares as it takes away."[4] Contentment is also enhanced as we are deliberately and consciously thankful for God's many blessings (1 Thess. 5:18).

THOSE WHO ARE HAPPIEST MAKE LONG-TERM HEAVENLY INVESTMENTS

Many Christians choose to reduce their lifestyle for the sake of investing in the kingdom of heaven (Matt. 6:19–21). They look to

2. www.monergism.com/thethreshold/sdg/contentment02.html.

3. J. C. Ryle, *Practical Religion: Being Plain Papers on the Daily Duties, Experience, Dangers, and Privileges of Professing Christians*, ed. J. I. Packer (Cambridge: James Clarke & Co., 1977), 209.

4. Ryle, *Practical Religion*, 215.

God to meet their material needs, but not all their desires. They so anticipate our glorious heavenly home that they can be content with simplicity in this present life (John 14:1–3).

SUMMARY

The solution to most financial problems begins not merely with a budget or a plan to get out of debt. Rather, we need to address our hearts. Are we growing in our ability to seek and find our ultimate joy and satisfaction in God? Are we more interested in storing up treasures in heaven than on earth? Are we willing to be content with what God sees fit to give us? If so, the practical application of biblical principles of wisdom should come easily.

— QUESTIONS FOR REFLECTION —

1. How can we say that most financial troubles are rooted in spiritual issues?
2. How has God used financial trials to help you to grow spiritually?
3. In what ways might you still need to grow when it comes to your attitude toward money?
4. How has God been faithful to you in the past when you faced financial troubles?
5. How can Christians learn to be content, even if they are financially poor?

PART 2

ACQUIRING MONEY

7

WHAT ARE SOME COMMON MISUNDERSTANDINGS ABOUT ACQUIRING MONEY?

Many people suffer from financial troubles because they have believed worldly myths about how to make money. The Bible mentions several legitimate sources of income and assets, including earnings for labor, an inheritance (Prov. 13:22; 2 Cor. 12:14), return on an investment (Matt. 25:14–30), and gifts (Prov. 18:16; 21:14; Phil. 4:15–17). Our main focus in this part 2 will be working in our vocations. Part 5 of the book will address investment and inheritance issues.

IS WORK A CURSE?

As we will see in more detail in the next chapter, work is designed by God to be a blessing for humankind. Our prefall purpose was not to merely sit around and eat chocolate. God put humans into the garden and charged them to work at subduing the earth (Gen. 2:15). Our fruitful labor is an aspect of our being in God's image. Through his work of creation, God established a pattern for human work and rest (v. 3; Ex. 20:8–11). During his earthly ministry, Jesus was devoted to completing the work that the Father had given him to do (John 17:4). Human sin, however, has made work, which God designed to be a blessing, difficult. But the gospel offers hope for our labor in a fallen world. As we see our work as being ultimately for Christ, our labor can become meaningful and significant, in spite of the effects of the curse (Eph. 6:5–8). The gospel also offers hope of a future new creation in which all the effects of the curse will be reversed: "There will no longer be any curse; and the throne of God and of the Lamb will be in it, and His bond-servants will serve Him" (Rev. 22:3). In heaven we will joyfully work to serve God. Chapter 8 will tell us why work is so important and how it can be a way in which we can serve God now.

ARE THERE LEGITIMATE WAYS TO MAKE LOTS OF MONEY WITHOUT HAVING TO WORK HARD?

As we will see in chapter 9, God's way is for us to make wealth by working hard and working smart. Schemes to make money without skill and effort seek to circumvent God's wisdom and will result in economic loss or dishonest gain, which will not be blessed. Sadly, many squander their time and money by pursuing get-rich-quick schemes and buying lottery tickets.

IS A COLLEGE DEGREE THE TICKET TO A LIFETIME OF HIGH EARNINGS?

While it might have been true a generation ago that a college degree put a person on a track to financial success, times have changed. While college graduates generally earn more money, some of them make much less than other people who have acquired valuable skills without getting college degrees.

AT COLLEGE, SHOULD SOMEONE MAJOR IN WHATEVER SUBJECT HE OR SHE MOST LOVES?

I remember at my college orientation in 1976 that a counselor told incoming students to major in whatever they most enjoyed while trusting that a job would be there when they graduated. Even then, I was not sure that this was wise advice. There were probably more people graduating with degrees in history, music, and philosophy than the market needed. I have many friends who wound up in careers that had nothing to do with what they had studied in college.[1]

The earning power of a degree today largely depends on its value in the marketplace of employers. Certain degrees from respected institutions can lead to a job offer at a very high salary right out of college. Many students, however, graduate from college with an education that hasn't equipped them with skills that are highly valued in the job market. When they realize that their degrees have very limited marketability, they wind up taking low-paying entry-level jobs outside their field of study in which little of their education is utilized. Their difficulties are compounded by high student-debt payments. They might wish that someone had advised them to choose a field of study that would have had greater earning potential. On the other hand, many high-paying jobs in the skilled trades will pay more than what many college graduates can earn. And those with entrepreneurial skills often make the most money by starting their own businesses or being self-employed, regardless of their lack of extensive formal education.

SHOULD EVERYONE HAVE A JOB THAT HE OR SHE LOVES?

Ideally, work should be fulfilling. Some enjoy the blessing of being excited to walk out the door every morning to do a job they love. As we saw earlier, however, the fall has impacted our work in such a way that work is often unpleasant and difficult. Certainly, we are free to pursue finding a vocation that utilizes our abilities and in which we find satisfaction. But there is no guarantee of having our dream job in this life. Paul probably didn't enjoy working with his hands to make tents as much as he enjoyed preaching the gospel, but did what he had to do to provide for himself (2 Thess. 3:7–9). In the same way, we must do

---

1. Some of my friends who teach in the liberal arts claim that there is research showing that liberal arts majors are often well qualified for high-paying jobs outside their academic field.

what is necessary to provide for ourselves and our families (1 Tim. 5:8). Some who are very picky about the work they are willing to do expect others to provide for them while they wait for an acceptable job. Paul warns: "For we hear that some among you walk in idleness, not busy at work, but busybodies. Now such persons we command and encourage in the Lord Jesus Christ to do their work quietly and to earn their own living" (2 Thess. 3:11–12 ESV). While we are free to pursue the best job situation that we can find, each of us is responsible to work.

IF A PERSON DOESN'T ENJOY A JOB, SHOULD HE OR SHE QUIT?

We should be thankful that we live in a time and place with vocational options. Someone who dislikes an employer or the nature of a job is free to search for another position. It is usually wiser for someone to keep his or her old job while looking for a better position rather than to take the risk of being unemployed and without income.

IS IT MOST FAIR FOR EVERYONE TO SHARE EQUALLY IN THE COMMUNITY'S OUTPUT?

Many are attracted to Karl Marx's slogan, "From each according to his ability, to each according to his needs."[2] Some promote socialism as the fairest and most just way to distribute income and wealth. Many resent it that entrepreneurs and managers get paid much more than their employees. The Bible, however, affirms the right of private property in the eighth commandment, "You shall not steal" (Ex. 20:15). Scripture also affirms unequal outcomes according to effort and ability. God has ordained that those who are lazy will experience poverty and that those who are diligent will prosper (Prov. 10:4). Socialism also fails to recognize human depravity, the fruit of which includes laziness. Bishop J. C. Ryle writes: "Universal equality is a very high-sounding

2. en.wikipedia.org/wiki/From_each_according_to_his_ability,_to_each_according_to_his_needs.

expression, and a favourite idea with visionary men. Men in every age have disturbed society by stirring up the poor against the rich, and by preaching up the popular doctrine that all men ought to be equal. But so long as the world is under the present order of things, . . . this universal equality cannot be attained. . . . So long as human nature is what it is, this inequality cannot be prevented."[3] He goes on to point out that if all the property in England were to be equally divided, before long "you would find things as unequal as before"[4] because "some would have been careless . . . . Some would have wasted, and others would have saved and at the end some would be rich and others poor."[5] History has shown that socialism and communism have not led to prosperity for anyone, especially the poor.[6] Yet the fact that socialism is not biblical and does not lead to prosperity does not (as we will see below) lead to the conclusion that unfettered capitalism is a perfect system.

DID THE EARLY CHURCH PRACTICE A FORM OF COMMUNISM?

The New Testament records remarkable acts of loving charity among the early Christians:

And all those who had believed were together and had all things in common; and they began selling their property and possessions and belongings and were sharing them with all, as anyone might have need. . . . And the congregation of those who had believed were of one heart and soul; and not one of them claimed that anything belonging to him was his own, but all things were common property

---

3. J. C. Ryle, *Practical Religion: Being Plain Papers on the Daily Duties, Experience, Dangers, and Privileges of Professing Christians*, ed. J. I. Packer (Cambridge: James Clarke & Co., 1977), 205.

4. Ryle, *Practical Religion*, 206.

5. Ryle, *Practical Religion*, 206.

6. The contrast between South and North Korea exemplifies the contrast between the results of the imperfect system of capitalism and the destructive system of socialism/communism.

to them. . . . For there was not a needy person among them, for all who were owners of lands or houses would sell them and bring the proceeds of the sales and lay them at the apostles' feet, and they would be distributed to each as any had need. (Acts 2:44–45; 4:32, 34–35)

The early church had an extensive ministry to care for widows (Acts 6), and the Gentile churches made great sacrifices to help their brethren in Judea (2 Cor. 8–9). These acts of charity, however, were voluntary and not compelled by any human or church government. When Ananias and Sapphira withheld some of the money from the sale of their property, they were punished—not for failure to be good communists, but for lying to the Holy Spirit (Acts 5:3–4). Peter, when rebuking them, acknowledged that the land and the proceeds legitimately belonged to the couple as their private property: "While it remained unsold, did it not remain your own? And after it was sold, was it not under your control?" (v. 4). When Paul sought financial support for the needy churches, he did not compel wealthier believers to give, but rather encouraged them to give voluntarily and cheerfully: "Each one must do just as he has purposed in his heart, not grudgingly or under compulsion, for God loves a cheerful giver" (2 Cor. 9:7). When Paul addressed the rich, he did not tell them to cease being rich, but rather encouraged them to practice voluntary generosity (1 Tim. 6:17–19).

IS PROFIT EVIL?

Some people (including many politicians) make it sound like profit is immoral. It is true that the Bible warns against taking sinful financial advantage of the desperate situations of others. This includes dramatically raising prices in a time of shortage ("He who withholds grain, the people will curse him," Prov. 11:26) and failing to pay a fair wage[7] ("He who oppresses the poor to make more for himself

---

7. We might take our knowledge of how fairly workers are treated into consideration when choosing which businesses to patronize.

. . . will only come to poverty," Prov. 22:16; also see James 5:1–6). And "the laborer is worthy of his wages" (Luke 10:7). But profit is not immoral when the other party in the exchange is treated fairly as someone provides valuable goods and services. The wise and virtuous woman of Proverbs 31 is an entrepreneur who engages in business and finds satisfaction in the profit she makes (Prov. 31:16, 18). Profit is a God-ordained reward for those who provide excellent goods and services. Competition for profit drives people to provide better goods and services: "The hard-working farmer ought to be the first to receive his share of the crops" (2 Tim. 2:6).

DOES GOD WANT ALL HIS PEOPLE TO BE RICH?

Sadly, this myth is propounded by so-called Christian preachers who claim that we can all be prosperous if we have enough faith. At best, they are confusing the promises of the heavenly kingdom with the realities of serving God in a fallen world. At worst, some are greedy liars. We have already seen that Paul, a most faithful and godly man, often lived a very meager lifestyle (Phil. 4:12). He describes his experience in serving the Lord: "in labor and hardship, through many sleepless nights, in hunger and thirst, often without food, in cold and exposure" (2 Cor. 11:27). Jesus, the one perfect man, lived a simple life without earthly riches. Jesus said, "The foxes have holes and the birds of the air have nests, but the Son of Man has nowhere to lay His head" (Luke 9:58). He warned that his followers would have trouble in this world (John 16:33). Our treasure and our mansions are in the world to come (Matt. 6:20; John 14:1–3).

SUMMARY

The world has expressed its counterfeit financial wisdom through many false myths that will lead only to loss. God's Word offers wisdom that first addresses our heart attitude toward our work and then gives practical advice about how to be successful and fruitful in our vocations to the glory of God.

— Questions for Reflection —

1. What are some wrong attitudes and beliefs that people hold about work?
2. When is it worthwhile to get a college degree?
3. How much fulfillment should we expect from our vocations in a fallen world?
4. How would you answer someone who claimed that the early church practiced a form of communism?

8

WHY IS OUR WORK SO IMPORTANT?

Many people falsely look upon work itself as a curse and a drudgery. Some dream of winning the lottery or inheriting a fortune so that they can march into the boss's office and quit their jobs. Many spend years planning and saving for retirement as they dream of fishing, enjoying their hobbies, playing golf, or traveling the world. Humankind, however, was not designed for mere leisure. God made us in his image to work and to be productive.

GOD WORKS

The Bible begins with work. God himself worked for the six days of creation and found satisfaction in his labor: "God saw all that He had made, and behold, it was very good" (Gen. 1:31; also see Prov. 8:24–31). God's work did not end at creation. Our Lord continues to exert effort to sustain what he has created: "In Him all things hold together" (Col. 1:17). And Jesus declares, "My Father is working until now, and I Myself am working" (John 5:17). So work cannot be a bad thing. God, who is good, works.

GOD CREATED HUMANKIND TO WORK

The garden of Eden was not meant to serve as a luxury resort at which Adam and Eve would do nothing but lie around and eat tropical fruit. God created humankind in his image (Gen. 1:26) with the intent that we work (and rest) in his image. The garden was not created to be self-sustaining. A farmer was required to keep it going and make it productive: "The LORD God took the man and put him into the garden of Eden to cultivate it and keep it" (Gen. 2:15). Humankind was to care for the garden and to maximize its fruitfulness. In this creation mandate God's intent is for humanity, through labor, to establish dominion over the earth. Just as God's work is good, humankind's labor is good. As we portray the image of God in our work, we honor him as we find satisfaction in being productive in establishing dominion over his creation. Our children will be happier when they are busy and productive—even the five-year-old who faithfully does his chores by putting away laundry. Even secular research shows that the greatest predictor of people's happiness and well-being is the satisfaction they take in their work.[1] "There is nothing better for a man than to eat and drink and tell himself that his labor is good. This also I have seen, that it is from the hand of God" (Eccl. 2:24; also see 9:7).

HUMAN SIN HAS MADE WORK TOILSOME

The blessing of human labor was adversely affected by humankind's fall:

> Cursed is the ground because of you;
> In toil you will eat of it
> All the days of your life.
> Both thorns and thistles it shall grow for you;
> And you will eat the plants of the field;
> By the sweat of your face
> You will eat bread,
> Till you return to the ground,
> Because from it you were taken;

1. https://getpocket.com/explore/item/the-strongest-predictor-of-men-s-well-being-isn-t-family-or-health.

For you are dust,
And to dust you shall return. (Gen. 3:17b–19)

In the fallen world, work itself has become unpleasant and difficult. The curse resulted in drought, pestilence, weeds, drudgery, pain, and risk. Some are limited in their ability to work as the result of disability.[2] Often, hard labor is frustratingly fruitless because of the hostile forces of nature or the acts of sinful people. What was meant to be productive and fulfilling becomes empty—vanity of vanities (Eccl. 2:17–23). In addition, human sin compounds the difficulties of our work. There is conflict between management and labor. Workers are oppressed by unjust bosses (James 5:1–6; 1 Peter 2:18–20). Some are tempted to resist work through laziness. Others idolize their vocation and neglect worship, rest, and family.

FALLEN HUMANKIND LABORS
TO ESTABLISH DOMINION

In spite of the effects of the fall on the creation and on human nature, humankind still bears the remnants of God's image. We are inwardly driven toward productivity and progress. In contrast to other creatures, which live from generation to generation without change or advancement, human beings progressively express their God-given dominion by subduing the earth. Civilizations are established. Cities are built. Advances take place in agriculture and technology, which improve our lives. Each generation builds on the accomplishments of those who came before. Even unbelieving human beings find fulfillment in what is accomplished through their labor.[3]

---

2. People with disabilities often find great joy and fulfillment in working according to the abilities that God has given them. I believe that it is much better for them to be productive, rather than remaining inactive. I especially appreciate businesses and churches that make special efforts to give such people opportunities for employment and voluntary service.

3. Scripture records that many advances in civilization, agriculture, culture, and technology came from the unbelieving line (Gen. 4:20–22).

As we see all that has been accomplished by fallen humanity's working to civilize the earth, it is hard to imagine what the world could have been like if we had not fallen, or what the new earth will be like when the effects of sin are removed. But human accomplishments over the centuries have been tainted by our sin. Advancements in technology that save lives and improve the quality of life have also been used to kill, shame, and oppress. Furthermore, rather than giving the Creator and Sustainer of all things glory, godless men arrogantly boast about their achievements and elevate themselves to the place of God. At Babel, humanity sought to unite in establishing human dominion independently of God by creating a great civilization (Gen. 11:1–9). Centuries later, King Nebuchadnezzar exemplified proud human dominion by declaring, "Is this not Babylon the great, which I myself have built as a royal residence by the might of my power and for the glory of my majesty?" (Dan. 4:30). Godless empire-builders of our day tend to demonstrate the same proud attitude, whether their empires be political, social, technological, or corporate. They fail to recognize that "God is opposed to the proud" (James 4:6) and that their ventures will succeed only if the Lord wills (vv. 13–17).

GOD REDEEMS OUR WORK

In the midst of a world in which human beings were striving to establish dominion in opposition to God, the Lord entered into a relationship with his people Israel and promised to establish them as his holy nation under the old covenant. Under his guidance, a better civilization would be established in the midst of a world full of Babel-builders. Through his law, the Lord regulated his people's labor and promised to bless it. The fourth commandment (Sabbath) not only provides for a day of rest, but also calls the Lord's people to work faithfully for six days a week in the image of God, who worked to create "the heavens and the earth, the sea and all that is in them" (Ex. 20:9–11). The Lord promised to bless the labors of his people as long as they remained faithful to his commandments (Deut. 28). Thus, the effects of the curse were partly rolled back, since the land of Israel was to be an outpost of God's kingdom on earth and a type of his eternal heavenly kingdom. The Old Testament also contains many examples of faithful individuals whose labor was especially blessed by God.[4]

Although under the new covenant no political nation experiences God's special covenant blessing, all believers are taught that their labor has significance in God's kingdom. Even slaves could find fulfillment in their toil because their work was ultimately done for Christ:

> Bondservants, obey your earthly masters with fear and trembling, with a sincere heart, as you would Christ, not by the way of eye-service, as people-pleasers, but as bondservants of Christ, doing the will of God from the heart, rendering service with a good will as to the Lord and not to man, knowing that whatever good anyone does, this he will receive back from the Lord, whether he is a bondservant or is free. (Eph. 6:5–8 ESV)

The gospel also calls masters (employers/bosses) to treat their workers with respect and fairness in light of the fact that the Lord is Master of us all (Eph. 6:9).

OUR WORK REFLECTS OUR CHARACTER

One's diligence and faithfulness in his or her work is important because it reveals the quality of the person's character. "He who gathers in summer is a son who acts wisely, but he who sleeps in harvest is a son who acts shamefully" (Prov. 10:5). Those who are godly and wise will work hard and will enjoy blessing from God, but those who are lazy and foolish will suffer the consequences: "Poor is he who works with a negligent hand, but the hand of the diligent makes rich" (v. 4; also see 15:19). The sluggard in Proverbs is a pathetic figure who wastes his life and the resources of others (6:6–11; 24:30–32). Work ethic is

---

4. These include Abraham, Joseph (as a servant, a prisoner, and prime minister), Daniel, and Nehemiah.

a crucial factor in choosing a spouse (31:10ff.). It would be miserable to be married to a sluggard, no matter how charming or attractive the person might initially appear to be.

The New Testament reaffirms the connection between godliness and a commitment to work hard to the glory of God. One mark of true conversion is the putting off of stealing from others (perhaps through laziness) and the putting on of diligent labor not only to meet one's own needs, but also to help others (Eph. 4:28). The apostle Paul went above and beyond what was required of him in order to set an example of hard work (2 Thess. 3:7–9). Professing Christians who refuse to work are not to receive charity, but rather are to be admonished (vv. 10–12). Paul regards someone who refuses to do what is necessary to provide for his family as "worse than an unbeliever" (1 Tim. 5:8).

GOD ESTABLISHES THE WORK OF OUR HANDS

Psalm 90 bemoans the brevity of human life, which, because of sin, fades away like the grass (Ps. 90:3–6). The psalmist acknowledges that the typical life span is relatively brief: "As for the days of our life, they contain seventy years, or if due to strength eighty years, yet their pride is but labor and sorrow; for soon it is gone and we fly away" (v. 10). But then he pleads with God to help us to grasp the brevity of life so that we will use our days wisely: "So teach us to number our days, that we may present to You a heart of wisdom" (v. 12). He concludes the psalm with a plea: "Let the favor of the Lord our God be upon us; and confirm for us the work of our hands; yes, confirm the work of our hands" (v. 17). God has built into humanity the desire to be productive. There is a sense in which ambition for success is a good thing. We want to accomplish something significant with our life's work. Sin and death threaten to keep us from being fulfilled. But as we are united with God, who is eternal (vv. 1–2), we have hope that what we do with our lives, including our vocations, will matter. Charles Spurgeon reminds us: "Man was not made for an idle life; labour is evidently his proper condition. Even when man was perfect he was placed in the garden, not to admire its flowers, but to keep it and to dress it. If he needed to work when he was perfect, much more does he require the discipline of labour now that he is fallen."[5]

Jesus addresses the desire for accomplishment that outlives us: "Do not store up for yourselves treasures on earth, where moth and rust destroy, and where thieves break in and steal. But store up for yourselves treasures in heaven, where neither moth nor rust destroys, and where thieves do not break in or steal; for where your treasure is, there your heart will be also" (Matt. 6:19–21). Godless people labor for a lifetime for that which will not last. Believers work—not just in ministry, but also in their homes and in their earthly vocations—for the glory of God and with the anticipation that the fruit of their labor will last forever.

WE WILL WORK IN HEAVEN

Many Christians view heaven as a luxury retirement resort where we will enjoy everlasting leisure. While it is true that we will enjoy the rest obtained for us by Christ (Heb. 4:1–11; Rev. 14:13), the Bible does not teach that heaven will be a place of inactivity. Just as the Lord charged humankind to be productive in Eden, we should anticipate that we will joyfully labor to the glory of God in the new heavens and the new earth. Revelation 22:3 tells us that we will continue to serve God: "There will no longer be any curse; and the throne of God and of the Lamb will be in it, and His bond-servants will serve Him." While I don't think it is wise to engage in extensive speculation about the nature of our heavenly service for the Lord, it is thrilling to consider that we will enjoy working in a world where there will be no more curse and where we will enjoy the personal presence of the Lord—"they will see His face" (Rev. 22:4).

5. www.spurgeon.org/resource-library/sermons/one-lions-two-lions-no-lion-at-all /#flipbook/.

SUMMARY

Work is important. Work itself is not a curse. God created human-kind in his own image, which includes our capacity to be productive and creative in our work and to establish dominion on the earth. One's approach to his or her vocation reflects the quality of the person's character. The fall has affected our work because both the creation and human nature have been corrupted. God's redemption of humanity is comprehensive. His covenant people labor for his glory in the present and anticipate the new heavens and earth, in which they will serve him with perfect joy and fulfillment.

— QUESTIONS FOR REFLECTION —

1. How would you answer someone who claimed that work is a curse?
2. How should a Christian view retirement?
3. How does your work reveal your true character?
4. How does the curse affect our work?
5. How does God work to redeem the earthly work of his people?
6. What do you think we will do in heaven?

9

WHAT ARE THE KEYS TO SUCCESS IN YOUR VOCATION?

Many individuals and families have a difficult time making ends meet. I have spent hours with counselees, poring over their budgets and trying to find ways to reduce expenses. Often, the only way that a budget can be balanced is to increase income. Others, while not experiencing financial distress, also recognize the benefits that could come from increasing their earnings. Financial goals such as saving for a down payment for a house or retirement could be met. Giving to serve the Lord and care for others could be increased. Many people feel stuck with their low-wage jobs. Why do some people earn more than others? What can be done to increase one's income from vocation? God's Word gives a simple twofold answer: work hard and work smart. Effort times skill produces income.

WORK HARD

Proverbs 10:4 tells us, "Poor is he who works with a negligent hand, but the hand of the diligent makes rich." In an agrarian society, the farmer who works long, hard hours in his field will usually enjoy a richer crop. The sluggard's field, in contrast, is unproductive, and its owner will experience poverty (Prov. 24:30–34). In the same way, a business owner will generally enjoy success in proportion to the effort that he puts into his enterprise: "The hand of the diligent will rule, but the slack hand will be put to forced labor" (12:24).

Employees are usually paid according to the time they spend on the job. The more hours you work, the more you will earn. A person who is in financial trouble should be willing to work long hours in order to meet his or her financial obligations. If an employee proves his or her value by working diligently and honestly, the employer might be eager to offer more hours or shifts. If one employer will not offer enough hours of work, then the employee might be wise to seek a second job or a different employer.

WORK SMART

Proverbs 22:29 declares, "Do you see a man skilled in his work? He will stand before kings; he will not stand before obscure men." The point of this wise saying is that those who are exceptionally skilled in their vocations will be most highly valued. Those whose labor is most highly prized will typically receive the highest pay.

We see how this principle works in our current economy. Employers are willing to pay only according to the benefit they anticipate receiving from the person whom they hire. Unskilled workers in fast food or retail are typically paid minimum wage. On the other hand, highly skilled workers are paid a much greater amount of money per hour of labor because they offer their employer a service that is more valuable.

For example, I had a friend who was an intellectual property lawyer and charged his clients $400 an hour. Those who required his services were willing to pay this very high wage because they expected to benefit at least that much from the work he did for them. My friend had not stumbled into this situation by chance. He gained his skills over time with hard work by earning multiple degrees, passing bar exams, and gaining experience in his specialized field. He earned a reputation for doing outstanding work, and his services were in high demand. On the other hand, the attorney might have a twenty-year-old son who lives at home and works at a fast-food restaurant where he earns $10 an hour to flip burgers and occasionally man the cash register. Each man might leave the house at the same time in the morning, work the same number of hours, and then return home at the same time each night. Each might work equally hard. Yet one has earned $80 at the end of the day and the other has earned $3,200.

Let's say that the twenty-year-old son wants to move away from his parents and get married. But he realizes that his income isn't nearly adequate to support a family. He could increase his income by working twelve hours each day, six days a week, but he would still be making only a fraction of what his father earns, and still not enough to support a family. More is needed than merely working more hours. He needs to improve his skills so that employers will be willing to pay him a higher wage that will multiply his earnings. Howard Dayton points out that an hourly wage increase of $2.50 would produce $250,000 over the course of a career.[1]

ACQUIRE "STAND BEFORE KINGS" SKILLS

Rather than complaining about his low wages, the wise worker will find a way to acquire skills that will make his services much more valuable to potential employers. This could be through formal education, vocational training, an apprenticeship, or other means. As a wise friend reminded me, "People pay for what you do and what you know."

PRACTICAL CONSIDERATIONS FOR TRYING TO INCREASE ONE'S VALUE IN THE JOB MARKET

1. How Has God Made You?

What skills and aptitudes do you have that could be honed and developed? Have you always been great with math, computers, and technology? You might be well suited for a career in computer science or engineering and could consider getting more training in those fields. On the other hand, if you struggle with math and are a technophobe, efforts to get a computer engineering degree would probably be in vain. Or God might have given you the ability to work well with your hands,

1. Howard Dayton, *Your Money Map: A Proven 7-Step Guide to True Financial Freedom* (Chicago: Moody Publishers, 2006), 94.

in which case a trade might be a lucrative vocation for you. Or God might have given you the creativity and drive to be an entrepreneur, in which case you could be well suited to start your own business.

2. What Skills Are Currently in Demand?

Do some research online about which vocations are going to experience growth in demand and income in coming years. For example, as the population in the United States ages, there will probably be a growing need for all kinds of medical professionals. Some of these job certifications can be acquired more quickly than a university degree. Also consider which of these jobs are expected to be in demand and pay well. Which of these careers match up with your aptitudes?

3. What Would It Take for You to Get the Job?

What training, experience, or certification is required for you to acquire the needed vocational skills? Skill acquisition always takes time and usually costs money. Sometimes the investment can be worth it. It takes many years and potentially hundreds of thousands of dollars to complete medical training, but the payoff in the end might make the effort and the money invested in education worthwhile for those who have the ability and opportunity. On the other hand, some people need to quickly improve their earnings potential. For example, a married man with limited vocational skills might not have several years to spend in earning a degree. He might need to discover the quickest path between his current earnings potential and a job that would provide more adequately for his family. In such a case, vocational training, an apprenticeship, or specialized training in a particular skill might work best to equip him to fulfill his obligations.

MONEY ISN'T THE ONLY CONSIDERATION WHEN IT COMES TO CHOOSING A VOCATION

A few qualifications must be pointed out about the "work times skill equals success" principle. While it is important that a person earn enough money to fulfill his or her God-given responsibilities (1 Tim.

5:8), financial reward is not the only factor in choosing a vocation. The most important consideration is determining how we can best serve God. We are also free to consider our own desires and interests while choosing our vocation. Some jobs pay only an adequate wage, but those who hold them are able to meet their financial obligations while finding great fulfillment. Many pastors and missionaries are highly skilled, having achieved advanced degrees and competence, yet these jobs are typically not high-paying. Most who serve in ministry could make more money in another vocation, but find great delight in serving the Lord. They are content with having just enough (Phil. 4:11; 1 Tim. 6:8). Not all work is paid. Some women (and men) choose to stay home as they devote their valuable God-given abilities to bring blessing to their children and their spouses.[2]

YOU ARE FREE TO LOOK FOR A BETTER JOB

It could be that you have "stand before kings" skills, but your employer is paying you an ordinary or inadequate wage. In other times and places in history, you would have been stuck as a slave or an indentured servant, not able to reap the just rewards of your valuable labor. In our day, however, you are perfectly free to make your labor available to others who would show more appreciation for your abilities and pay you a "stand before kings" salary.

In years past, someone graduating from college or high school might go straight to work for a corporation. Both sides would anticipate a mutually loyal relationship that would last until retirement. My father went to work for IBM right out of college in the late 1950s. When business was booming, the employees worked extra hard, and the corporation sought to reward their loyalty by sharing the business's prosperity. During times of economic recession, IBM avoided layoffs. While my father was free to leave and work for a competitor, he

---

2. For one spouse to stay at home usually requires that the other spouse work very hard and work very smart in order to earn enough income for the family's needs to be met.

happily stayed with IBM until he retired in his early 60s, at which time he received a generous pension. Such situations, however, are exceedingly rare in the private sector these days. Now it is common for a skilled employee to have to change employers several times throughout his career in order to earn what his abilities deserve. A person who continues to accept an unfair wage should not merely hope that his boss will come to his senses and offer him a raise. Nor is there benefit in complaining about the injustice of his situation. Rather, he should seek an employer that will gladly pay him what his skilled labor is worth.

SUMMARY

The truth recorded in Proverbs three thousand years ago is still true today. The key to being paid well for your labor is working hard and working smart. It is wise and commendable for godly people to maximize their income so that they can meet their own needs and those of their families. In addition, as they prosper they are able to serve the Lord by giving more resources to his work and those in need. Wise people will be proactive in seeking to improve their skills (value in the labor marketplace) and to actively seek employment that will give them opportunity to fully use their abilities.

— QUESTIONS FOR REFLECTION —

1. What is the basic biblical formula for financial success?
2. What concrete steps can one take to increase income?
3. How should one choose a career?
4. When is it wise and right to look for another job?
5. What considerations, other than money, should one take into account when choosing a career?
6. What actions can you take to pursue fruitfulness in your vocation?

10

WHAT DISTINGUISHES THE WISE WORKER FROM THE SLUGGARD?

We have already seen that your work reflects your character and that the biblical formula for vocational success is to work hard and to work smart. God's Word contains more specific vocational wisdom, both positively in the characteristics of the wise worker and negatively in terms of the sluggard, who is one of the most pathetic examples of the fool in the book of Proverbs.

Proverbs 6 brings out the contrast between the ant and the sluggard:

> Go to the ant, O sluggard;
> Observe her ways and be wise,
> Which having no chief,
> Officer or ruler,
> Prepares her food in the summer
> And gathers her provision in the harvest.
> How long will you lie down, O sluggard?
> When will you arise from your sleep?
> "A little sleep, a little slumber,
> A little folding of the hands to rest"—
> Your poverty will come in like a vagabond
> And your need like an armed man. (Prov. 6:6–11)

THE WISE WORKER, AS PORTRAYED BY THE ANT

1. The Wise Worker Doesn't Merely Work

He or she always works hard. You have never seen an ant standing still (unless she is dead). We have all been in situations in restaurants or stores in which we received poor service because the employees seemed uninterested in their work. You are waiting for your food while they are talking to each other. I have spoken to business owners who have complained that it is hard to find workers who will show up on time and put forth a full day's effort. Some workers are motivated to work hard only when the boss is around to notice them. The New Testament elevates our motivation to work hard because we are serving Christ through our labor, whether or not the boss sees and recognizes our efforts, "not by the way of eye-service, as people-pleasers, but as bondservants of Christ, doing the will of God from the heart, rendering service with a good will as to the Lord and not to man" (Eph. 6:6–7 ESV).

2. The Wise Worker Takes Initiative and Works Well without Supervision

As the ant labors on, "having no chief, officer or ruler" (Prov. 6:7), so the wise worker blesses his or her employer by recognizing what needs to be done and taking action. Immature workers must be micromanaged. After they have finished one assigned task, they will stand around until someone tells them the next thing to do. Employers value workers who stay busy, figure out what needs to be done, and solve problems on their own.

3. The Wise Worker Plans for the Future

As the ant gathers and stores food in the harvest, the wise worker thinks ahead. Recently, my wife ordered a salad at a local fast-food restaurant. As we sat down to eat, we noticed that her meal had not come with any utensils. When we asked for a fork, we were told by an uninterested employee that they had run out. Someone had not planned ahead. Being prepared for the future could include anticipating such needs in the workplace. It could also involve planning for one's future career by improving one's value in the job marketplace through enhancing skills and education.

4. The Wise Worker Patiently Builds Wealth through Hard Work

"He who tills his land will have plenty of food, but he who follows empty pursuits will have poverty in plenty" (Prov. 28:19). The ant, through painstaking diligence, has enough to eat. The wise worker shuns get-rich-quick schemes and diligently engages in his vocation so that over time, "little by little" (13:11 ESV), he can build a measure of financial security for his family.

5. The Wise Worker Is a Good Steward of Resources

"Know well the condition of your flocks, and pay attention to your herds; for riches are not forever" (Prov. 27:23–24). In an agrarian economy, long-term financial success depended on taking care of one's animals, fields, and tools. In contrast, the sluggard's field has been neglected and is no longer productive, thus leading to poverty (24:30–34). Many people today engage in business that requires maintenance of equipment or organization of a work space in order to ensure ongoing success. For many of us, our tools are our skills, which must be maintained and honed through ongoing education.

6. The Wise Worker Is Content with His or Her Wages

When John the Baptist was asked by Roman soldiers what they should do in order to express their repentance toward God, his reply included an exhortation to be content with their wages (Luke 3:14). The opposite of contentment is grumbling, which Scripture treats as a significant sin against God (1 Cor. 10:10; Phil. 2:14). Many workplaces are characterized by employees' complaining about wages and working conditions, even in front of customers. Thankfully, we are not slaves, as many of the early Christians were. As we have already observed, in our day, if one believes that he or she is not being paid a fair wage or being treated fairly, the person is free to ask for a higher salary in keeping with his or her value to the employer. If the employer is not willing to pay a fair wage and treat workers with respect, then their employees are free to offer their services to a different employer that will value their work.

7. The Wise Worker Views His or Her Vocation as Having Significance before God

Many have heard the story of a traveler who came upon three men working. He asked the first man what he was doing, and the man replied that he was laying bricks. The traveler asked the second man the same question, and he said that he was putting up a wall. When the traveler got to the third man and asked him what he was doing, he stated that he was building a cathedral.[1] A more modern version of the same parable involves a janitor, sweeping floors at NASA, who is asked what he is doing. His reply might be, "I am helping to send a man to the moon." For Christians, our work is fulfilling God's call to subdue the earth (Gen. 1:28; 2:15) and to serve Christ (Col. 3:23). The Reformer Martin Luther recaptured the idea that all legitimate vocation (not just monks or those in full-time ministry) is significant; he asserted that the milkmaid and the manure hauler have noble vocations because they do God's work in the world.[2] Tim Keller points out that our work also fulfills the second greatest commandment as an act of love of neighbor, who benefits from our skilled labor.[3] As the Israelites were to be a blessing when they were exiles in Babylon, we can be a blessing as we dwell in the city of man, awaiting the revelation of the City of God (Jer. 29:7).

THE SLUGGARD IS THE OPPOSITE OF THE WISE WORKER

I have counseled in many very hard cases with people who have been depressed, angry, anxious, and so on. I have never been more

1. www.huffpost.com/entry/are-you-laying-bricks-or_b_12387634.
2. www.thegospelcoalition.org/article/the-power-and-danger-in-luthers-concept-of-work/.
3. Timothy Keller, *Every Good Endeavor* (New York: Dutton, 2012), 74–76.

frustrated than when counseling a sluggard. Proverbs accurately por-
trays his poor character in a way that is full of biting sarcasm—which
is sometimes humorous in a somewhat pathetic way.

1. The Sluggard Loves Rest and Recreation

"As the door turns on its hinges, so does the sluggard on his bed"
(Prov. 26:14; also see 6:9–10). While the door hinges might have a
useful purpose, the sluggard is completely worthless. Sluggards might
be up on all the latest movies and TV shows. They might be passionate
about their video games. But they are failures at work.

2. The Sluggard Hates Hard Work

"The sluggard buries his hand in the dish, but will not even bring
it back to his mouth" (Prov. 19:24). "A lazy man does not roast
his prey" (12:27). We have already seen that he is lazy, refusing to
emerge from his bed to earn a living. Now it appears that someone
has given him food, but he is too lazy even to cook it. If someone
else cooks it for him, he won't even elevate his hand from the plate
to his mouth.[4]

3. The Sluggard Is Proud

"The sluggard is wiser in his own eyes than seven men who can
give a discreet answer" (Prov. 26:16). A sluggard will not listen to wise
counsel or rebuke (9:8). When you try to reason with him about why
he needs to apply himself to find a job and to provide for himself, he
will exhaust you with reasons why he cannot or should not have to
work hard. He is picky about the work that he would accept. The right
situation never seems to come along.

---

4. Not all who need to receive food are lazy or sluggards. Food shortages, famines,
crop failures, extreme poverty, homelessness, war-caused geographic disruption, and
other causes may result in the need for the church, private and public charities, or the
government to provide food or the means to obtain it. Compassion for the poor and
hungry is a biblical, godlike virtue (Deut. 15:11; Lev. 23:22; Job 22:7; Prov. 22:9; Ps.
146:7; Isa. 58:10; James 2:14-17).

4. The Sluggard Is a Talker, Not a Worker

"In all labor there is profit, but mere talk leads only to poverty" (Prov. 14:23). The sluggard might talk about the business that he plans to start or the career that he expects to launch, but nothing ever comes of it. Charles Spurgeon, speaking from Proverbs 26:13, declares of the sluggard, "You first notice about him that his tongue is not slothful:— 'The slothful man saith.' The man who is lazy all over is generally very busy with his tongue."[5]

5. The Sluggard Is Full of Excuses

"The sluggard says, 'There is a lion outside; I will be killed in the streets!'" (Prov. 22:13). In contrast to other sinners, such as drunks and adulterers, who will at least admit that they have a problem, I have never met a sluggard who admits that he is a sluggard. There is always a reason why he isn't able to perform a certain job or why he can't even rouse himself out of bed (or off the couch) to seek work. I have often thought that many sluggards, if they worked as hard at a job as they work at avoiding real work, could be wealthy. Spurgeon adds, "When a man is thoroughly eaten up with the dry rot of laziness he generally finds some kind of excuse, though his crime is really inexcusable. 'There is a lion in the way.'"[6]

6. The Sluggard Procrastinates

"The sluggard does not plow after the autumn, so he begs during the harvest and has nothing" (Prov. 20:4). He puts off until tomorrow what should have been done today (such as looking for a job).

7. The Sluggard Is a Destroyer

"He also who is slack in his work is brother to him who destroys" (Prov. 18:9). "Like vinegar to the teeth and smoke to the eyes, so is the lazy one to those who send him" (10:26). Woe to the employer that

5. www.spurgeon.org/resource-library/sermons/one-lions-two-lions-no-lion-at-all /#flipbook/.

6. www.spurgeon.org/resource-library/sermons/one-lions-two-lions-no-lion-at-all /#flipbook/.

hires a sluggard. Businesses are destroyed by lazy, apathetic employees. Even national economies are damaged by unproductive people who take from those willing to work.

8. The Sluggard Expects Others to Provide for Him

As we have already seen from Proverbs 20:4, after the sluggard has refused to work for himself, he asks others to meet his needs. The early church also faced the problem of lazy busybodies who refused to work and then expected the church to offer them charity (2 Thess. 3:6–12).

GOD HAS ORDAINED
CONSEQUENCES FOR SLUGGARDS

"The way of the lazy is as a hedge of thorns" (Prov. 15:19). Those who are lazy will be poor (6:11; 10:4). They will suffer many regrets as they see others succeed and enjoy the blessings of their labors with families, houses, businesses, and possessions. "The soul of the sluggard craves and gets nothing, but the soul of the diligent is made fat" (13:4). I have counseled lazy men who were frustrated that they were not married because the women they desired were wise enough to recognize their bad character. One hope for sluggards is that their poverty will drive them to change: "A worker's appetite works for him, for his hunger urges him on" (16:26). If they are able to get any job at all, it will be low-paying with limited responsibility: "The hand of the diligent will rule, but the slack hand will be put to forced labor" (12:24).

DON'T ENABLE SLUGGARDS

While it is generally appropriate to help the poor, it is unwise, unjust, and even unhelpful to give resources to those who refuse to work. We once saw a sign on the pier at San Clemente, California: "Please do not feed the birds. Feeding creates a dependent population. There is a potential health hazard, and it makes a costly mess." What is true of birds is true of sluggards. For churches, governments,[7] and individuals to give resources to sluggards circumvents the God-ordained consequences of laziness and actually keeps them in poverty.

In contrast, a primary Old Testament approach to helping the poor was gleaning, which allowed those in need to work for what they would eat (Lev. 19:9–10; Ruth 2). Offering productive work is usually the best way to help a person in need and can be a good test of whether the person's need is genuine or whether he or she is a sluggard.

The gospel gives hope even to sluggards, who can be transformed from those who take to those who give in light of God's gift to them (Eph. 4:28).

SUMMARY

When we think of significant virtues and vices, issues such as sexual immorality and substance abuse immediately come to mind. Scripture teaches that excellence in work is an important virtue and that laziness is a great vice. In counseling with young couples who are considering marriage, one of the most important issues to be covered is the work ethic of the prospective spouse. In the old days, the girl's father might expect a young man to demonstrate his commitment to working hard to provide for his bride. The wise mother in Proverbs 31 advises her son to marry a woman of excellence, which means that she would also be a woman of diligence who doesn't "eat the bread of idleness" (Prov. 31:12–27).

— QUESTIONS FOR REFLECTION —

1. How do you measure up to the biblical standards for a wise worker?

---

7. Some government policies create disincentives for work. I have read news reports about unemployed persons who refused work because they were better off keeping their government benefits.

2. How does Jesus exemplify the biblical standards for a wise worker?
3. How should society deal with sluggards?
4. How should the church deal with sluggards?
5. How would you counsel a sluggard?

11

WHAT ARE ILLEGITIMATE WAYS OF MAKING MONEY?

While it is good and wise to be concerned about earning enough money to meet one's financial obligations, there are many temptations to sinfully or unwisely pursue wealth. "Ill-gotten gains do not profit" (Prov. 10:2). The sinful pursuit of wealth is caused by sins of the heart, including pride, greed, idolatry, and unbelief. Scripture makes it clear that the sinful pursuit of wealth will never profit in the long run.

DON'T BE IN A RUSH TO GET RICH

We have seen that God's way for us to earn money is by working hard (Prov. 10:4) and working smart or skillfully (22:29) and that such an approach will grow one's wealth gradually over time (13:11). Many, however, are impatient and greedy. They are unwilling to put forth the effort to acquire and apply valuable skills in the workplace. They insist that they must acquire wealth quickly. Scripture warns, "He who makes haste to be rich will not go unpunished. . . . A man with an evil eye hastens after wealth and does not know that want will come upon him" (28:20b, 22). Such people are vulnerable to get-rich-quick schemes that prey on the impatience and pride of those who are unwilling to follow God's wisdom for vocational success. They allow themselves to be convinced that they have discovered a secret for obtaining wealth without skillful labor. Almost invariably, such schemes leave people worse off financially (12:11; 28:19).

DON'T BUILD YOUR WEALTH
BY ANY FORM OF THEFT

When we read the eighth commandment, which forbids stealing (Ex. 20:15), what first comes to mind might be shoplifting, pickpocketing, burglary, embezzlement, and armed robbery. But there are more subtle ways of stealing from one's neighbors. One common sin of the ancient world was that merchants would keep two sets of weights—one for buying and another for selling. The problem was so bad that archaeologists who have dug up weights are not sure what the accurate value should be. "Differing weights are an abomination to the LORD, and a false scale is not good" (Prov. 20:23). It would be like a gas station where the pumps dispensed only three quarts and charged for a gallon, or like a grocery store where the produce scales were inaccurate. Similar ways of stealing would be to accept pay for eight hours when you worked only six, to cheat on your income taxes, or to bill a client for more materials and labor than you had actually provided. Believers who come under conviction for stealing should make restitution (Luke 19:8).

Another form of stealing takes place when sluggards refuse to work and then expect others (the church, family members, and friends) to provide for them. When sluggards are converted, the power of the gospel transforms them into diligent workers who are givers rather than takers (Eph. 4:28). Many would regard the government practice that takes resources away from those who are diligent and productive to give to those who are unwilling to take responsibility to provide for themselves as a form of theft.

DON'T DECEIVE OTHERS IN FINANCIAL MATTERS

We might also be tempted to deceive others in order to gain wealth. "The acquisition of treasures by a lying tongue is a fleeting vapor, the pursuit of death" (Prov. 21:6). This happens when a salesman misleads a client about his product (or his competitor's) or when a contractor cuts corners by using materials inferior to what he had promised. Another way of deceiving others is to trick them out of the value of their goods and services. "'Bad, bad,' says the buyer, but when he goes his way, then he boasts" (20:14). This verse makes me think of people who go on the TV program *Antiques Roadshow* and brag about how they had knowingly bought a rare, valuable item at a garage sale for a fraction of its true value, thus taking advantage of the seller's ignorance. Such a transaction might be legal, but it does not reflect biblical morality of loving one's neighbor as oneself.

DON'T MISTREAT OTHERS FOR GAIN

While Scripture acknowledges that making a profit by providing valuable goods and services is good, economic power should not be abused in exploiting the weak: "He who oppresses the poor to make more for himself or who gives to the rich, will only come to poverty" (Prov. 22:16). Jesus said that the laborer deserves his wages (Luke 10:7). The Old Testament law required that workers be paid their wages on a timely basis (Deut. 24:15). Scripture warns that God will judge employers that mistreat their workers: "Behold, the pay of the laborers who mowed your fields, and which has been withheld by you, cries out against you; and the outcry of those who did the harvesting has reached the ears of the Lord of Sabaoth" (James 5:4). While the general principles of supply and demand are useful in setting reasonable wages and prices, the godly are expected to treat others fairly and to resist the temptation to take advantage of their distress. For example, in times when there are shortages of certain necessities, "he who withholds grain, the people will curse him, but blessing will be on the head of him who sells it" (Prov. 11:26).

DON'T PURSUE WEALTH AT THE EXPENSE OF YOUR RELATIONSHIP WITH GOD, YOUR FAMILY, AND THE CHURCH

While the sluggard is tempted to ignore six-sevenths of the fourth commandment, "Six days you shall labor and do all your work," the workaholic is tempted to neglect worship and rest because he has made an idol of his vocation (Ex. 20:8–11). My first job after college was with a consulting firm. I was confident that my commitment to a biblical work ethic would contribute to my success and would make me stand above my peers. I was surprised, however, to find that my coworkers so idolized their careers that I could not keep up with them. They would work on weekends and late into the evening on weekdays, even when such long hours weren't necessary. While I sought to work hard and was willing to work overtime when necessary, I was newly married and wanted to spend time with my wife. I was very much involved in our church and was unwilling to miss worship on the Lord's Day. Sadly, I observed that some of my coworkers appeared to suffer as a result of their workaholism. During my first year with this company, both my boss and his boss were in the process of divorce. A few years later, the head of our division suddenly died of a heart attack at a relatively young age. "There was a certain man without a dependent, having neither a son nor a brother, yet there was no end to all his labor. Indeed, his eyes were not satisfied with riches and he never asked, 'And for whom am I laboring and depriving myself of pleasure?' This too is vanity and it is a grievous task" (Eccl. 4:8). Don't invest your time merely toward making money. Invest yourself in your own soul, in your family (9:9), and in your church.

Setting aside the Lord's Day for worship and rest takes faith, which thereby honors God. Just as the Israelites trusted God to supply sufficient manna on the sixth day to feed them on the seventh day, our decision to follow God's creation pattern of weekly rest expresses our faith that he will provide for our needs without our having to work seven days a week. Making worship a priority instead of using Sunday as merely one more day in which to pursue money honors God and demonstrates that we value heavenly treasure (Matt. 6:24). God's gift of a day of rest is also beneficial for our souls and our bodies (Mark 2:27).

GOD WILL NOT ALLOW THOSE WHO
SINFULLY PURSUE WEALTH TO PROSPER

The biblical prohibitions against the sinful pursuit of wealth are accompanied by warnings that such wealth will be lost: "Wealth obtained by fraud dwindles" (Prov. 13:11a). "Bread obtained by falsehood is sweet to a man, but afterward his mouth will be filled with gravel" (20:17). "He who profits illicitly troubles his own house" (15:27). In addition, those who oppress the poor and take advantage of others through exacting usurious interest will not profit in the long run (22:16; 28:8). This is because God is sovereign and just. Psalm 73 reminds us that while it is true that the wicked might seem to prosper in this life, which can be vexing to the righteous, God will ultimately enact justice. We need not envy them. "When I pondered to understand this, it was troublesome in my sight until I came into the sanctuary of God; then I perceived their end" (Ps. 73:16–17).

THE SINFUL PURSUIT OF WEALTH
IS A SPIRITUAL PROBLEM

Jesus teaches that sinful behavior comes from a sinful heart: "And He was saying, 'That which proceeds out of the man, that is what defiles the man. For from within, out of the heart of men, proceed the evil thoughts, fornications, thefts, murders, adulteries, deeds of coveting and wickedness, as well as deceit, sensuality, envy, slander, pride, and foolishness. All these evil things proceed from within and defile the man" (Mark 7:20–23). The main spiritual issues behind financial sins are idolatry and pride. Greedy (or covetous) people make money more important than God, which Paul says amounts to idolatry (Col. 3:5). They look to money to bring them the happiness and satisfaction that only God offers (Isa. 55:1–2). They devote their lives to pursuing that which they most value instead of pursuing God (Matt. 6:19–21). They are willing to sin in order to gain their idol (1 Tim. 6:10).[1] They

---

1. Biblical examples of fatal greed are Achan (Josh. 7), Gehazi (2 Kings 5), Judas

are also proud to think that they can get rich by defying the financial wisdom that God has revealed. Their pride is further manifested by their denial of God's sovereign justice in their belief that they will get by with their financial sins and avoid God's judgment.

SUMMARY

Though thousands of years have passed since Scripture was written, human nature has not changed. People are still tempted to make wealth an idol, and they are still tempted to pursue riches in the same kinds of sinful and foolish ways. While it is good for believers to know about the specific biblical warnings against ill-gotten gains, so that they will neither be exploited nor be guilty of exploiting others, it is more important that our hearts be right. The cure to financial sin and folly is not merely to change outward behavior by acting less sinfully and living more wisely. There must be a change of heart to repent of pride and idolatry and to value God above all else while trusting that his ways are best.

— QUESTIONS FOR REFLECTION —

1. What are some examples of ways in which people have been led astray by get-rich-quick schemes?
2. How might it be possible to legally defraud others?
3. What are the root heart sins that lead to sinful and foolish financial actions?
4. How do sluggards and workaholics each break the fourth commandment?

(Matt. 26:15), Ananias and Sapphira (Acts 5:1–11), and Simon the sorcerer (Acts 8:20).

12

MAY CHRISTIANS GAMBLE?

Grace and Gil phoned, saying that they urgently needed to meet with us. When they arrived and sat down, Grace was weeping and Gil had his head down. I was wondering what Gil could have done. Adultery? No. It turns out that Gil had lost his job, but hadn't told Grace. Each day he would act as though he were going off to work, but he really went to the local casino. He had been convinced from a book he purchased that he could win at blackjack by following a certain system. It wasn't working, yet he wasn't losing faith. But he had run his credit card up past its limit. Grace found out when the debt collectors started calling the house. Then she looked at their credit-card bills and saw thousands of dollars in charges to the local casinos. Grace wept because she felt that Gil had deceived her, and she wondered whether she could ever trust him again. Gil just looked down at the floor, despairing of ever being able to pay off his debts and regain his wife's respect.

As of this writing, government-run lotteries take in $80 billion a year in the United States,[1] amounting to well over $200 per capita or nearly $1,000 a year for a typical family. An equal amount is spent in other forms of gambling, including casinos, online gambling, and sports gambling.[2] Is gambling an innocent pleasure in

1. www.bloomberg.com/news/articles/2018-09-12/the-poorest-americans-risk-the-most-in-hopes-of-striking-it-rich.
2. www.onlineunitedstatescasinos.com/usa-gambling-facts/.

which Christians can participate freely? Or is gambling unwise or even inherently sinful?

GAMBLING AND LOTTERIES PLAY ON PEOPLE'S GREED

Gambling is the ultimate get-rich-quick scheme by which people hope to instantly gain incredible wealth. Yet they are almost always poorer for their efforts. Lotteries and casinos play on the bankrupt values of worldliness as they encourage us to envy the winners, as though suddenly gaining a fortune would solve all our problems and bring lifelong happiness and fulfillment. Jesus warns, "Beware, and be on your guard against every form of greed; for not even when one has an abundance does his life consist of his possessions" (Luke 12:15).

GAMBLING AND LOTTERIES SUBVERT THE WORK ETHIC

Scripture teaches that wealth is gained over time through hard work and skill. Many poor people have been convinced that the most likely path to wealth and privilege is through gambling. "Lotteries have become an alternative mechanism of social mobility—a way of achieving financial success in an economy that's increasingly bereft of those opportunities," said Jonathan Cohen, a PhD candidate at the University of Virginia who's completing his dissertation on American lotteries. "There's an understandable belief that the economy is rigged and your best chance of making it out and getting rich is through the lottery, not through your job or savings."[3] People who should be working to advance their careers through gaining more valuable skills and working harder put their hope in picking the right lucky numbers. I have counseled men who thought they could dig out of their financial troubles through gambling, rather than pursuing gainful employment.

---

3. www.bloomberg.com/news/articles/2018-09-12/the-poorest-americans-risk-the-most-in-hopes-of-striking-it-rich.

GAMBLING AND LOTTERIES DO THE MOST HARM TO THOSE WHO CAN LEAST AFFORD IT

"The lowest-income households in the U.S. on average spend $412 annually on lottery tickets, which is nearly four times the $105 a year spent by the highest-earning households. . . . Low earners spend 2.5 percent of their take-home pay on lottery tickets."[4] These funds could be spent on groceries, put toward better healthcare, or saved for the future. Gambling is by nature psychologically addictive, and many gambling "games" (such as slot machines) are designed to keep the player engaged as long as possible.[5] Gambling causes much greater harm to those who become addicted, often resulting in personal financial disaster and significant costs to society in general.

GAMBLING AND LOTTERIES EMPLOY DECEPTION

In addition to the moral lie that money brings happiness, the gambling industry employs other forms of deception to get people to participate. Lotteries and casinos advertise: "You could be next. Keep dreaming." The odds of winning a large prize, however, are minuscule. Many extremely unlikely events, including being literally struck by lightning, are more likely to happen to you than winning a huge lottery prize.[6] Another subtle form of deception is employed when a casino tries to create a more positive or innocent image for its business, calling it *gaming* rather than *gambling*.

The lottery is often promoted as benefiting children through funding public education. The reality is that less than a third of what is spent on lottery tickets goes back into education and other government programs.[7]

---

4. www.bloomberg.com/news/articles/2018-09-12/the-poorest-americans-risk-the-most-in-hopes-of-striking-it-rich.

5. Many have noticed that most people sitting at the slot machines in a casino appear sad, dazed, and sullen.

6. www.independent.co.uk/news/uk/home-news/11-things-that-are-more-likely-than-winning-the-lottery-a6798856.html.

7. money.com/money/4912284/powerball-money-funds-education/.

It is also ironic that the lottery, which is supposed to promote learning, is rooted in intellectual irrationality and moral greed. Many children from impoverished homes are negatively affected when their parents waste money on lottery tickets—money that could have been used instead to provide for the children's needs.

GAMBLING DOES MORE THAN JUST CAUSE FINANCIAL HARM

In addition to the evils listed above, gambling is typically accompanied by an increase in substance abuse/drunkenness, sexual immorality/prostitution, theft, suicide, traffic fatalities, involvement of organized crime, and family breakups.

EVEN IF YOU WIN, YOU LOSE

Only two things can happen when you gamble, and both are bad. You will probably lose money, which is bad stewardship, but it can be equally harmful if you win. Rather than gaining money through hard work that provides value to those who pay you, winning at gambling defrauds the losers by taking their money without offering them any benefit. God will not bless ill-gotten gains: "Ill-gotten gains do not profit, but righteousness delivers from death" (Prov. 10:2; also see Ps. 62:10).

Many years ago I had a connecting flight through the Las Vegas airport, where I saw a slot machine that claimed to have a potential payoff of tens of millions of dollars. The thought passed through my mind, "What would it hurt to put in a few quarters?" Then I said to myself, "But what if I were to win? Would I really be better off? Or would the riches be a snare to me (Prov. 30:8–9)? Furthermore, what would happen to my testimony? I can just see the headlines: 'Pastor wins slot jackpot.'" I imagined my picture on billboards throughout Nevada. I didn't play the machine.

I have had counselees who believed that they could earn a living by playing poker in casinos against other gamblers. They were probably proud and self-deceived to think that they could outwit a table full of people who had also convinced themselves that they were going to come out on top. Even if they were to succeed, they would have made money not through earning it in a biblical way by providing benefit to others, but through exploiting the pride and foolishness of others.

It has been well documented that many lottery winners have foolishly squandered their winnings and have wound up in poverty,[8] illustrating the biblical principle that ill-gotten gains suddenly obtained do not endure: "Do not weary yourself to gain wealth. Cease from your consideration of it. When you set your eyes on it, it is gone. For wealth certainly makes itself wings like an eagle that flies toward the heavens" (Prov. 23:4–5; also see 10:2; 13:11; 28:22).

WHAT ABOUT GAMBLING A LITTLE BIT JUST FOR RECREATION?

While some of us would like to forbid all Christians from all forms of gambling, many regard very limited gambling as a matter of Christian freedom. Some Christians contend that there is no harm in buying a few lottery tickets or gambling a little bit in a casino for fun, as long as we don't spend so much money that it negatively affects our ability to meet our financial obligations. They argue that almost all of us spend more money than necessary on clothes, meals, sporting events, entertainment, and so on.

While I do not believe that someone should undergo church discipline because he or she bought a lottery ticket, played penny-ante poker with friends, or put a quarter into a slot machine, I believe that one should consider certain questions before engaging in gambling: Do you really want to support a system that relies on deception and does so much harm to others? Given that gambling is designed to be addictive, are you certain that you can resist the temptation? "Therefore let him who thinks he stands take heed that he does not fall" (1 Cor. 10:12;

8. www.cnbc.com/2017/08/25/heres-why-lottery-winners-go-broke.html.

also see Matt. 5:29). Can you do this to the glory of God (1 Cor. 10:31)? Does Ephesians 5:11 apply ("Do not participate in the unfruitful deeds of darkness, but instead even expose them")?

IS INVESTING IN THE STOCK MARKET GAMBLING?

I have known people who view buying and selling stocks as a form of gambling. As we will see in part 5 of this book, providing capital in a long-term investment that helps to enable a corporation to provide useful goods and services is a legitimate way to make money. On the other hand, certain risky investment schemes are no better than gambling. I have known men with little education or experience in the stock market who became convinced based on a book, seminar, or website that they could employ some supposedly proven method to make a killing in the market. Day trading appears to be a get-rich-quick scheme that has some of the same problems as trying to make a living at playing poker. The focus is on outsmarting the other players/investors, as opposed to wisely investing long term in a solid business that offers value to its customers. It is proud and foolish for an inexperienced investor to think that he can outwit educated, experienced investors who manage billions of dollars.

SUMMARY

Gambling can be a great temptation for some people and a dangerous distraction for others. Gambling harms many people in addition to those who participate and has a negative impact on society in general. A casino in our area once put up a billboard with the slogan, "We make our money the old-fashioned way. We win it." The real old-fashioned way to make money is to follow the three-thousand-year-old wisdom of Proverbs by working hard and smart to earn your money from those who benefit from your labor.

— Questions for Reflection —

1. What harm is caused to society by gambling?
2. What harm is caused to individual Christians who gamble?
3. Should church leaders confront members who gamble? If so, when and how?
4. How can certain kinds of investing be like gambling?

13

SHOULD CHRISTIANS PARTICIPATE IN MULTILEVEL-MARKETING ORGANIZATIONS?

Many Christians are attracted to multilevel marketing (MLM), also known as network marketing, as a way to improve their finances. Many stay-at-home mothers join these organizations as a way to supplement family income without having to take jobs outside the home.[1] These "businesses" always involve direct sales to family and friends of products or services on which the seller receives a commission. But the real money in MLM is made when you get others to sell the product or services as a part of your network so that you receive a percentage of their sales.[2] Then your network and income can exponentially expand as those selling under you enlist others to sell under them, who get others to sell under them, and so on. Some people successfully build very large networks and thereby make a great deal of money through

1. "Women make up 75 percent of MLM participants overall; in some jewelry and health-and-beauty-companies that number is more like 95 percent." www.christianity today.com/ct/2015/december/divine-rise-of-multilevel-marketing-christians-mlm .html.

2. Personal-finance expert Dave Ramsey tells his listeners, "MLM success is about recruiting and retaining a sales team, not selling products." www.christianitytoday .com/ct/2015/december/divine-rise-of-multilevel-marketing-christians-mlm.html.

MLM. Some of the products sold through network marketing are soaps, kitchen products, cosmetics, cleaning products, essential oils, vitamins, and other health-enhancement products. One key component of a successful MLM is that the product or service sold has to appear unique and not readily available through normal retail channels such as Amazon, Walmart, or the warehouse club.

Many of those who succeed at MLM are Christians. One reason for this is that Christians typically have a large network of friends in their churches who are potential candidates to buy their products or join their sales networks. Many Christians also enjoy their involvement in MLM because they build enjoyable new relationships through their organization. Those who are most successful in MLM tend to be outgoing and self-motivated and to enjoy working with people.

GENERALLY SPEAKING, CHRISTIANS ARE FREE TO ENGAGE IN NETWORK MARKETING

We have already seen that profit is not unbiblical, as long as one offers something of value to the customer. The Bible commends the virtuous woman who engages in business creating valuable goods and makes a profit (Prov. 31:16–18, 24). Many customers are well satisfied with their purchases from their friend's MLM business. Some are glad to learn of a low-risk business opportunity that has the potential to enhance their family's income. Some successful MLMers have given generously to churches and charities.

POSSIBLE RISKS ASSOCIATED WITH MLM

1. Most People Who Join MLM Organizations Don't Make Money

Almost half lose money,[3] often winding up with a closet full of unsold product. Three-quarters of those who get involved in MLM don't make any profit. Most of those who do come out ahead earn

---

3. www.aarp.org/content/dam/aarp/aarp_foundation/2018/pdf/AARP%20 Foundation%20MLM%20Research%20Study%20Report%2010.8.18.pdf, 8.

less than $500 a month.[4] The percentage of participants who make a significant income from MLM is small. It is estimated that fewer than 1 percent can earn a living through their MLM.[5] Many would do well to seek to earn or supplement their income in more traditional ways (Prov. 12:11).

2. Most People Who Join MLM Organizations Are Dissatisfied with Their Experience

One research study showed that "knowing what they know now, 65% of the MLM participants would not join the same MLM organization that they first became involved with compared to 16% who would re-join."[6]

3. The Products Sold through MLM Organizations Might Not Be a Good Value

Such products tend to be much more expensive than similar products available online or in large stores. One reason for this is that direct sales is an inefficient method of delivering goods to consumers. The markup on a product must cover the time spent by the salesperson to acquire and deliver the product plus the commissions earned by the people above her in the network. MLM organizations explain the higher cost of their product by claiming that cheaper products available online or in stores are vastly inferior. They have to convince consumers that their products are unique. For example, it might be that the laundry soap that costs 20 cents a load at Walmart is just as good as the soap sold through MLM for 50 cents a load.

4. It Is Awkward to Try to Recruit or Sell to Family and Friends

This is a major reason why many people drop out of MLM.[7]

---

4. www.aarp.org/aarp-foundation/our-work/income/multilevel-marketing/.

5. www.epm.org/blog/2019/Feb/25/multilevel-marketing.

6. www.aarp.org/content/dam/aarp/aarp_foundation/2018/pdf/AARP%20 Foundation%20MLM%20Research%20Study%20Report%2010.8.18.pdf, 12.

7. www.aarp.org/content/dam/aarp/aarp_foundation/2018/pdf/AARP%20 Foundation%20MLM%20Research%20Study%20Report%2010.8.18.pdf, 12.

SINS THAT CAN BE ASSOCIATED WITH MLM

1. Greed

While any of us can be tempted to covetousness, MLMs are especially adept at motivating their members to sell and recruit more diligently by emphasizing the material rewards. When my wife and I were first married, we house-sat for a nice couple who were involved in a major MLM organization. Everywhere in the house and in their vehicles we saw pictures of exotic vacation spots, luxury cars, and treasure chests filled with gold jewelry, with accompanying sales slogans. It was overwhelming and brought to mind this warning: "But those who want to get rich fall into temptation and a snare and many foolish and harmful desires which plunge men into ruin and destruction. For the love of money is a root of all sorts of evil, and some by longing for it have wandered away from the faith and pierced themselves with many griefs. But flee from these things, you man of God, and pursue righteousness, godliness, faith, love, perseverance and gentleness" (1 Tim. 6:9–11; also see Col. 3:5; Heb. 13:5).

2. False or Misleading Claims Made by Some MLMs

Scripture exhorts us concerning the importance of truth, especially among Christian brothers and sisters: "Therefore, laying aside falsehood, speak truth each one of you with his neighbor, for we are members of one another" (Eph. 4:25). Greed, or eagerness of success, can tempt us to fall short of our obligation to be completely honest with those whom we are seeking to recruit. For example:

A. Overstating the likelihood of financial success. As we have already observed, most people who engage in MLM don't make any money. Very few make a significant amount of money. A majority of MLM participants believe that the organization misrepresented the chances of achieving financial success.[8]

---

8. www.aarp.org/content/dam/aarp/aarp_foundation/2018/pdf/AARP%20 Foundation%20MLM%20Research%20Study%20Report%2010.8.18.pdf, 10.

Some MLM companies have faced legal complaints for deceptive recruiting practices.[9]

B. Overselling the products in terms of their value and potency. In order to get people to pay the higher prices charged through direct sales, marketers have to convince consumers that their products are unique and provide spectacular benefits. I have been particularly concerned when MLMs claim that their products provide spiritual benefits of setting users free from anxiety, fear, and worry and that they can experience calm and peace.

C. Overstating claims of expertise. Some who sell health-related MLM products present themselves as experts whose mission is to educate consumers about how their products can solve various health issues (from snoring to back pain to more severe medical issues such as cancer). They often rely on anecdotal stories or research funded by the manufacturer that doesn't meet accepted scientific standards (double-blind studies).

Once people are committed to an MLM, their loyalty to their organization may prevent them from objectively considering the concerns above. They might become defensive or hostile when challenged.

3. Misusing Relationships with Other Christians

We are called to sincerely and selflessly love one another as Jesus loved us (John 13:35). Those involved in MLM succeed by recruiting family and friends to buy their products and to recruit others for their networks. They are taught to fully utilize their networks, which for Christians includes church. This can tempt salespeople to see others as prospects for their businesses. A young couple who were new to a church were glad to receive a few dinner invitations from church members. They were disappointed, however, to find that some of these invitations were primarily aimed at introducing them to a "business

---

9. www.christianitytoday.com/ct/2015/december/divine-rise-of-multilevel
-marketing-christians-mlm.html.

opportunity," and that when they didn't express interest in the MLM, their hosts seemed to lose interest in them. It can be very awkward to be invited by a friend to a "party" at which expensive products will be sold. One might not be interested in or be able to afford the products, but still feel pressure to support the friend's business. In recent years, MLMs have relied on social media for their marketing efforts, advertising to their "friends" through testimonials and special offers. Randy Alcorn wisely states, "Nobody likes to find out that an apparent friendship is nothing more than a sales strategy."[10] Some churches have had to make policies discouraging people from conducting MLM business between (or even during) services or using the church directory for leads.

4. MLM Community's Substituting for Church

MLMs often use the language of mission, seeing the use of their products as a kind of ministry to others. Recruiting new members can be seen as a form of evangelism, introducing others to the good news of the MLM.[11] Converts are celebrated. New participants in one's network are viewed as disciples. Testimonies are shared. The organization and its leaders can achieve almost messianic status when they are credited with changing lives (or even changing the world). Sometimes the MLM becomes the primary community for its members. They might even shun those who are in competing MLMs, or those who question the claims made by their products. Or they can become a clique within a local church. MLM organizations often demand and obtain significant commitments of time, energy, and loyalty from their members. Some become so obsessed with their MLM mission that they neglect participation in their local church (as can also happen in other professions).

10. www.epm.org/blog/2019/Feb/25/multilevel-marketing.
11. When meeting someone new, which "good news" will you first share with that person—Christ or the MLM?

SUMMARY

Christians are free to participate in network marketing, but they should be cautious. There are pitfalls that could be spiritually dangerous. Do some independent research using sources outside the MLM organization regarding the quality of its products and the integrity of its practices. If you choose to be involved, be careful not to let your commitment to your organization adversely affect your relationships in the church.

— QUESTIONS FOR REFLECTION —

1. What are some of the possible attractions of being involved in direct MLM?
2. What are some of the spiritual dangers of being involved in MLM?
3. What are some of the financial dangers of being involved in MLM?
4. When might a church need to make a policy regarding members' promoting their MLM?
5. What particular problems might emerge when a church leader becomes involved in an MLM organization?

14

WHAT PRACTICAL WISDOM CAN BE OFFERED TO THOSE WHO NEED MORE INCOME?

Many find themselves in the position of needing more money. Salary increases are not keeping up with rising expenses. You have tried to cut back, but no matter how hard you try, you put a little more on the credit cards each month. Or you have been laid off from your job and need to find work soon or you won't be able to make your house or rent payment.

IF YOU ARE UNEMPLOYED,[1] YOUR JOB IS TO GET A JOB

Losing one's job can be heartbreaking. Being rejected by potential employers can be extremely discouraging. Unemployed people can be tempted to become depressed and lazy. These spiritual temptations must be fought by turning to the Lord through prayer and meditation on his life-giving Word. It is also important to continue to press on in your job search with the strength that God gives you. Sinfully wasting time can cause the cycle of depression to spiral down and can make your financial problems much worse.

1. By "unemployed" I am not referring to a full-time stay-at-home spouse/parent who is working hard but not being paid.

94

1. Work Hard at Finding Work

One common mistake that unemployed people make is to simply email a résumé to a possible employer or two and then to wait for a response. In some cases, they might have had what seemed to be a promising interview, so they stop searching, hoping to learn that they got the job. The reality is that many job-seekers send out dozens of résumés and have several interviews before receiving a suitable job offer. Don't put all your hope in one possible employer. Keep searching until the job is secured. Ecclesiastes 11:6 offers wisdom for the unemployed person: "Sow your seed in the morning and do not be idle in the evening, for you do not know whether morning or evening sowing will succeed, or whether both of them alike will be good." A person who needs work should spend as much time pursuing a job as he or she would spend working at a job. Many seeds might be sown before the harvest comes.

2. Work Smart at Finding Work

In addition to working hard at seeking work, one should work smart in pursuit of employment. Time invested in networking usually produces much better results than merely submitting numerous job applications.[2] This could drive the job-seeker out of his comfort zone as he reaches out to coworkers and supervisors from previous jobs to see whether they are aware of any suitable openings. Often colleges and training schools help graduates find jobs, especially through networking with employers who are graduates. Some have successfully found work by visiting potential employers rather than merely relying on online communication. If you get an interview, follow up immediately with a thank-you note that expresses your enthusiasm for the employer. The person in need of work should also let the need be known to friends and family members, who might know of an available job. Time can also be wisely spent in investigating where the best job

---

2. Ken Coleman observes, "Finding opportunities to do what you love is as simple as getting around the right people and being in the right places." *The Proximity Principle: The Proven Strategy That Will Lead to the Career You Love* (Brentwood, TN: Ramsey Press, 2019), 8.

opportunities might be in terms of both the kinds and the locations of potential employment.

3. Make Yourself More Attractive to Potential Employers

Get help in creating an attractive, eye-catching résumé. Make sure that there are no typos in whatever you give to a potential employer. Craft the résumé to fit particular jobs for which you apply. Work on your interviewing skills by doing research and practicing with helpful friends and family members. Develop your "elevator speech" to be able to summarize in less than a minute the message you would want to convey to a potential employer. What unique qualities and skills has God given you that would help the business to thrive?

4. Pray That God Will Send a Boaz to Employ You

When Ruth went out to glean in order to feed herself and her mother-in-law, Naomi, she needed the Lord to provide a godly man who would allow her to work in his field. Humanly speaking, for a Moabitess to find a worthy benefactor during the days of the judges seemed extremely unlikely. But all things are possible with God. In the same way, a believer today who needs work should pray for a "Boaz" who would give the person an opportunity to work for a living. I have seen God answer this particular prayer by providing a Boaz employer for a believer who was having a very difficult time finding work.

IF YOUR CURRENT WORK ISN'T PROVIDING WELL ENOUGH, YOU NEED TO BE PROACTIVE

Some people complain that their job doesn't pay enough, living in the hope or expectation that their present employer will increase their pay. In such situations, it is usually wise (and necessary) to take matters into your own hands. If you believe that you are being underpaid for your skilled labor, you can actively look for a better job. Often an employer that realizes that it is on the verge of losing a valued team member will be motivated to substantially increase an employee's pay in order to keep that person. It is usually not wise to quit your current job until you have the new and better situation. Also, there is a risk that your employer will let you go if you threaten to look for another job. Another way to potentially raise income is to obtain further training or certification in your field that would make you more valuable to your employer or other potential employers.

YOU MIGHT NEED TO TAKE SOME DRASTIC STEPS

If the job search is not producing suitable results, you might need to think outside your original parameters so that you can fulfill your responsibilities to provide for yourself and your family. First Timothy 5:8 warns, "If anyone does not provide for his own, and especially for those of his household, he has denied the faith and is worse than an unbeliever." This means that a godly person will do whatever it takes to feed his family.

1. You Might Need to Consider Changing to a Different Line of Work—Where the Well-Paying Jobs Are

This will be difficult because you might prefer your previous job function or because you invested a lot in your education for that particular work. For example, I have seen several cases of men who trained for the ministry but were unable to find full-time ministerial work.[3] They had to go into different careers in order to earn a living. Others have pursued advanced degrees in a field with very few jobs. The decision to change careers will often involve getting retrained for your new vocation and having to work your way back up the ladder in terms of both responsibility and finances.

2. You Might Want to Get Some Extra Training to Upgrade Your Skill Set to Make Yourself More Attractive to Potential Employers

A friend who was out of work stayed busy every day, following the Ecclesiastes 11:6 principle of sowing in many ways. He not only

3. Just because one is not in paid full-time ministry does not mean that his training and gifts are useless. The apostle Paul often found himself in the position of having

diligently searched for a job, but also took a class related to his field. The course gave him a new skill and certification. When he finally got a job, he learned that the employer needed someone with that particular certification. The employer was also impressed that he had used his downtime during a job search to improve his professional qualifications. Such training can be expensive, so one would want to research to make sure that the possibilities are good that the time and effort will pay off.

3. You Might Need to Consider Moving Out of the Area Where You Live to a Place Where You Can Find Suitable Employment

It might be hard to leave your family, friends, and church. Sometimes job opportunities dry up in one town, making it necessary for many to find work elsewhere.

4. You Might Have to Take On Temporary (and Less Desirable) Work in Order to Make Ends Meet

The gig economy, including ride-share and delivery services, provides opportunity for many to make money during flexible hours. Such work could be done full time while searching for a more suitable job. It could also serve as part-time work to supplement a job that isn't (yet) paying enough to provide for the family. Those with practical skills (from coding to carpentry) can take on side jobs on evenings and Saturdays. But every effort should be made to set aside the Lord's Day for worship and rest.

5. You Might Be Able to Raise Money by Selling Assets

This is not a long-term income solution, however.

6. You Might Consider Obtaining Regular Income by Renting Out One or More Rooms in Your Home

---

to make tents in order to support himself (Acts 18:3; 1 Thess. 2:9). God often uses tent-making (self-supported) ministers and missionaries for great spiritual good.

7. You Might Need to Downsize Your Lifestyle

If you can't increase income sufficiently to meet expenses, then you might be able to reduce spending as you learn to live within your means. We will discuss budgeting, lifestyle choices, and debt in subsequent chapters.

8. A Stay-at-Home Spouse Might Need to Find Ways to Contribute to Family Income

I respect the commitment of many families to have one spouse, usually the wife, stay at home in order to care for children. While I agree that this is often ideal (Titus 2:4–5), it is not always possible. Some men[4] are not capable of earning enough money to meet the family's needs. Many wives are able to supplement the family income by running a home-based business (e.g., teaching music lessons or creating and selling crafts, Prov. 31:24). Some wives can take on a part-time job that works around the husband's schedule, while other couples find that both spouses have to work full time outside the home in order to survive economically. In such cases, a couple would need to be very intentional about planning time together to maintain the health of their marriage. On the other hand, in cases in which the breadwinner is earning a good salary, the addition of a second income might not improve their lifestyle enough to justify the economic benefits of a second income (especially when additional tax, daycare, and work expenses are considered).

BEWARE OF DANGEROUS SHORTCUTS

Those in financial need are often tempted to attempt to circumvent the biblical formula that hard work times skill produces income (Prov. 10:4; 22:29). The more valuable the goods and services we create through our labor, the more money people will be willing

---

4. I speak of the husband as the spouse who works outside the home because this is the more common situation. I acknowledge that in many families the wife is the primary breadwinner. Each couple has to work out how they can best serve God and each other in their marital roles.

to pay us. Those in desperate need of income are often deceived by hucksters promising significant financial rewards with minimal amounts of skill and effort. Those promoting ways to make easy money try to enrich themselves by employing flattery as they appeal to the pride of their victims. Those in financial trouble waste time and money on such schemes, thus digging themselves into a deeper financial hole. Such scams are not new. Proverbs 28:19 warns, "He who tills his land will have plenty of food, but he who follows empty pursuits will have poverty in plenty." If it sounds too good to be true, it almost certainly is.

A WORD TO EMPLOYERS

While a fellow believer in the church can be a source of financial help to those in need through charity (Acts 2:44–45), an even greater way of blessing a brother or sister might be to provide an opportunity for employment in business. And when a fellow Christian provides a job, one should work especially hard to be a blessing in thankfulness to that person and to God (1 Tim. 6:2).

SUMMARY

The person who is unemployed or underemployed cannot afford to be a procrastinator. If you are receiving unemployment benefits or have savings, be thankful to God, but don't wait until your situation is desperate before seeking work. Diligently seek a job that will provide adequately for your needs, praying that God will open the right doors.

— QUESTIONS FOR REFLECTION —

1. What are some of the most serious mistakes made by unemployed people?
2. What are some of the most serious mistakes made by underemployed people?
3. When is it wise to change jobs?

4. What wisdom does Scripture offer to the person who is unemployed?
5. How can a Christian employer be a blessing to other believers?
6. What might be the risks of a Christian's hiring a friend from church?

PART 3

SPENDING MONEY

15

WHAT ARE SOME COMMON MISUNDERSTANDINGS ABOUT SPENDING MONEY?

Many people spend money unwisely. Often this is due to greed. Sometimes it is due to ignorance. God's Word wisely dispels the many common misunderstandings that people have about how to use their money.

WILL SPENDING MONEY MAKE YOU HAPPY?

Some people escape sadness, stress, and boredom through substance abuse. Others attempt to relieve the same pressures by spending money on new possessions (new clothes, jewelry, or the even bigger super-giant-screen television), exotic vacations, fancy vehicles, or even a new home. We have known couples who were struggling in their marriages who put their hope in a major purchase (a better house) to unite them and solve their marriage problems. As we have already seen in previous chapters, money will not bring the satisfaction that people long for (Eccl. 5:10; Isa. 55:1–2). Greed (covetousness) is idolatry (Col. 3:5)—pursuing the glory that God alone possesses in the wrong places. We have never seen a new house fix a broken marriage. Some overspend out of envy, trying to keep up with friends and family members who have the latest phones, the most impressive home-entertainment systems, and the biggest boats. The idolatry of what money can buy often leads to excessive debt, hoarding, and even greater sadness. The buzz of a new "toy" wears off, often long before the bills are paid.

IS IT WRONG FOR CHRISTIANS TO ENJOY WHAT MONEY CAN BUY?

Wrong ideas about spending money can go to another extreme, which says that the only worthwhile pleasures in life are spiritual and that it is wrong for committed Christians to enjoy earthly things. This mentality (asceticism) is sometimes accompanied by the idea that believers must live an extremely meager lifestyle so that almost all their money can be given away for the poor and for missions. This error crept up in the early church, and the apostle Paul had to warn against people who sought to impose legalistic restrictions on all believers, "men who forbid marriage and advocate abstaining from foods which God has created to be gratefully shared in by those who believe and know the truth. For everything created by God is good, and nothing is to be rejected if it is received with gratitude; for it is sanctified by means of the word of God and prayer" (1 Tim. 4:3–5). Paul teaches that God approves of our enjoying good food and other legitimate pleasures as long as we do so with thankfulness. Scripture offers a balanced approach to our enjoyment of earthly things: "Instruct those who are rich in this present world not to be conceited or to fix their hope on the uncertainty of riches, but on God, who richly supplies us with all things to enjoy" (6:17). Notice that Paul doesn't rebuke the wealthy for being rich or require them to give up all their wealth. He even acknowledges that God richly supplies us with good things to enjoy in this life. Yet he warns the rich not to be proud or to put their hope in their wealth, which is fleeting, rather than in God.

ARE YOU DOING WELL IF YOU GET BY FROM MONTH TO MONTH ON YOUR PAYCHECK?

The main problem when someone lives from paycheck to paycheck is that the person is unprepared for major expenses that don't occur as regularly. Such expenses include major car repairs, medical bills not covered by insurance, and significant household expenses, such as replacing a major appliance or the HVAC system. Some expenses should be anticipated. I have known people who thought that they were doing well until their semiannual car-insurance bill arrived. When bills such as these or unanticipated expenses come up, such people then rely on credit-card debt, which often puts them in a deep financial hole (see part 4 on debt). Major expenses should be anticipated and preparations should be made. These include replacing aging vehicles, children's education, and retirement (also see part 5 on saving and investing). Budgeting can help a family to be prepared for the future.

IS THERE NO POINT TO CREATING A BUDGET FOR PEOPLE WITH EXTREMELY LIMITED INCOME BECAUSE ALL THE MONEY GETS SPENT ON NECESSITIES AS SOON AS IT COMES IN?

We should certainly sympathize with the plight of those who are barely earning enough to survive. Some have the idea that budgets are for people who get to make financial choices and that the poor don't have options. My experience has been that people who are in the midst of financial hardship often stand to benefit the most from a carefully made budget. Putting all their expenses down on paper gives them the opportunity to face reality, which might involve identifying where money is being wasted or the need to take steps to increase income (see previous chapters). In chapter 18, we will show you how to create and follow a budget.

ARE PEOPLE ON VERY LIMITED INCOMES FREE FROM THE OBLIGATION TO GIVE TO THE LORD'S WORK?

Some Christians who are struggling financially believe that they are not under any obligation to give. Yet Scripture commends the generous poor. Paul commends the churches in Macedonia "that in a great ordeal of affliction their abundance of joy and their deep poverty overflowed in the wealth of their liberality. For I testify that according to their ability, and beyond their ability, they gave of their own accord" (2 Cor. 8:2–3). Jesus also commends the widow who gave generously out of her poverty (Luke 21:1–4). So Scripture would encourage those who are poor who choose to sacrificially give even a small amount to the Lord's work. On the other hand, I strongly advise against going deeper into debt in order to give.[1]

SUMMARY

When money is tight, we especially need to act wisely when allocating our limited funds. During seasons of prosperity, we need to be good stewards of the blessings from God. When it comes to spending money, as with everything else, the wisdom of God's Word surpasses worldly wisdom.

— QUESTIONS FOR REFLECTION —

1. In what ways are you tempted to spend money in order to deal with stress or sadness?
2. How can one maintain the balance between enjoying the good gifts from God through our money and not making wealth an idol?
3. How should a person who is poor decide how much to give to the Lord's work?
4. How could a budget help a family that has been living on the edge financially?

---

1. I also warn against false teachers who entice the poor to give more than they can afford by promising that their giving will lead to earthly prosperity. Paul was confident that God would meet the needs of those who gave generously, not their every material desire.

16

HOW MUCH OF YOUR MONEY BELONGS TO GOD?

While there is a God-given sense of accomplishment when we work hard and develop skills, many who are wealthy are tempted to take full credit for their success. In their pride, they reason that because they have worked harder and smarter than others, they deserve all that they have. Yet they should heed the warning that God often chooses to humble the proud (James 4:6), as in the case of the parable of the rich fool (Luke 12:16–21) and the humiliation of King Nebuchadnezzar (Dan. 4). In contrast, God's people are told, "But you shall remember the LORD your God, for it is He who is giving you power to make wealth" (Deut. 8:18).

GIVE GOD THE CREDIT HE DESERVES FOR YOUR SUCCESS

Those who produce financial wealth should acknowledge that God has given them the skills and talents that have produced their success. God has also been kind to give them life and health, without which they could not work. God has put them into his world, which has tremendous potential for fruitfulness. He has showed them kindness by allowing them to live in a situation of political and social stability as well as an infrastructure that allows them to succeed. Scripture often warns that financial success can tempt people to godless pride (Prov.

30:9a; Mark 10:25). As they consider all that they have accomplished, they can fall into the sin of Nebuchadnezzar, who boasted, "Is this not Babylon the great, which I myself have built as a royal residence by the might of my power and for the glory of my majesty?" (Dan. 4:30).

ULTIMATELY, GOD OWNS EVERYTHING

Christians should acknowledge that whatever they have is from God, who gives every good gift and ultimately owns everything. We are not autonomous. "The earth is the LORD's, and all it contains, the world, and those who dwell in it" (Ps. 24:1). He asserts his ownership over "the cattle on a thousand hills" (50:10). We are stewards of our wealth and possessions, seeking to employ them in a way that pleases God, who owns everything and is our Master. When speaking of each family's inheritance in the promised land under the old covenant, the Lord reminded his people that "the land is Mine" (Lev. 25:23). In a sense, we are all sharecroppers, working for our gracious Master. In his parables, Jesus teaches us the importance of being good stewards over all that God has given to us (Matt. 25:14–23).

WE ARE STEWARDS WHO
ANSWER TO OUR MASTER

The idea of God's owning everything has some radical implications. For example, many Christians think that the tithe implies that if 10 percent of what we earn belongs to God, then we are free to spend the other 90 percent as we please. The biblical standard is that we are to utilize 100 percent of what we earn and own in a way that glorifies God (1 Cor. 10:31).[1]

This higher standard of stewardship gives us both more responsibility and more freedom. It might seem easier to live by a mathematical

1. A related implication is that all our time belongs to God and should be used in a manner that pleases him. Spending time, like spending money, should be carefully planned, because both belong to God.

formula so that we can be confident that our financial management is pleasing to God, as long as we give our full 10 percent. Instead, we have to consider every purchase in light of his ownership of us and our possessions. We have to live with the tension between using our resources for the Lord's work and to help the poor versus our freedom to enjoy the material blessings that God provides (1 Tim. 6:17) and our responsibility to save for the future (see part 5). Different people will work this out in different ways. We are free to make many of these choices without fearing the judgment of those who can't afford what God has given us (Prov. 29:25). We also acknowledge the freedom of others to enjoy more than we can afford without judging them: "Do not speak against one another, brethren. He who speaks against a brother or judges his brother speaks against the law and judges the law; but if you judge the law, you are not a doer of the law but a judge of it. There is only one Lawgiver and Judge, the One who is able to save and to destroy; but who are you to judge your neighbor?" (James 4:11–12).

SUMMARY

The idea that God owns only 10 percent of our income is not biblical. Everything we own is from God, which means that we are to utilize all our income and resources for his glory. This does not mean that we are obligated to give everything away to the poor or to judge those who don't. Rather, we seek God's wisdom as we enjoy what his resources supply while also being generous to meet the physical and spiritual needs of others.

— QUESTIONS FOR REFLECTION —

1. Why is it hard for some people to acknowledge God's ownership over all their possessions?
2. What is wrong with saying, "I will give God his 10 percent, and then I am free to spend the rest as I please"?
3. How would thinking of God as the owner of everything affect how you spend your money?

4. How can we decide how to divide our income among lifestyle choices, saving for the future, and giving to the Lord's work?

5. How is our stewardship of our time similar to our stewardship of our money?

17

HOW MUCH SHOULD YOU GIVE?

Some of us come from church backgrounds in which giving is publicly emphasized in every single worship service. Others come from churches that rarely talk about money. Some come from families that have faithfully tithed. Others grew up without even learning about giving to the Lord's work.

GIVING SHOULD BE A PRIORITY

"Honor the LORD from your wealth and from the first of all your produce" (Prov. 3:9). This proverb envisions an agrarian society in which a farmer is beginning to harvest his crops over which he has worked long and hard. Rather than waiting until the harvest is complete, he gives to the Lord from the beginning of what he brings in. An analogous situation would be a family's demonstrating its priorities by giving to the Lord's work from the beginning of their budget or paycheck, rather than waiting to see whether anything is left over after all their other expenses have been paid.

GIVING IS WORSHIP

We honor the Lord when we give to his work (Prov. 3:9a). By devoting what is precious to us (our money), we demonstrate how highly we value God as we acknowledge his ownership of us and all that we have. As we make giving a priority, we also express faith that

113

God will continue to provide for us, even if we no longer possess what we have devoted to him. Over the course of a lifetime, a faithfully giving Christian will have given away a very large sum of money, which would amount to many years' salary if the person tithed. We genuinely believe that our souls are better off because of our giving (Matt. 6:19–21). Giving generously loosens our grip on earthly treasures as we demonstrate our hope in heavenly riches.

WE DO NOT GIVE BECAUSE GOD IS NEEDY

It grieves me to hear certain Christian fundraisers make it sound as though the work of God's kingdom will grind to a halt unless we call today and make a large donation. Scripture makes it very clear that God does not need our money in order to accomplish his purposes (Acts 17:24–25; Rom. 11:35). He will accomplish all his good plans with or without our help. When we give, we enjoy the privilege of participating in God's work.

GIVE TO THOSE IN NEED

Scripture emphasizes our responsibility to help the poor: "One who is gracious to a poor man lends to the LORD, and He will repay him for his good deed" (Prov. 19:17; also see Deut. 15:10). The great majority of the references to giving in the New Testament deal not with fundraising for buildings and staffing, but with the faithfulness of the early church in providing for widows and other needy believers (e.g., Acts 2:45; 6:1; 2 Cor. 8–9; Gal. 2:10; Eph. 4:28; 1 Tim. 5:3–8). And our giving is not limited to those in our own local church. Much of the giving in the early church involved believers from one region of the world helping needy believers in another region. You might give to your church's benevolence fund or to parachurch agencies that offer help to believers in need in other countries. When you become aware of a need, you might choose to meet it directly, rather than going through the church. As a pastor, I have found joy when a member of the church hands me an envelope containing cash and asks me to deliver it anonymously to another member who is in financial trouble. One of the very best ways in which you can help someone in need is to give the person opportunity to earn money by giving him or her work to do. Under the old covenant, needy individuals who were healthy were provided for, not by receiving a handout, but by working at gleaning from the fields of those who were more prosperous (Lev. 19:9–10). We previously observed how Boaz graciously gave Ruth the opportunity to gather grain among his harvesters (Ruth 2).

GIVE TO THE LORD'S WORK

The New Testament teaches that those who work hard at serving the Lord in ministry should be paid by the church (1 Cor. 9:13–14; 1 Tim. 5:17–18). This resembles the system under the old covenant in which the Levites were supported by the tithes and offerings of God's faithful people. The generous financial gifts of church members enable many important ministries to take place. Missionaries are sent out. Needed facilities are purchased. Men and women are equipped for a lifetime of ministry. College students are discipled. Those in financial need are rescued from homelessness.

GIVE WISELY

Many years ago, a member of our church who had recently immigrated to America and was of limited financial means asked my wife whether she had to give to all the organizations that wrote to her asking for help. My wife explained that she was not obligated to give to all of them. Furthermore, it might be unwise to give to some of them. As good stewards, we want to give generously to churches and ministries that are faithfully and effectively serving the Lord. It is wasteful to give to religious organizations that have unsound doctrine or unsound leadership or that squander the Lord's resources. Similarly, we are not to give to every person who claims to have financial need. Many unscrupulous hucksters and sluggards prey on tenderhearted

Christians for money. This is not a new problem. Paul warns, "For even when we were with you, we used to give this order: if anyone is not willing to work, then he is not to eat, either. For we hear that some among you are leading an undisciplined life, doing no work at all, but acting like busybodies. Now such persons we command and exhort in the Lord Jesus Christ to work in quiet fashion and eat their own bread" (2 Thess. 3:10–12). If you hand money to someone begging at a traffic intersection, you might be helping that person to buy drugs or alcohol or to avoid the responsibility of work. We once had a friend who offered prepackaged food instead of money to people standing by the road who claimed to be hungry. The best ways to offer help to the poor are found in situations in which you know well that the need is genuine and in which there is accountability—family and church. On the other hand, if you can look back over many years and can't think of any time when your generosity might have been taken advantage of, then you have probably been too cautious. "So then, while we have opportunity, let us do good to all people, and especially to those who are of the household of the faith" (Gal. 6:10).

Wayne Grudem suggests that one of the wisest ways to help the poor, whether at home or abroad, is through providing work or helping people to establish their own businesses (e.g., through microloans). Grudem applies this principle to our giving: "The only solution to world poverty is business. That is because businesses produce goods, and businesses produce jobs."[1]

MUST CHRISTIANS TITHE?

Tithing was part of the old covenant law for Israel (Lev. 27:30; Num. 18:24; Deut. 14:22). Many believe that because different tithes were required, the Israelites were actually expected to give an average of more than 20 percent a year. Some argue that we are no longer required to tithe because the Mosaic civil and ceremonial laws no longer apply

---

1. Wayne A. Grudem, *Business for the Glory of God: The Bible's Teaching on the Moral Goodness of Business* (Wheaton, IL: Crossway, 2003), 80.

under the new covenant. Furthermore, the command to tithe is not explicitly repeated in the New Testament. On the other hand, there is a record of God's faithful people devoting a tithe (10 percent) to the Lord long before the law of Moses was given (Gen. 14:17–20; 28:20–22). While I don't believe that we can explicitly command that every believer must give exactly (or at least) 10 percent, throughout the years many Christians have found the tithe to be a helpful guideline (or baseline) for giving. Randy Alcorn refers to tithing as "The Training Wheels of Giving."[2] Beginning this practice early in your life can lead to generosity far above 10 percent over a lifetime.

GIVE PROPORTIONATELY AND GENEROUSLY

Even though the New Testament does not specify a percentage, we are repeatedly told to give in proportion to how God has materially blessed us: "Now concerning the collection for the saints, as I directed the churches of Galatia, so do you also. On the first day of every week each one of you is to put aside and save, as he may prosper, so that no collections be made when I come" (1 Cor. 16:1–2). Those whom God has richly blessed materially are expected to be exceptionally generous in good works (1 Tim. 6:17–19). Paul commends the generosity of the Macedonians, who gave not merely proportionately "according to their ability" but even "beyond their ability" (2 Cor. 8:3). As we apply this in our day, for those of limited means, 10 percent could involve great sacrifice. Those who are wealthy might be able to give far more than 10 percent of their income to the Lord's work without suffering much financial pain. It is distressing that statistics show that only a small percentage of professing Christians give as much as 10 percent.[3] My advice is to make 10 percent a starting point and then throughout your life to try to increase the percentage of income that you have the privilege of devoting to the Lord's work. As you earn more, limit your

2. Randy Alcorn, *Money, Possessions, and Eternity*, 2nd ed. (Wheaton, IL: Tyndale House, 2003), 173.

3. www.barna.com/research/new-study-shows-trends-in-tithing-and-donating/.

consumption so that you can give more. You will not regret it. I am blessed to have friends who are "rich in this present world" (1 Tim. 6:17) whose chief financial goals revolve around their desire to give large sums of money to important Christian ministries. Such people have an important role in God's kingdom because they provide needed major funding to churches, seminaries, and missions. God also uses the faithful gifts of those who have much less but are eager to participate as partners in the work of the gospel (Phil. 1:5; 4:15–17).

GIVE WILLINGLY AND CHEERFULLY

The believers in the early church didn't need to be pressured and cajoled into giving. Rather, they saw giving as a blessed opportunity. Paul says of the Macedonians that "they gave of their own accord, begging us with much urging for the favor of participation in the support of the saints" (2 Cor. 8:3b–4). Paul later declares, "Each one must do just as he has purposed in his heart, not grudgingly or under compulsion, for God loves a cheerful giver" (9:7). The motivation for giving is not to receive recognition or glory from men. Nor is there an expectation of a reward of earthly wealth. Rather, Paul bases our giving on God's giving: "For you know the grace of our Lord Jesus Christ, that though He was rich, yet for your sake He became poor, so that you through His poverty might become rich" (8:9). We who have received the gift of God find joy in sharing his gifts and grace with others. Paul also writes, "In everything I showed you that by working hard in this manner you must help the weak and remember the words of the Lord Jesus, that He Himself said, 'It is more blessed to give than to receive'" (Acts 20:35).

GIVE HUMBLY

Jesus warns against giving in order to impress other people (Matt. 6:1–4). Dr. Martyn Lloyd-Jones, when commenting on this text, asserts that the depth of human depravity is not merely seen in the drunk in the gutter, but rather seen in fallen man at his best, trying to worship God, yet still sinning.[4] My wife and I went to a Christian college where every building, classroom, and even chair was named after a donor. I suggested more than once, tongue in cheek, that along with the donor's name, a plaque from Matthew 6:2b should be inscribed: "They have their reward in full." Instead of giving to be seen by men, Jesus teaches, we should give in secret, trusting that God sees and that God will honor our faithfulness in his way and in his time.

GIVE HOPEFULLY

Scripture frequently tells us that God blesses those who give generously and wisely. Under the old covenant, there was a direct correlation between Israel's faithfulness to God's law (including paying the tithe and caring for the poor) and her material prosperity (Deut. 28). The book of Proverbs teaches that generous individuals will be blessed (Prov. 3:10; 11:25; 19:17; 22:9). The New Testament also offers hope that God will bless those who make financial sacrifices for people in need and for the advancement of the gospel. This does not imply, as some false teachers claim, that those who give to the Lord's work will be rich in this world (like some spiritual pyramid scheme). Paul tells his generous loved ones in Philippi that God will meet their needs, not that they will be rich: "My God will supply all your needs according to His riches in glory in Christ Jesus" (Phil. 4:19). When he writes to the Corinthians, Paul states that he trusts that as God continues to bless them materially, they will use God's blessing for God's purposes: "Now He who supplies seed to the sower and bread for food will supply and multiply your seed for sowing and increase the harvest of your righteousness; you will be enriched in everything for all liberality, which through us is producing thanksgiving to God" (2 Cor. 9:10–11). Therefore, as we give, we can trust that God will care for our earthly requirements, as the psalmist states: "I have been young and now I am old, yet I have not seen the righteous forsaken or his descendants

4. D. Martyn Lloyd-Jones, *Studies in the Sermon on the Mount* (Grand Rapids: Eerdmans, 1993), 2:22.

begging bread" (Ps. 37:25). As we put God's kingdom first, we can be confident that we will have food and clothing (Matt. 6:33). But the treasure that we seek and expect by faith as we generously give is in heaven (vv. 19–21).

SUMMARY

Giving is the financial subject most spoken of by churches and parachurch ministries. Yet much of what is said does not reflect biblical teaching on giving. Those who love Christ will not need to be cajoled into giving. They will make giving a priority as they cheerfully contribute, knowing that it is a great privilege to participate in God's work. Bishop J. C. Ryle exhorts us, "I ask no man to neglect his worldly calling, and so to omit to provide for his family. . . . But I ask all to look around continually as they journey on and to remember the poor,—the poor in body and the poor in soul. . . . Might we not lay out less upon ourselves and give more to Christ's cause and Christ's poor?"[5]

— QUESTIONS FOR REFLECTION —

1. What are some common false teachings about giving?
2. What priority should helping the poor have in our giving? What is the best way to do this?
3. What are some common mistakes that Christians make with their giving?
4. What should motivate our giving?

5. J. C. Ryle, *Practical Religion: Being Plain Papers on the Daily Duties, Experience, Dangers, and Privileges of Professing Christians*, ed. J. I. Packer (Cambridge: James Clarke & Co., 1977), 220.

18

WHAT STEPS CAN BE TAKEN TO SUCCESSFULLY CREATE A BUDGET?

Perhaps the most powerful initial step that many people could take in order to get their finances under control would be to make and follow a budget. Without a budget, you are flying blind with reference to your finances. Those without a budget are usually poor stewards of the resources that God has entrusted to them.

IS THERE A BIBLICAL BASIS FOR MAKING A BUDGET?

"The plans of the diligent lead surely to advantage, but everyone who is hasty comes surely to poverty" (Prov. 21:5). A budget is a detailed plan for how you will seek to be an excellent steward of the financial resources that God gives you. Because we are finite, all our plans are made tentatively, in submission to God's sovereign control: "The mind of man plans his way, but the LORD directs his steps" (16:9; also see James 4:13–17). But it is still wise to plan. Jesus also reminds us of the importance of making realistic plans: "For which one of you, when he wants to build a tower, does not first sit down and calculate the cost to see if he has enough to complete it? Otherwise, when he has laid a foundation and is not able to finish, all who observe it begin to ridicule him, saying, 'This man began to build and was not able to finish'" (Luke 14:28–30).

WHY DON'T PEOPLE MAKE A BUDGET?

If a budget is the financial plan made by a diligent person (Prov. 21:5), then failure to budget is a form of laziness. For some people, it seems like too much trouble to live by a budget. Many plead that they are bad at math, so they can't create a budget. Some grew up in homes where their parents never budgeted and were always under financial pressure. These are poor excuses for bad stewardship. Those who feel overwhelmed by the idea of creating a budget can seek help from a godly deacon or financial counselor[1] who can help them walk through the steps of making and keeping a budget. They can learn the disciplines of living within a budget and keeping good financial records. It is possible to create a budget in a few hours and then to maintain it in less than thirty minutes a week.

WHAT IS THE HARM OF NOT HAVING A BUDGET?

People who don't live by a financial plan typically wind up in financial trouble or "poverty" (Prov. 21:5b). You often hear people in financial distress complain, "We don't know where all our money goes." They find themselves caught unprepared for major unexpected expenses. Many end up going deeply in debt or even bankrupt because they have failed to wisely and responsibly make and keep financial plans.

Steve and Sally came to me for counsel concerning their financial problems. It seemed that no matter how hard they tried, Steve and Sally weren't able to make ends meet. Some months would go well, but then the next month a major expense would arise, and they would have to put a few hundred dollars more on their credit cards. I took the following approach with them.

1. See mentoring.crown.org.

WHAT PRACTICAL STEPS CAN BE TAKEN IN ORDER TO SUCCESSFULLY LIVE BY A BUDGET?

1. Attempt to Estimate Your Monthly Income and Expenses in Each Budget Category (See Appendix A for a Blank Worksheet, along with Some Sample Budgets).[2]

Because neither Steve nor Sally had experience with making a budget, I sat with them during a counseling session, and we created a rough estimate of their regular income and expenses.

A. Your budget should include setting aside money as provision for irregular major expenses such as medical/dental bills and car repairs.

B. It is also wise to budget to save for future major purchases, such as vehicle replacement.

C. It is also helpful to have a miscellaneous category (not too big) for items that don't easily fall into other categories.

D. Giving to the Lord's work should be a priority in your budget.

E. Your budgeted expenses must be less than or equal to expected income.

F. See Appendix A for some guidelines on what percentage of your income to put in each budget category, along with some sample budgets.

G. If you are having a hard time balancing your budget, you might need to identify areas in which you can cut back in order to make ends meet (see below).

2. Refine Your Budget by Going Over Recent Income and Expenses

After helping Steve and Sally to make their initial budget, I sent them home to compile and categorize all their expenses over the past three months by looking through receipts and credit-card and bank statements.

---

2. You might find it easier to use an app or a computer spreadsheet to create your budget. See jimnewheiser.com/financial-resources/.

A. A review of your recent financial transactions will help you to know how much to budget in various categories.

B. For most people, the great majority of transactions will be reflected in bank statements (checks and debit-card transactions) and credit-card statements.

C. Allocation of your cash transactions may be estimated by listing your cash withdrawals (ATM transactions) and trying to determine where that money was spent (coffee, fast food, tolls, tips, and so forth).

D. Russ Crosson points out that the two most common mistakes people make when creating a budget are underestimating in certain categories (e.g., eating out) and failing to account for other categories altogether (e.g., children's allowances).[3]

E. You should be able to account for the spending of every dollar of your income. If not, you need to do further investigation to discover and plug some financial leaks. Steve and Sally have a combined monthly take-home income of $5,400, but in the past month they could account only for where $5,100 had gone. They had no idea of how the other $300 had been spent. Part of their assignment for the following month was to keep an exact record of every single expense so that there would be no more financial leaks.

3. After You Have Created Your Budget, Keep Track of Your Income and Expenses by Recording Every Dollar Spent or Received

With my help, Steve and Sally created a balanced budget, but their work was not yet done. They still needed some way to see whether they were keeping to their budget.

A. A budget written but not followed will do you no good.

B. This will necessarily involve some effort. As Proverbs 21:5 notes, it is the plans of the *diligent* that succeed.

C. Keeping track of your expenses will help you to see whether your budget is realistic and to modify it if it is not.

3. Russ Crosson, *Your Money Made Simple* (Eugene, OR: Harvest House, 2019), 62.

D. Monitoring expenses should also help you to live within your budget. For example, if your entertainment budget is $100 a month and you have spent $97 by the end of the first week, you have to limit yourself to $3 in this category for the rest of the month (self-control is a fruit of the Spirit, Gal. 5:23) or find money that you can take from another category (e.g., clothing) and transfer to the entertainment category.

4. There Are Many Possible Methods by Which You Can Monitor Your Expenses and Income

A. Many have successfully used what is called the envelope system, in which a family at the beginning of each month puts cash into several envelopes representing their expense categories. Purchases are made by taking money out of that category's envelope. And when the money is gone, no more money can be spent from that category until next month, when it is replenished. In practice, it might work to use cash envelopes for variable discretionary spending, such as clothing and eating out. It isn't convenient or practical, however, to pay major fixed expenses (such as mortgage or rent payments) in cash. Steve and Sally started by using the envelope system because of its simplicity. They also discovered that paying cash for discretionary items, instead of using a card, helped them to have more financial self-control.

B. One could also accomplish the same thing through a virtual envelope system in which budget and expenses are monitored on an app or spreadsheet that shows how much is left to spend in each category. Every expense lowers the remaining budget in a given budget category. No more may be spent from that category until it is refilled when the next month begins.

C. Some old-fashioned people do best by keeping track of their finances on multicolumned accounting paper. They put the budgeted amount for each category on the top of each column and then write down the expenses as they occur.

D. The same recordkeeping function can be accomplished through a simple computer spreadsheet created through a program such as Excel.

E. People who are more tech-savvy enjoy using specially designed personal budgeting programs and apps that allow them to create a budget and then categorize bank and card transactions by budget category. After several months of using the envelope system, Steve and Sally heard from friends about an app that functioned a lot like envelopes. They found the program easy to use as they sought to maintain the same financial self-discipline they had exercised while they were on the envelope system.[4]

F. Many have found that it helps to get a receipt for each purchase, especially cash transactions, and to keep the receipt until the expense has been recorded.

WHICH SPOUSE SHOULD OVERSEE THE BUDGET?

While I fully affirm the complementary biblical roles of husband and wife in marriage,[5] I do not think that the husband's headship is compromised if his wife creates and monitors the budget (and investments). If she is more capable than he in financial matters, he should be grateful for how God has gifted his "helper" (Gen. 2:18). No matter who does the bookkeeping, it is important that husband and wife respectfully cooperate in financial matters.

SUMMARY

While we can't command someone to use a particular budgeting system, God's Word does teach that it is wise to plan and that a failure to plan is likely to create significant hardship. For many people, the decision to live by a budget is a major new life commitment, like

4. See mvelopes.com; mint.com.
5. See Jim Newheiser, *Marriage, Divorce, and Remarriage: Critical Questions and Answers* (Phillipsburg, NJ: P&R Publishing, 2017).

going on a new diet or exercise program. Similarly, it can be very hard to get started, but once new habits are formed, keeping a budget becomes part of one's routine. I have seen the finances of individuals and couples, including those with relatively low incomes, transformed by making and keeping a budget. One of the greatest benefits of managing our money more wisely is that we are enabled to give more of our resources to the Lord's work.

— Questions for Reflection —

1. What is the biblical basis for saying that we should live by a budget?
2. What excuses do people offer for not living by a budget? How would you refute these?
3. What harm results from failing to live by a budget?
4. What are the benefits of living by a budget?
5. What practical steps could you take to better plan your finances?

19

WHAT STEPS CAN BE TAKEN TO BALANCE YOUR BUDGET?

I worked with Nate and Sonya[1] on their budget during a counseling session and then sent them home to refine their budget based on their recent spending history. But as I continued to work with them, we faced a problem: their monthly expenses exceeded Nate's take-home pay by over $300.

There are essentially two ways to balance an out-of-balance budget: either increase income or decrease expenses. We discussed options for increasing income in chapter 14. Now we will consider some options for decreasing expenses. For many people, the best way to reduce expenses is to get rid of debt, which will be discussed in chapter 30.

CAN DISCRETIONARY EXPENSES BE REDUCED?

Some people have trouble balancing a budget because they are overspending in discretionary categories that could be significantly reduced without overwhelming pain. Some of these categories are entertainment, eating out, travel, electronics, and clothes. It is not necessarily wrong to enjoy fine dining, new clothes, and the latest smartphones— if one has the resources to afford them. But someone whose current

1. The case examples used are based on various people I have counseled over the years, with some names and details changed.

expenses exceed income could save hundreds of dollars a month by cutting back on these expenses, which could lead to a balanced budget.

Here are some of the steps I suggested to Nate and Sonya:

1. Nate and Sonya have the gold package with their cable TV company, which costs $120 a month. They could downgrade to the silver plan, which is $75, or they could choose to cut the cord altogether, at least until their financial situation improves. Savings: $45–120 per month.
2. Sonya gets a latte each morning after she drops off the kids at school. It costs $4, including tip, which amounts to $80 per month. She could cut this expense out entirely, or she could limit herself to one per week. Savings: $64–80 per month.
3. Nate typically grabs fast food for lunch during work at an average of $10 a day, which amounts to $200 a month. He could pack a lunch four days a week and eat out once a week. Savings (taking into account the cost of the packed lunch and allowing for a few times when Nate can eat out): $120 per month.
4. Nate gets his hair cut once a month at Guido's Fancy European Salon, which costs $80. He could try a traditional barbershop. Savings: $55 per month.
5. After two years, Sonya has just finished paying off her phone at $50 per month. She has been attracted to the newer model with the 3D camera, which would cost $1,320 ($55 per month for two years). She could decide to make do with her old phone for two more years. Savings: $55 per month.
6. Nate and Sonya had been planning to take their kids to Disney World for a week this summer, which was expected to cost $4,800 (requiring them to put aside $400 a month). They could choose to enjoy a beach vacation ($2,400 or $200 a month) or to go camping in a national park ($1,200 or $100 a month). Savings: $200–300 per month.

Others might find different places to cut back. Some might choose to buy their kids' clothes at Target instead of Macy's. Others could save money each month by adjusting the thermostat a few degrees, by doing their own lawn care, or by getting their nails done less often. The point is that the budget must balance (including making provision through savings for anticipated future expenses).

In the case of Nate and Sonya, we had identified over $700 in potential monthly expense reductions, and they needed to take advantage of only $300 worth in order to get their budget to balance. They also had the option of choosing to make more reductions in order to reduce debt or increase savings (see parts 4 and 5).

SOME PEOPLE ARE FORCED TO MAKE A MORE DRASTIC CHANGE TO THEIR LIFESTYLE

I have run into some cases in which every imaginable discretionary expense has been reduced, but the budget still can't be balanced. Assuming that everything possible has been done to earn more income, the next step is to consider making some very hard choices in order to reduce major fixed expenses. The biggest budget items for most people are housing and transportation. Some people pay far more in rent or mortgage payments than their income can afford. This could be because of a reduction of income after a job change, or a family might have purchased more house than their income could afford. In any case, it might be necessary to investigate downgrading or downsizing to an affordable dwelling (as painful as that may be). Similarly, many people drive a vehicle that costs more than they can afford, in which case they might need to get by with a much more modest ride.[2]

MANY PEOPLE HAVE TO DEAL WITH AN IRREGULAR INCOME STREAM

Some, such as those in seasonal work or sales, have income that varies widely from month to month. While it is easier to manage a

2. One of the negatives of buying a vehicle on credit is that one might owe more than the car is worth, which makes it very difficult to get out from under the

budget when monthly income is steady, budgeting could be all the more important for those with variable income. Just as Joseph led the Egyptians to save during their "fat cow" years in preparation for the "skinny cow" years (Gen. 41), people with variable income need to save during the prosperous months in order to pay the bills that will continue during the lean months. In such cases, I recommend that they make a conservative estimate of expected income based on previous experience and budget accordingly. Such people might benefit by creating a separate budget to reflect the realities of each month of the year, rather than relying on the same budget for each month. They might need more money in short-term savings to cover income fluctuations.

DEBT IS THE GREAT ENEMY OF A BALANCED BUDGET

I have counseled many people who could easily balance their budget if they weren't encumbered by credit-card payments, student debt, and personal loans. We will discuss ways to avoid and eliminate debt in part 4.

A WORD OF CAUTION FOR COUNSELORS

Many budgeting and lifestyle issues are matters of wisdom and personal choice rather than absolute biblical command. We need to be careful not to overstep our authority. As a counselor, I cannot demand that a family open up their finances to me. But I can offer to take a look if they want my help. Nor can I tell someone where to shop for clothes, which Internet package to buy, or whether they should order a double latte every morning. I can tell them that they need to live within their means while meeting their financial obligations. I can warn them that overspending and debt will lead to financial ruin.

I can also make suggestions about where they might be able to cut expenses. While I may suggest that they downgrade their cable TV

---

unaffordable payment. We will discuss this further in part 4, which deals with debt.

plan or eat out less often, they are free to make other choices as long as general biblical principles are followed.

SUMMARY

Making and following a budget takes time and effort. Many families realize, once they begin the budgeting process, that they will need to make some changes and exercise self-control in their spending. The benefits make budgeting worthwhile. Those who plan well are able to save more, give more, and enjoy more of the earthly blessings for which money can pay.

— QUESTIONS FOR REFLECTION —

1. What are some of the most common ways that people could cut their expenses in order to balance their budget?
2. What steps can someone take if the person can't find any more "fat" to cut out of his or her budget?
3. Why is it wrong for a counselor to tell someone what expenses the person must reduce?
4. Can financial mismanagement ever be grounds for disqualification of a church officer? Or church discipline?

20

WHAT CAN BE DONE TO HELP PEOPLE WHO ARE FAILING TO FOLLOW THEIR BUDGET?

Bob earns a good income as an accountant. His work skills have helped him to create a balanced budget for him and his wife, Miriam. But Miriam habitually overspends, especially on clothes for herself and the children, and on gifts for family and friends. Bob has repeatedly tried to explain the importance of following the family budget, but Miriam's spending habits haven't changed. While Bob and Miriam are not deeply in debt, Bob is getting frustrated because their savings goals are not being met. Recently, they have had some heated arguments about money. Their nine-year-old has asked Miriam if this means that her parents are divorcing.

MANY BUDGETING PROBLEMS HAVE SPIRITUAL ROOTS

1. Greed: Materialism and Covetousness

Paul Tripp writes, "We don't have a budget problem; we have a treasure problem."[1] Many people overspend because they have bought

---

1. Paul David Tripp, *Redeeming Money: How God Reveals and Reorients Our Hearts* (Wheaton, IL: Crossway, 2018), 97.

into the world's lie of materialism, that possessions and experiences will make you happy. We have already seen how Paul warns that covetousness is a spiritual problem and amounts to idol-worship (Col. 3:5). The idol of greed is never satisfied; thus, people spend more money than they can afford, chasing the illusion that these things will bring them joy and satisfaction (Luke 12:15). As we discussed in previous chapters, a key to financial success is to find our greatest satisfaction in the Lord (Isa. 55:1–2).

2. Envy

"A tranquil heart gives life to the flesh, but envy makes the bones rot" (Prov. 14:30 ESV). Miriam's sister is married to a surgeon, who earns a lot more money than Bob. Thus, Miriam's sister lives in a luxurious home and shops at the finest stores without worrying about the cost. Miriam is tempted to overspend as she tries to keep up with her sister.

3. Indulgence

Many need to learn the "secret" of contentment (Phil. 4:11–13; Heb. 13:5). Phoebe grew up in a wealthy family that lived in an exclusive neighborhood. She went to the best private schools. When she was a teenager, her father gave her a credit card, which she used at the mall. No questions were ever raised about her spending. During college she became a Christian. A few years later, she fell in love with and married Henry, whose life goal was to be a pastor. While they were in seminary, Phoebe struggled while they had to live on very limited means. There was almost no money for eating out or shopping for nonessentials. She had never before had to live on a budget and was having a hard time keeping her spending within the agreed-upon limits. Henry, who had grown up in a very frugal family, was tempted to become impatient and angry when Phoebe overspent.

4. Man-Pleasing

Some spend too much money as a way of trying to gain the acceptance and love of others. A grandmother who lives far away from her grandchildren might be tempted to show her love by spending more than she can afford on gifts. We once had a case in which a woman had stolen a great deal of money from a Christian ministry. We learned that she had spent all of it on family members and friends so that they would love her.

5. Laziness

Some people just don't want to exert the effort it takes to keep track of their spending. Sadly, the laziness and poor stewardship of such people will most likely result in financial troubles and possible conflict with family members. "Poor is he who works with a negligent hand" (Prov. 10:4a).

SOME BUDGETING PROBLEMS ARE RELATIONAL

Money is one of the most common issues over which married couples fight. Often the financial problems cannot be solved until their deeper marriage issues are addressed.

In one couple's case, the husband, Alvin, worked long hours in order to make a good income for his young family. But it seemed that no matter how much money Alvin made, his wife, Katy, spent more, often on expensive designer fashion items. As we explored Katy's motives, we came to realize that her overspending was not because she believed that those possessions would make her happy. Rather, it was as an act of revenge because Katy was angry and jealous that Alvin was working so much and had little time for her. We had to work with Alvin to help him to learn to better care for his wife in a Christlike way. We also had to counsel Katy to repent of her sinful jealousy and anger, and then to learn how to express her concerns to Alvin in a godly way (Gal. 6:1). Each had to seek forgiveness from the other and to show grace for past sins (Eph. 4:31–32).

1. Selfishness and Jealousy Lead to Many Financial Battles

The husband resents how much money the wife spends on getting her hair and nails done. The wife is angry over how much the husband spends on hunting and fishing gear (or theology books). Rather than humbly seeking to look out for the interests of the other (Phil. 2:3–4), they each fight for their own financial rights and thus "bite and devour one another" (Gal. 5:15). In practical terms, it is wise to allow each spouse some "pocket money" within the budget for his or her personal hobbies and interests. But if the relational sin issues are not first addressed, this technique probably won't make things much better.

2. Some Couples Experience Conflict When the Primary Wage-Earner Thinks That He or She Has Greater Say in How the Finances Are Managed, Reasoning That "It's My Money"

In a healthy marriage, each partner is working hard in his or her sphere, and resources are managed and shared in equal partnership. If your wife is a "fellow heir of the grace of life," then she surely is a coheir of your finances (1 Peter 3:7).

3. One Spouse's Failure to Stick to the Budget Can Undermine Trust in Marriage

When a couple makes a budgetary plan, they are making a commitment to each other. When one spouse doesn't follow the budget, that person is breaking his or her promise. Often the problem is compounded when the guilty spouse tries to hide the spending from the other. "Therefore, laying aside falsehood, speak truth each one of you with his neighbor, for we are members of one another" (Eph. 4:25).

4. Many Couples Have Significant Unresolved Personal Conflicts in Their Marriage That Spill Over into Financial Conflicts

Often bitterness has built up over many years. Such a couple probably need comprehensive marriage counseling for biblical peacemaking so that they can be right with God and with each other before they can get their financial house in order.[2] To illustrate, you can't grow many flowers in your garden if it is infested with weeds.

---

2. For a biblical approach to resolving marital conflicts, see chapters 15–18 in Jim Newheiser, *Marriage, Divorce, and Remarriage: Critical Questions and Answers* (Phillipsburg, NJ: P&R Publishing, 2017).

SOME PEOPLE NEED HELP KEEPING A BUDGET

Many people have never before successfully lived by a budget. Others are not very good at math. We can sympathize because most of us are tempted to avoid doing things at which we think we are likely to fail. A humble believer will admit his or her weaknesses and seek help from someone who is stronger—a spouse or a kind, capable friend from church—who can try to help the person to get into the habit of spending his or her money according to a wise plan. The financially savvy helper needs to be patient and would do well to find ways to simplify recordkeeping for the one who has a hard time understanding financial matters.

Several years ago, Ferdinand and Vicki came to us for financial help. They both worked low-wage jobs and were constantly under financial pressure. They had never before lived by a budget. We sat with them and helped them to create one. About a year in, Vicki proudly showed me how she was keeping track of their expenditures and said that they were experiencing a lot more financial freedom. About two years after that, Ferdinand and Vicki wanted to meet again to discuss their finances. This time, their problem was that they had over $20,000 saved and wanted to know how to invest it (see part 5 to find out about investing).

SUMMARY

When someone is failing to follow his or her budget, rather than giving up, the person should seek to find and address the cause(s) of the failure. Often, deeper spiritual or relational issues need to be addressed. Many require someone to walk patiently alongside them through the process of getting their finances in order.

— QUESTIONS FOR REFLECTION —

1. What are the most common causes of people's failing to keep within their budgets?

2. How can those who are bad at math and finances be helped in keeping their budgets?
3. Why is it difficult for a couple with unresolved conflicts to work together on finances?
4. What sins might be involved when someone overspends?

21

WHAT ELSE CAN BE DONE IN PRACTICAL TERMS TO AVOID OVERSPENDING?

DON'T LIVE BEYOND YOUR MEANS

"He who loves pleasure will become a poor man; he who loves wine and oil will not become rich" (Prov. 21:17; also see 23:20–21). While we are free to enjoy legitimate earthly blessings as our income allows (1 Tim. 4:3–4), we need to guard our hearts from the temptation to overspend. Many small economic indulgences can add up to a lot. By forgoing some luxuries in the present, we will have more that we can give away to worthy causes and more that we can save for the future.

DON'T COMPARE (ENVY)

I remember that when our kids were growing up, our best friends purchased a new minivan. I was impressed with how our three children could be spread out over three rows in separate seats, instead of fighting for real estate in the back seat. I dreamed of being able to put on a video that would calm them on long road trips. Suddenly I thought, "I need a minivan." And: "If he can afford a new minivan, so can I." We also tend to notice how often our friends and family members eat out, the kinds of phones they use, and the cars they drive. We want to keep up. It has been said that we often spend money we don't have to buy things we don't need to impress people we don't even like. Often those whom we are tempted to envy are living on the edge financially as they use debt to finance their lifestyle.

DON'T MAKE IMPULSIVE PURCHASES

Many have found it wise to make a shopping list before going to the grocery store, the mall, or the warehouse club and then to commit not to buy anything not on the list without careful budgetary consideration (including spousal agreement). This can be a challenge because stores carefully plan their layouts in order to get you to buy more than you had planned. For example, you go into the shoe store, planning to replace your worn-out pair of street shoes, but then learn that you can buy a second pair for half off. Some of us have closets filled with hundreds of dollars' worth of items purchased on impulse but never or rarely used. Randy Alcorn points out some important general principles for buying: "Nothing is a good deal if you can't afford it" and "You don't save money by spending money."[1] If you buy a $100 item you didn't need for $60, you didn't so much save $40 as much as you spent $60. Online shopping is designed to entice you to keep shopping and to buy more. If you exit the website, you will likely receive further enticements to buy on social media and through email. Some have suggested that when considering a purchase, you convert the price into the number of hours you would have to work to buy it. For example, if you make $20 an hour after taxes, it would take you ten hours of labor to buy $200 worth of clothes. Randy Alcorn suggests instead that every purchase should be prayerfully evaluated in light of its alternative use or ministry potential.[2]

1. Randy Alcorn, *Managing God's Money* (Carol Stream, IL: Tyndale House, 2011), 173.
2. Alcorn, *Managing God's Money*, 173.

BE ESPECIALLY CAREFUL WITH MAJOR PURCHASES AND COMMITMENTS

Salespeople are trained to get you to spend more than you had planned, often on products that you had not previously considered. They will tell you that you must buy today or your opportunity for a deal will be lost. "The naive believes everything, but the sensible man considers his steps" (Prov. 14:15; also see 22:3). It is wise to research products and prices from objective sources before talking to a salesperson.

BEWARE OF TIME-SHARES

There is probably no financial commitment that more people have regretted more deeply than committing to time-share vacation ownership.[3] Potential customers are enticed to attend a sales presentation by the offer of free meals, tickets, or lodging. Such presentations typically involve high-pressure sales tactics. The salespeople have an answer for every objection and try to get you to make a major financial commitment on the spot. You should be very wary whenever any salesperson pressures you to act immediately or else the opportunity will be lost. An honorable time-share offer would allow the purchaser time to do research and to ponder the decision before making a commitment. Many who have purchased these time-share products have been saddled with budget-busting monthly payments (which typically include maintenance fees over which they might have no control, in addition to the cost of the unit itself). Purchasers have also found that it is extremely difficult and expensive to get out of these contracts. Some find that they don't even utilize their time-share when it is available to them. Because salespeople can be so persuasive, my advice is not to be enticed by the "free" offers. The salespeople are betting

---

3. I heard a story about a guy who was asked how he felt about his recent time-share purchase. He said, "Ever since I committed, I have slept like a baby—up every three hours crying!"

that they can overcome your sales resistance. They often win. They know that most people plan to take the free stuff they offer without buying anything, but are confident that they can make enough sales to more than pay for whatever they give you. "A prudent man sees evil and hides himself, the naive proceed and pay the penalty" (Prov. 27:12).

Some people are happy with their time-share. Those who are most satisfied tend to have significant financial resources so that the time-share is not a financial burden. They enjoy going to the same place year after year or taking advantage of the ability to swap for different locations.

SHOP AND SPEND WISELY

I have been impressed by families with limited income who have saved a great deal of money through being frugal. They stock up on sale items at the grocery store and use coupons. They find bargains at garage sales and thrift stores. They aren't afraid to negotiate when a price seems too high. Others believe that they are so well off that they don't need to shop for sales and use coupons. Yet many have observed that those who are wealthy continue to be very careful with their money, choosing a lifestyle well below their means[4]—which is probably one of the reasons they became rich to begin with.

THE BEST THING YOU CAN DO FOR YOUR BUDGET IS TO BE DEBT-FREE

Money spent on interest payments is generally unproductive. When debt is eliminated, money is freed up for expenditures for lifestyle improvement, for giving, and for saving. (See part 4.)

4. Thomas J. Stanley and William D. Danko, *The Millionaire Next Door: The Surprising Secrets of America's Wealthy* (Lanham, MD: Taylor Trade Publishing, 2010), 27.

SUMMARY

Some people dig themselves into a deep financial hole by making major financial mistakes. Most of these can be avoided if you stick to your budget plan. It is also important that a couple be united in making major financial decisions. A wise budget-keeping saver who hates debt might help to keep his or her free-spending spouse from making unwise, impulsive financial decisions.

— QUESTIONS FOR REFLECTION —

1. How does one decide at which standard of living to live?
2. When have you been tempted by envy when you have observed the lifestyle of family and friends?
3. What are some practical things you could do to spend less?
4. When is it no longer worthwhile to chase sales and bargains?

PART 4

DEBT

PART 4

REST

22

WHAT ARE COMMON MISUNDERSTANDINGS ABOUT DEBT?

Many of the major financial mistakes that individuals, corporations, and governments make have to do with borrowing money. Debt can be like a drug because it offers the benefits of spending without the disciplined effort of earning and saving. A debt addiction, like a drug addiction, can come to dominate and then ultimately ruin the user.

IS WHAT YOU CAN SPEND DETERMINED BY HOW MUCH CREDIT YOU HAVE?

Many people decide how much to spend on a house or a car based on the amount of money that the bank is willing to lend them, without adequate concern about the risk of one day being unable to make the payments. Credit cards, when not paid off every month, allow people to make an extended sequence of smaller purchases beyond current income, which can lead to large and often overwhelming debt. We will address these basic issues about debt in chapters 23–24.

DO YOU NEED SOME DEBT SO THAT YOU CAN ESTABLISH A GOOD CREDIT RATING?

Because so much of our financial system revolves around debt, it is important to have a good credit rating.[1] While I strongly believe that debt should be minimized or avoided altogether, good credit can help you qualify for loans, such as a mortgage. Bad credit can prevent you from being able to borrow money, or will cause you to pay very high interest. *Bad credit can even cause your auto-insurance premiums to go up.* Some people carry a balance on a credit card or borrow money in some other way, in the hope that establishing a good record of making timely payments will boost their credit rating. Sadly, this can be expensive, in terms of interest paid, and unnecessary. There are ways in which one can establish good credit without running up debt and paying interest. Simply pay your bills on time and avoid having high amounts of debt in proportion to your income. This is also a key element in repairing bad credit from the past.

DOESN'T EVERYONE HAVE TO BORROW MONEY TO BUY A CAR?

A much better strategy would be to save money so that you can pay cash for your next car, thus avoiding interest expenses. We will explain this and discuss whether leasing a car makes financial sense in chapter 26.

ARE YOU IN GOOD SHAPE IF YOU CAN MAKE THE MINIMUM PAYMENTS ON YOUR CREDIT CARDS?

If you are making the minimum payments on your credit cards, you will be paying too much for what you have purchased, and you could be in big financial trouble for many years to come.

1. One of the most widely used credit ratings is the FICO score, which can range from 300 to 850. Lenders use this score to determine how great a risk it would be to lend you money, which will guide their decision whether to issue credit to you and what interest rate to charge.

ARE OFFERS OF ZERO PERCENT FINANCING WORTH TAKING?

Home-improvement stores often entice customers to make major purchases, such as mattresses, televisions, and flooring, with "zero interest and no payments until next year." You are still incurring debt and having to make payments for something that you might not be able to afford within your budget. In addition, the fine print on the contracts for such purchases often states that high interest will be charged from day one if the buyer doesn't make the required payment in full on time.

IS STUDENT DEBT WORTH IT BECAUSE OF THE FINANCIAL BENEFITS OF AN EDUCATION?

Those who incur significant student debt often don't realize how hard it will be to pay it back and spend many years, if not decades, regretting the financial choices they made when they were young. We will discuss student debt in chapter 25.

IS IT WISE FOR FAMILY AND CLOSE FRIENDS TO HELP EACH OTHER BY LENDING MONEY AND COSIGNING FOR EACH OTHER?

Involving yourself in the debts of those to whom you are close often leads to both financial and relational disaster. As Dave Ramsey writes, "Loaning money to a friend or family member is a bad decision. Someone who lends money to a loved one has their heart—not their head—in the right place. It is okay to give money, but loaning money to someone with whom you have a relationship will lead to broken hearts and broken wallets. . . . Thanksgiving dinner tastes 100% better when friends or relatives don't owe one another money! Eating with your master is different than eating with your family."[2] In chapter 29,

---

2. www.daveramsey.com/blog/the-danger-zone#:~:text=Loaning%20money%20to%20a%20friend,broken%20hearts%20and%20broken%20wallets.

we will explain why it is generally unwise to become entangled in financial matters with family members. We will also make some suggestions about what you can say to them when you turn them down.

IS IT ALWAYS FINANCIALLY ADVANTAGEOUS TO BUY, RATHER THAN RENT, YOUR HOME?

Home ownership can be expensive. In some situations, buying a home can be much costlier than renting. In chapter 27, we will explain the many things you should consider when making this important financial decision.

IS DEBT CONSOLIDATION THROUGH BORROWING AGAINST THE EQUITY IN YOUR HOME A GOOD WAY TO REDUCE DEBT?

Debt consolidation often prolongs the cycle of overspending and can result in financial ruin. We will also discuss this in chapter 27.

SUMMARY

In spite of the conventional wisdom in our culture, debt is neither wise nor inevitable. The Bible offers wisdom that will help you to avoid debt, to get out of the debt you have, and to enjoy the blessings of being debt-free. The questions raised above will be answered in detail over the next eight chapters.

— QUESTIONS FOR REFLECTION —

1. What misconceptions do many people have about debt?
2. What are some of the biggest mistakes you have seen other people make with debt?
3. What mistakes have you made with debt?

23

WHAT DOES THE BIBLE
TEACH ABOUT DEBT?

Debt is a part of every aspect of economic life. Governments at every level borrow money, typically by issuing various kinds of bonds, in order to fund both capital projects and ongoing expenses. Corporations finance expansion and ongoing operations by borrowing either from banks or from investors. (We will discuss government and corporate debt in chapter 28.) Individuals and families use debt to pay for houses, cars, education, and even everyday expenses. Borrowing in our society is viewed as both inevitable and beneficial. As of this writing, the average American has about $40,000 in consumer debt, which does not include mortgage debt.[1] Only about one in four persons is debt-free.[2]

WHY DO PEOPLE GET INTO DEBT?

Some people get into debt after experiencing financial calamity, such as a huge unexpected medical bill or the loss of a job. Others incur debt because they have been unwise with income or expenses (see parts 2 and 3). Debt can be attractive because you can have what you

1. www.cnbc.com/2018/08/20/how-much-debt-americans-have-at-every-age.html #:~:text=The%20average%20American%20now%20has,27%20percent) .%E2%80%9D.
2. www.cnbc.com/2018/08/20/how-much-debt-americans-have-at-every-age.html #:~:text=The%20average%20American%20now%20has,27%20percent) .%E2%80%9D.

want today without having to postpone gratification, and then you can worry tomorrow about how you will pay for it. Lenders and retailers, eager to make sales, often make borrowing easy, even for those whose ability to pay back is questionable. Many people get deeply into debt like they gain weight—one small bad decision at a time over a period of many years, during which they are living in denial.

DEBT IS OFTEN PRESUMPTUOUS

In the old Popeye cartoon, the character Wimpy was famous for saying, "I'll gladly pay you Tuesday for a hamburger today." When I was a kid, I watched a lot of Popeye cartoons, but I never once saw Wimpy pay anyone back. Individuals incur debt under the optimistic assumption that they will be able to pay when their income increases. Governments and corporations borrow money with the expectation that the economy will continue to expand. Scripture warns, however, "The mind of man plans his way, but the LORD directs his steps" (Prov. 16:9). We cannot expect uninterrupted stability and prosperity in a fallen world. Individuals lose their jobs. Corporations lose market share. National economies go into recessions and depressions. Famines, droughts, and pandemics occur. Those who are deepest in debt suffer the most when hard times come. In January 2020, the economy was booming with full employment and prosperity. Stock markets were at record highs. When the pandemic hit, shutting down the economy, many businesses, from small family ventures to large corporations, went into bankruptcy or permanently ceased operations. Many of these businesses failed because they had what the financial press called "a millstone of debt" hanging on them. They had borrowed money for expansions and acquisitions on the assumption that the good times would continue. They were totally unprepared for an unexpected dramatic economic downturn. Financial guru Warren Buffett points out, "When the tide goes out, you can tell who was skinny-dipping."[3]

3. Quoted in Dave Ramsey, *The Total Money Makeover*, 3rd ed. (Nashville: Thomas Nelson, 2009), xxiii.

DEBT HAS CONSEQUENCES

The Bible warns against taking on debt: "The rich rules over the poor, and the borrower becomes the lender's slave" (Prov. 22:7).

1. Debt Is Enslaving

It is very hard to get rid of debt. In previous centuries, a person who couldn't pay his debts could have literally been made a slave to the debtor or be put into debtors' prison until he or his friends and relatives could pay off what he owed. Debt still turns people into slaves. Debt forces you to spend much of your hard-earned income on unproductive interest expenses, thus leaving much less for both the necessities and the luxuries of life. Your debt might be like shackles that prevent you from fulfilling your God-given responsibilities to provide for your family (1 Tim. 5:8) and to give to the Lord's work. Paul writes, "You were bought with a price; do not become slaves of men" (1 Cor. 7:23).

2. Debt Is Costly

It lowers your standard of living. In addition to paying the cost of what you buy, you are paying interest. Debt makes everything you buy more expensive. People often incur debt for the purpose of enhancing lifestyle, but in reality debt invariably reduces lifestyle because in the long run you spend money on interest, which could have been allocated to other more desirable budget categories. Many families spend a large percentage of their monthly income to pay interest on their debts. We have seen debt prove to be costly in another way: the ending of a courtship because one party decided that the excessive debt of the other was reason to break off the relationship. The person believed that the debt was most likely indicative of a lack of self-control and was a burden that he or she didn't want to bear and a marriage risk that he or she didn't want to take.

3. Debt Can Cause You to Lose What You Have

Scripture vividly warns of this consequence of debt: "If you have nothing with which to pay, why should he take your bed from under you?" (Prov. 22:27; also see Neh. 5:3–5). When people can't pay, cars are repossessed and houses go into foreclosure.

4. Debt Is Stressful

Those who are in debt will often be tempted to worry about how they will make all their payments (Matt. 6:25ff.). Excessive debt has robbed many people of a good night's sleep.

5. Those Who Are Deeply in Debt Are Always Behind Financially

This reality was expressed in the 1950's bestselling hit song *Sixteen Tons*, sung by Tennessee Ernie Ford, which poignantly depicted coal miners who labored all day to load sixteen tons of coal each but only ended up deeper in debt to the coal company's general store. Those stuck in the cycle of debt find themselves going deeper into debt every day—not to the company store, but to Mastercard, Visa, and American Express. A growing number of the hours of their daily labor are spent merely to service their debts. The worse their predicament, the more desperate they become, resulting in their paying even higher interest rates to those who are still willing to lend to them.[4]

DEBT IS GENERALLY AN INDICATION OF THE ABSENCE OF GOD'S BLESSING

Under the old covenant, the nation of Israel was told that debt is a curse of covenant disobedience: "He shall lend to you, but you will not lend to him; he shall be the head, and you will be the tail" (Deut. 28:44). This goes along with Proverbs 22:7, which says that the borrower is the lender's slave. Those who borrow are in a position of weakness and dependence. The lender has a certain amount of power over them. Their financial freedom is limited by their debt. This is true of nations, corporations, and individuals.

---

4. Payday loans, which allow one to borrow against a future paycheck, often have extremely high interest rates. The underworld is famously involved in debt as loan sharks prey on the desperate, charging exorbitant interest rates.

IS IT ALWAYS SINFUL TO INCUR DEBT?

Given all that Scripture says against borrowing, some wonder whether it is always wrong to borrow. While debt is often incurred sinfully, borrowing or lending money is not always sinful. Some borrow from sinful motives because they are covetous, discontent (not being satisfied with what God has supplied), and impatient because they believe that in order to be happy, they must immediately possess what they can't currently afford. Some people wind up in debt because of a sinful failure to wisely plan/budget (Prov. 21:5). Some people borrow money while deliberately planning not to repay it (Ps. 37:21), which amounts to stealing. Some borrow out of ignorance, thinking that because everybody does it—my parents did it, my government does it, my friends do it, even my church does it—therefore it must be normal.

So while the Bible teaches that debt is generally unwise, incurring debt is not always sinful. The most common example is a home purchase. Few people can pay cash for a suitable house. There is often little financial difference between a rent payment and a mortgage payment. (See chapter 27 for more on borrowing to buy a home.) One might also choose to borrow money for other major purchases.

WHAT ARE SOME GENERAL PRINCIPLES ABOUT BORROWING?

If you must borrow, you want to do all that is in your power to avoid putting yourself in a position of being unable to meet your obligations.

1. Make the maximum down payment and borrow as little as possible.
2. Ensure that your monthly payments are well within your budget.
3. Avoid borrowing money for depreciating items.
4. If you are borrowing money in order to pay for consumption items such as groceries, you have significant debt troubles.

5. Debt makes everything more expensive and reduces lifestyle. The higher the interest rate, the greater the harm done.
6. Make loan payments in full and on time (Prov. 3:27–28).
7. Do all that you can to meet your debt obligations (Ps. 37:21).
8. Ensure that you have sufficient short-term savings (see part 5) to make up for periodic budget shortfalls so that you won't get behind on debt.
9. Avoid putting yourself in a position in which you owe more for something than you could quickly receive if you had to sell the item quickly.
10. Make it your goal to be completely debt-free.

SUMMARY

Scripture exhorts us to avoid debt: "Owe nothing to anyone except to love one another" (Rom. 13:8a). Just as debt produces slavery and grief, being debt-free results in financial freedom and happiness. As Dickens's troubled character Micawber famously stated, "Annual income twenty pounds, annual expenditure nineteen nineteen and six, result happiness. Annual income twenty pounds, annual expenditure twenty pounds ought and six, result misery."[5]

— QUESTIONS FOR REFLECTION —

1. Is debt always sinful? Why or why not?
2. How might debt be sinfully incurred?
3. What are some of the possible consequences of debt?
4. In what sense is debt a curse?
5. When might it be allowable or even wise to take on debt?

5. Charles Dickens, *David Copperfield* (1849–1850; repr., Hertfordshire, UK: Wordsworth Editions, 2000), 153.

24

IS THERE A WISE WAY TO USE CREDIT CARDS?

Credit and debit cards have replaced cash as the most common form of payment both in brick-and-mortar business and in online commerce. Many businesses, including my seminary's bookstore, won't even accept cash as payment. Yet credit and debit cards can be dangerous.

CREDIT CARDS ARE PROBABLY THE MOST COMMON WAY THAT PEOPLE BECOME ENSLAVED TO DEBT

Research studies have shown that people tend to spend much more when they are using a credit card, as compared to paying cash.[1] There might be something about physically handing over the money for a purchase that helps the buyer to grasp the real cost, compared to swiping or inserting a card. This could be a reason that credit-card issuers and retailers make it increasingly convenient to pay with a card or with an app on your phone. They want you to maximize your spending while feeling as little immediate financial pain or anxiety as possible in the process. The bills will arrive later.

---

1. www.forbes.com/sites/billhardekopf/2018/07/16/do-people-really-spend-more-with-credit-cards/#4370f4081c19.

BEWARE OF AUTOPAY

Many companies try to get their customers to put expenses on autopay from a credit or debit card or bank account for the sake of convenience. Sometimes you are offered a discount if you enroll in autopay. This practice can decrease your awareness of expenses, thus increasing your risk of wasting money. Thus, it might be much more convenient for the merchant than for you. I have known people who put certain expenses such as memberships (clubs and gyms), streaming services, and subscriptions on autopay and then stopped using them, but continued to be charged for years. They had wasted hundreds of dollars without receiving any benefits. Expenses on autopay can be financial vampires that gradually drain your dollars.

ARE THEY TRYING TO KEEP YOU IN THE DARK?

Banks and credit-card companies also encourage or even require you to receive your monthly statements online.[2] This makes it less likely that your expenses will be carefully reviewed (compared to paper statements received in the mail). The end result is that the consumer no longer has a good grasp of where his money is going as his finances gradually bleed out.

CREDIT-CARD DEBT MAKES
EVERYTHING MORE EXPENSIVE

Several years ago, we made a major purchase of $7,000 using a credit card, with the intent to immediately pay it off by using money we had saved. I was astonished when our credit-card statement arrived to read that if we were to make the minimum payments (of about $200 per month) on our $7,000 debt, it would take us twenty-eight years

---

2. I have noticed that the same banks that claim to "go green" by no longer mailing you a monthly bank or credit-card statement still send plenty of snail mail with new credit-card offers.

to pay off this debt. Credit-card interest rates are very high, which adds to the cost you pay for whatever you purchased. In addition, if you make a late payment, you pay draconian fees and the interest rate goes up even more. In this case, if we had made only the minimum payments, we would have been paying literally double, $14,000 for a $7,000 item.

YOU CAN DIG YOURSELF INTO A VERY DEEP FINANCIAL HOLE WITH CREDIT CARDS

We have counseled many families who have built up tens of thousands of dollars of credit-card debt over years of financial indiscipline. We have even counseled college students who had already incurred huge credit-card debt in addition to their student loans, even before embarking on their careers. And the debt problem often becomes much worse. In my example above, the credit-card company's estimate of $14,000 over twenty-eight years assumes that we would incur no additional credit-card debt. In most cases, this would be a false assumption. People who make only the minimum payment typically continue to overspend, thus digging a much deeper hole of debt (or building a higher mountain of manure that must be removed). Sooner or later, they might hit their credit limit and no longer be able to borrow. Or they might reach the point at which they can no longer make even the minimum payment. Financial disaster, including bankruptcy, could soon follow. Approximately one in three credit-card holders make only the minimum payment each month.[3]

CREDIT CARDS CAN HAVE BENEFITS

Because of the dangers of credit-card debt, many financial experts insist that their followers not use credit cards at all. While I agree that this is probably the safest course for those who can't manage credit-card

3. www.nytimes.com/2016/11/12/your-money/the-persistence-of-the-minimum -payment.html.

debt well, it is possible to use credit cards responsibly. Furthermore, there can be benefits to making purchases with credit cards. Credit cards are much more convenient than cash. If you carry large amounts of cash, you are at risk of theft. In contrast, if your credit card is stolen, you are protected from fraud. Credit-card transactions can be automatically downloaded to an app, which can make it easy to keep track of your budget. One of the best benefits of using credit cards is that many cards offer benefits such as airline miles for travel or a percentage of purchases back in cash. Of course, you should realize that these incentives are designed by the credit-card companies to get you to spend more.

WHAT CAN BE DONE IN PRACTICAL TERMS?

1. When Making Major Purchases, Look Into Whether You Can Get a Discount for Paying Cash

Credit-card issuers charge merchants a percentage for each transaction. Many merchants will give as much as a 3 percent discount for cash or check or will place a surcharge to cover the fees they pay for credit-card transactions.

2. Carefully Discipline Yourself to Spend Only What Is Allowed by Your Budget When Using Credit Cards

3. Record Every Financial Transaction Immediately So That What You Have Spent Is Taken from Your Budgeted Amount, Showing What Remains for the Current Month

There are apps that can help you do this.

4. Carefully Review All Credit-Card and Bank Statements to Be Sure That All Transactions Are Valid and Within Your Budget

Look out for autopay vampires. Insist on receiving paper statements in the mail so that you won't miss any statements.

5. Pay Off Your Credit Cards in Full Each Month—No Exceptions

6. If You Can't Stick to Your Budget While Using Credit Cards, Then Get Rid of Them

I regard this as an application of Jesus' words, "If your right eye makes you stumble, tear it out and throw it from you; for it is better for you to lose one of the parts of your body than for your whole body to be thrown into hell" (Matt. 5:29). Use cash as much as possible. In situations in which cash isn't an option, use a debit card (which immediately deducts the cost from your bank account) instead of a credit card.

WHAT ABOUT DEBIT CARDS?

Debit cards have the advantage of being tied to the cash you have in the bank, which should limit how much you can spend, as opposed to credit cards, which allow you to go deeply into debt. On the other hand, the convenience of debit cards can lead to overspending, which would wipe out your bank balance.

SUMMARY

While credit cards have made shopping very convenient, their misuse has led to massive amounts of consumer debt. If one chooses to use these as a form of payment, extra care needs to be taken to avoid overspending, which leads to unmanageable debt.

— QUESTIONS FOR REFLECTION —

1. Why do you think that people overspend when using credit cards?
2. What steps can be taken to ensure that your credit cards are not abused?
3. What are some benefits of using credit cards?
4. What counsel would you give to someone who is misusing credit cards?
5. May we tell someone that he or she must not use credit cards? Why or why not?

25

IS IT WISE TO INCUR DEBT TO FINANCE YOUR EDUCATION?

Jane was an excellent student and graduated near the top of her class. She was accepted into two highly selective universities. Each offered some scholarship money, but also expected her parents to contribute several thousand dollars a year. And Jane was expected to take out tens of thousands of dollars' worth of student loans over the course of her four-year education. She and her parents agonized over what decision they should make. As of this writing, student-loan debt is the second-highest debt category in the United States, behind only mortgage loans and surpassing auto loans and credit-card debt.[1] Most college graduates are burdened by tens of thousands of dollars in loans. Some owe over $100,000. In some cases, education debt can be worthwhile because of the resulting increase in earning power.

WHAT MISTAKES DO PEOPLE MAKE WITH STUDENT DEBT?

1. Borrowing Large Sums of Money without Carefully Thinking through Whether Incurring So Much Debt Is Wise and Whether Repaying It Is Feasible (Prov. 27:12)

The typical pattern for American students has been to attend the best college that will accept them, to major in what they love, and then to worry about paying for it later.

1. www.forbes.com/sites/zackfriedman/2020/02/03/student-loan-debt-statistics

2. Paying More Than the Education May Be Worth and More Than Students Can Afford

The cost of attending American universities has skyrocketed in recent decades at a rate far surpassing the rate of inflation. A major cause of the increased cost of education has been that there has been virtually no pressure from consumers to keep prices down. Students compete to be accepted into the best universities, which makes education a seller's market, especially in the best schools. Though most students and their families could never afford to pay cash for the exorbitant cost of education, government-backed loans are available so that virtually every accepted student will be able to attend, no matter how high the price. In this system in which acquiring education debt is so easy, students and their parents often fail to take the cost of a particular school into account. After all, payments don't start until after graduation. Only then might people realize that they have become enslaved to their debt (Prov. 22:7).

3. Assuming That University Degrees Always Pay for Themselves

Some college majors have limited value in the marketplace. Many graduates discover that their newly minted degrees do not offer the prospect of high-paying jobs. Many college graduates are unable to find jobs in their chosen fields and wind up working in jobs for which a high school graduate could qualify.[2] The result is that a young adult might be saddled with a very expensive monthly loan repayment that must be paid out from a very limited income.

4. Assuming That Everyone Who Starts College Will Finish

Those who don't finish college wind up with the burden of college debt, but no degree or job prospects to go along with the debt. Once they are no longer students, monthly loan repayments begin.

/#3a7e3006281f.

2. Sometimes they find themselves being supervised by the high school graduate who got work experience while they were in college.

CONSIDER OTHER OPTIONS TO
AVOID OR MINIMIZE STUDENT DEBT

1. Save and Invest for College Education

There are numerous programs for saving and investing for college education.[3] Every family with children should attempt to work this into their budget during the children's growing-up years. Grandparents may fund accounts for their grandchildren.

2. Let the Military Pay for Your College Education

Many get a good education by taking on a debt of service to our country rather than taking on a financial debt. Some qualify to enter the military academies, which provide an excellent education. Others get their education paid for through joining the ROTC at their universities. In each case, the government pays for their education. After graduation, they have an obligation to serve in the military for a certain number of years. While working for the military, they receive pay and benefits. Some join the military out of high school, and then when their service is complete they take advantage of the GI Bill in order to pay for their education.

3. Comparison-Shop among College Options

Many high school students are determined to go to the college of their dreams without serious consideration of cost. It may be that an education is offered at a comparable college at a much more reasonable price. Students can sometimes negotiate with financial-aid departments for more direct aid (scholarships) and fewer loans, especially when various colleges are competing to enroll them.

4. Diligently Investigate Your Eligibility for All Kinds of Scholarships, and Then Apply for Them

These could be through an employer, a community organization, or a group with which you are affiliated.

---

3. See www.savingforcollege.com.

5. Establish Wise Financial Habits While in College

The ease with which college students can borrow money often leads to their incurring far more debt than is necessary (often due to excessive eating out, travel, and entertainment expenses, Prov. 21:17). They should be careful with their money, making wise financial choices and living according to a reasonable budget. They should develop an aversion toward debt and strive to minimize the debt they incur during college. They should remain constantly aware of their loan balance and the future cost of repayment.

6. Consider Less Expensive Ways to Earn College Credit

Many high school students take advanced college-level courses that allow them to take AP exams that give college credit. Some students enter a four-year college with a year's worth of credits, which can save thousands of dollars.[4] A college student can also save money by taking some core courses through inexpensive online courses or at a local community college before enrolling in a much more expensive university program. Money can also be saved by finding a college in a location where the student can live with family or friends.

7. Research the Job and Earning Prospects That You Would Have upon Graduation from the Various Universities and Majors You Are Considering

Choosing an education program is, at least in part, a consumer decision. While it is desirable to pursue studies in a field for which you have aptitude and that offers work you would enjoy, you must also consider financial realities.

WHEN MIGHT IT BE WISE TO TAKE ON EDUCATION DEBT?

1. Education Debt Can Be Worthwhile When It Pays for Itself

Certain degrees or certifications lead to high earnings that would make the cost worthwhile and the debt payments manageable. For

---

4. This was what my wife, Caroline, and I did. Our parents were most grateful!

example, medical school is typically very expensive, and few can pay in cash. But doctors usually earn a great deal of money, thus making the debt repayment manageable. This principle can be true of other kinds of training. For example, it could be worthwhile for someone who is making $3,000 a month to spend (or if necessary borrow) $10,000 for a reputable training course at a trade school that would give the person a certification and make him or her employable at $5,000 a month. The person would want to carefully investigate the training course and the claims of increased earnings before committing. Some people incur debt for education that doesn't fulfill its promise to equip them for a more lucrative career. Another risk is not being able to complete the course—perhaps due to a lack of aptitude for that particular work. Such people could end up incurring debt without gaining the increased income.

2. Borrowing Could Allow You to More Quickly Complete a Program That Leads to a Much Higher-Paying Job

For example, I knew a young man who wisely wanted to graduate from college debt-free. He was working full time in the service industry, making $2,500 a month while going to school less than half time. He was pursuing a degree in a technical field for which the starting pay was over $5,000 per month. At that rate, it would have taken him at least four more years to graduate. I encouraged him to consider the option of going to school full time while working only part time. This would force him to borrow several thousand dollars, but it would enable him to finish school two years earlier. If his assumptions about his job prospects upon graduation were correct, he would be better off financially to complete his education sooner because of the increased earnings from his new job.

ON THE OTHER HAND, IT IS UNWISE TO BORROW MONEY FOR AN EDUCATION THAT WILL NOT PAY FOR ITSELF

One example is theological education. Thirty-three years ago, I left my career in the business world to attend seminary. The ministry jobs I have had using my seminary degrees pay much less than I was previously making while working in business. The Lord provided for me to complete my theological education without incurring debt. Now I teach in a seminary, preparing students for future church, missions, and parachurch ministries. I believe that theological education is very valuable—spiritually, if not economically. I strongly advise seminary students to make every effort to avoid debt as they complete their educations because it is likely that the jobs they obtain after seminary won't pay enough to service major student-loan debt. I encourage those aspiring to ministry to earnestly pray that God will provide a way that they can complete their training without incurring a great deal of debt. Sadly, I have seen seminary students whose prospects for ministry employment upon graduation were limited because they graduated with a large amount of debt from both their undergraduate and graduate studies. The ideal solution to this particular problem would be for local churches to make significant contributions to the seminary educations of those whom they believe to be gifted and called to ministry so that these students can one day serve Christ without the encumbrance of debt.

SUMMARY

While it is true that certain degrees or certificates can lead to higher earnings that would make the cost worthwhile, many people have been significantly burdened financially by taking on education debt. Students and their families often don't consider whether the education they are considering is worth the future cost. Universities and the government contribute to the problem by making it convenient for students to borrow large amounts of money. Students and their families would be wise to make debt avoidance a major consideration when making the major financial decision of choosing a college. If you must take out a student loan, borrow the least amount possible for the least amount of time and at the lowest interest rate.

— Questions for Reflection —

1. What are some of the biggest mistakes that people make with student debt?
2. How can students avoid or minimize student debt?
3. When might education debt be worth it?
4. What are the risks of taking on student debt?
5. May we tell someone that taking on student debt is sinful?

26

IS IT WISE, OR EVEN NECESSARY, TO USE DEBT TO BUY A VEHICLE?

Another major category of debt for many individuals is vehicle loans. Next to a home purchase, vehicle purchases are the largest single expenditures made by most people. Many people can't imagine life without a car payment. Just when they are on the verge of paying off their current vehicle, they start browsing in the dealer showrooms, dreaming of their new nicer ride. There is a better way.

WHY IS IT DESIRABLE TO AVOID BORROWING MONEY TO BUY A VEHICLE?

1. People Tend to Spend Much More for Vehicles When They Buy on Credit as Opposed to Paying Cash

Their eyes get big as they admire the shiny new models and consider the various options. Salespeople will often encourage the buyer to focus on the amount of the monthly payment rather than the actual cost of the car or truck that will be paid over a period of several years.

2. Banks and Car Dealers Are Often Willing to Lend Consumers More Money Than They Can Afford to Repay

High monthly payments strain their budget. Car loans typically are for four to as many as seven years, which is a long time to have a significant debt payment.

3. Vehicles Cost More When You Have to Pay Interest

You are paying both for your car and for the use of the bank's money. For example, you could pay over $35,000 for a $30,000 car.

4. Vehicles Depreciate

Unless you make a very large down payment, you will owe the bank much more than the car is worth as soon as you drive it off the lot. And your car will continue to depreciate. If for some reason you want to sell your car, you will probably need to come up with the difference between the sales price and what you still owe on it, which could amount to thousands of dollars.

5. New Vehicles Are Usually Expensive to Own because They Cost More in Depreciation

Typically, a new car loses at least 20 percent of its value in the first year. Because depreciation slows after that, some people prefer to buy a car that is one to three years old.

6. Vehicles Deteriorate (Being Destroyed by Rust, etc., Matt. 6:19)

The best day you will have with your new car will almost certainly be the first day. Over time, dings will appear and the interior will get stained. Some of the optional gadgets will break. But the last payment in year six is the same as the first payment in year one.

HOW CAN YOU AVOID VEHICLE DEBT?

1. Buy and drive an older, less expensive car that you can pay for with cash.
2. Learn to do some basic maintenance yourself to save even more money.
3. Make a car payment to yourself each month as part of your budget while you save for a nice car for which you will pay cash.
4. Enjoy being debt-free as you save for the next car after that.

BUT ISN'T IT A DEAL TO PURCHASE
A CAR WITH VERY LOW INTEREST RATES?

Car dealers often entice buyers with special deals on financing.

1. Low-interest loans still put you into debt and have you spending income on interest. Debt always involves bondage (Prov. 22:7).
2. In most cases, the cost of the interest that the buyer is avoiding is built into the price of the car. If you walk into the dealership with cash, you will often get a much better price than the person buying on credit, even with a zero-interest deal.

WHAT ABOUT LEASING
INSTEAD OF BUYING A CAR?

When you lease a car, you get a monthly car payment, but at the end of the lease you don't get to keep the car. Leases have limitations and upcharges in case of excessive mileage. Some businesses find that there are tax advantages to leasing corporate vehicles. Many prefer to lease so that their employees will always be driving reliable cars that are under warranty. For individuals, however, leasing is usually the most expensive way to have a car.

ISN'T IT CHEAPER TO BUY A NEW CAR THAT
WON'T REQUIRE EXPENSIVE MAINTENANCE?

1. It Is True That Cars Require More Repairs as They Age, and at Some Point a Broken Car Is Not Worth Fixing

As a general rule, that is when the repairs exceed the value of the vehicle.[1]

1. The hard thing about choosing to do an expensive repair on an old car is that you don't know when and how expensive the next repair might be. Also, car makes and models vary in their reliability. Often it is wise to ask a trusted mechanic whether he thinks the car is worth repairing.

2. Usually It Is Much Cheaper to Repair the Old Vehicle Than to Replace It

Most repairs cost less than one car payment on a new car, and far less than the amount that the new car will depreciate in the first year (the new $30,000 car will have lost as much as $6,000 of its value in the first twelve months). But some people think it makes sense to take on a new $25,000 debt rather than pay for a $500 repair.

3. Some People Are Looking for an Excuse to Buy an Expensive New Car

It could be that someone who claims to be worried about repair expenses is tired of his or her perfectly good older vehicle and is looking for a justification to buy a shiny new one, even if doing so doesn't make financial sense.

SUMMARY

How much to spend buying a car is determined by what one can afford and what one values. Even if you have enough money to buy a fancy late-model vehicle, the amount you spend will not be available for savings, giving, and other lifestyle options. A starting place for most people is to avoid vehicle debt. One of the best ways to eliminate debt long term is to drive a vehicle for which you have already fully paid. By making a car payment to yourself toward your next vehicle purchase, you will be well ahead of those who make car payments, with interest, to the bank.

— QUESTIONS FOR REFLECTION —

1. What are some significant problems with using debt to pay for a vehicle?
2. How can someone avoid vehicle debt?
3. Are people free to borrow money to buy a car or truck? If so, what guidelines would you recommend?
4. When is it no longer worthwhile to keep an older vehicle?

27

IS HOME OWNERSHIP
ALWAYS A GREAT INVESTMENT?

ISN'T IT BETTER TO OWN THAN RENT?

For generations, home ownership has been part of the American dream. But sometimes people are better off renting. Home buyers often come out far behind financially. Many home buyers have suffered deep regrets and have incurred significant losses when they sell.

While debt is generally to be avoided, few people can pay cash for a home, so almost everyone has to borrow money in order to purchase one. Generally speaking, houses are appreciating, not depreciating, assets, so they can be a good investment (as compared to vehicles). The amount of money spent on a mortgage payment is often similar to the money that one would have otherwise spent on rent. An advantage of a mortgage is that equity is built up as debt on the house is gradually being wiped out.

While home ownership can be a great blessing, I disagree with the conventional wisdom that says to make the minimum down payment on as much house as you can afford because you can't go wrong with owning a home.

AN ETERNAL PERSPECTIVE ON HOME OWNERSHIP

Remember that there is no ultimate stability or permanence in this world. Apparently, our Lord Jesus did not own a house: "The foxes

Debt

have holes and the birds of the air have nests, but the Son of Man has nowhere to lay His head" (Luke 9:58). This world is not our permanent home (Heb. 13:14), but rather, we anticipate going to the place that our Lord has prepared for us (John 14:2–3). Our true home is with him (2 Cor. 5:8). Furthermore, our earthly houses are not truly permanent. One day they, along with our other earthly treasures, will cease to exist (Matt. 6:19–21; 2 Peter 3:10). So there is a sense in which we are all "renting."

HOW CAN YOU DECIDE
WHETHER TO RENT OR TO BUY?

People who are renting often feel a great deal of pressure to buy a house. Landlords keep increasing the rent, and it feels that the money is being wasted. Renters are afraid that they will miss out on potential gains as home prices continue to rise. They see that family and friends own their own homes, so they feel that they are behind in life. There are questions that need to be addressed before purchasing a house:

1. Is Your Financial House in Good Order?

Are you living within your means and following a budget? Are you well established in your career with stable income? Have you paid off all other debts? After you make the down payment, do you still have three to six months of emergency savings in place? With the new mortgage payment in your new budget, will there still be room for saving up for other major purchases (such as your next car) and investing? (More about investing in part 5.) "Prepare your work outside and make it ready for yourself in the field; afterwards, then, build your house" (Prov. 24:27).

2. Do You Anticipate Living in Your New Home for at Least Five Years?

If it is likely that you will move because of a job change, or to purchase a large home, it might be better to wait. You can lose a lot of

174

money by owning a home short term. There are at least three reasons for this:

A. It typically takes years to recover the transaction costs of buying and selling a house. Transaction costs include realtor fees, loan fees, inspections, title costs, and necessary repairs. These ordinarily total at least 10 percent of the value of your house. For example, if you were to buy a home in year one for $250,000 and had to sell it in year two for $255,000, you would come out $20,500 behind, assuming that you had $25,500 in transaction costs. If you didn't have sufficient equity in your home to cover this amount, you would owe the difference to the bank. Owning a house over a longer period ordinarily allows sufficient time for the value to go up so that you can come out ahead (or at least cover transaction expenses) when you sell.

B. Short-term home ownership leaves you vulnerable to a drop in the housing market. In the long term, houses tend to go up in value at approximately the rate of inflation (with variance according to region). But in the short term, housing markets can be volatile, experiencing steep rises and drops. For example, some homes in Southern California that were valued at $650,000 in 2007 dropped in value to less than $400,000 in 2009. Over the next several years, prices gradually recovered. But those who bought at the peak and then had to sell were "upside down" (having to sell at far below the purchase price).

C. Renting allows for much more flexibility in terms of your location and your budget. Buying a home is a big commitment personally and financially. Don't buy until you are personally and financially ready.

3. Do You Have a Sufficient Down Payment?

If you don't have enough money to make a large down payment, you can't yet afford to buy a house. While I suggest a minimum of

20 percent of your home's cost, others suggest that 10 or 15 percent is sufficient. There are at least four reasons for making a large down payment:

    A. If housing prices drop, a large down payment is a cushion that will help to prevent your home from being worth less than the amount for which you could quickly sell it.

    B. A larger down payment will lower your loan amount, thus lowering your monthly mortgage payment.

    C. A sufficient down payment (usually at least 20 percent) will enable you to have sufficient equity in your home to avoid mortgage insurance, which can cost several hundred dollars a year.

    D. A large down payment will bring you closer to owning your home free and clear.

    E. Don't make a down payment so large that you leave no money in emergency savings (see chapter 32).

4. Can You Afford the Ongoing Costs of Home Ownership?

    A. Can you afford the monthly mortgage payment? Realtors sometimes encourage buyers to stretch their finances in order to buy nicer, more expensive homes. Mortgage lenders are often willing to allow buyers to borrow more money than they can afford to repay. Buyers sometimes qualify for a mortgage based on the incomes of both husband and wife, which might not be reasonable if they plan to have one parent stay at home when children come along. Buying more house than you can afford is presumptuous (Prov. 16:9; James 4:13–17) and could put you into a more stressed financial situation with risk of losing your home to foreclosure (Prov. 22:27).

    B. Just being able to pay for the mortgage is not enough. First-time home buyers often fail to consider that owners pay many expenses not ordinarily incurred by renters, including maintenance, repairs, taxes, HOA fees, and insurance. HVAC units, roofs, and appliances break and sooner or later must be replaced. Walls need painting. Flooring wears out. "Through indolence the rafters sag, and through slackness the house leaks" (Eccl. 10:18).

5. Is This a Great House?
A. Does it seem to be a good value?
B. Is the neighborhood safe?
C. Is it in an area where the neighbors take good care of their homes and home values are appreciating?
D. Is it in a good location in relation to your church, your work, and your children's school?
E. Will the home meet your family's needs in terms of rooms, layout, outdoor space, and the like for the next several years?
F. If you can't afford a home that would be suitable, it might be wiser to grow your income and savings than to buy a house that is too small or in the wrong neighborhood. Renting can be part of a great financial plan to buy a house correctly.

WHAT ARE THE BENEFITS OF HOME OWNERSHIP?

1. The Greatest Economic Advantage of Home Ownership Is That You Are Working toward Being Completely Debt-Free

Many hate paying rent, since they feel that they are throwing money away because they have nothing to show for it. The same could be said for the interest you pay on a mortgage. The money in your mortgage payment that goes toward loan principal increases your net worth and benefits you in the long term. Every payment brings you closer to owning the house.

2. Government Has Encouraged Home Ownership by Offering Financial Incentives

Mortgage interest is tax-deductible, and most homeowners are able to avoid capital gains taxes when they sell their homes at a profit.

3. Home Ownership Also Offers Many Nonfinancial Benefits

One gains a sense of satisfaction with owning a house. You can plant gardens and trees, which you can anticipate enjoying for many years to come. You can decorate and paint without worrying about what the landlord will say. A home can be a place of connection as your family builds memories there.

MAKING WISE MORTGAGE CHOICES[1]

1. Variable-Rate Mortgages Are Risky and Usually Unwise

Such mortgages charge interest based on the market rate, which can rise or fall. The risk to the homeowner is that his or her payment can rise, possibly to an unaffordable level if interest rates go up. A fixed-rate mortgage is much safer because your payment is stable for the life of the mortgage.

2. There Is a Great Advantage to Shorter Mortgage Terms If You Can Afford the Payments

    A. Typically, the interest rates on fifteen-year mortgages are lower than those on thirty-year mortgages.

    B. In addition, you will pay off your loan in half the time, with more of each payment paying down your principal. Thus, you will reach your goal of owning your home free and clear much sooner.

    C. As of this writing, the total payments on a $300,000 loan would be approximately $485,000 on a thirty-year mortgage and $368,000 on a fifteen-year mortgage—a difference of over $100,000.

3. Lower Interest Rates Significantly Lower Your Mortgage Payment

This enables you to put more of your income into other categories or even afford a more expensive house. For example, for a loan of

---

1. For a mortgage calculator, see www.crown.org/resources/crown-calculators/.

$300,000, the mortgage payment on a thirty-year loan would be about $1,350 at 3.5 percent interest, but at 5 percent interest the payment would be $1,610. This can make buying a house more attractive at times of low interest rates, but low rates can also contribute to driving up housing prices. On the other hand, high interest rates can make a home more difficult to sell and can drive down prices.

4. If Possible, Pay More Than Your Required Mortgage Payment

When you pay more than your normal mortgage payment, all the additional money goes toward reducing the loan amount, which reduces your ongoing interest expense and can lead to your house being paid off much sooner. People who have regularly added to their monthly mortgage payment have shaved years off their mortgages and saved tens or even hundreds of thousands of dollars.

OTHER CONSIDERATIONS IN HOME OWNERSHIP

1. Your House Is a Home Much More Than It Is an Investment

Even if its value goes up, you still need a place to live, so you aren't pocketing the cash. The primary reason to purchase and keep a house is so that it will function as a blessing for your family and ministry.

2. Not All Homeowners Come Out Ahead Financially

Housing markets vary according to time and place, and the future is difficult to predict. Homes in hot real estate markets appreciate at a rate much higher than inflation, sometimes pricing ordinary families out of those areas. Home values in cold markets[2] remain flat or even decline, thus creating distressed sellers. Sometimes when housing markets go cold, houses remain on the market for many months or even over a year. Sellers are then unable to move or forced to make two monthly house payments while they wait for a buyer.

---

2. Housing markets might grow cold when a factory or industry moves out of an area, or when a particular neighborhood deteriorates.

A. Even when the sales price significantly exceeds the asking price, the gain might not be great when you consider what has been invested in home improvements.

B. Housing bubbles (and crashes) often occur when unqualified buyers are able to enter the market to purchase homes they can't afford. This increase in demand, along with the entrance of speculators into the market, drives up housing prices. Then a point comes at which the unqualified buyers start defaulting on their loans, leading to foreclosures and short sales. This flood of foreclosed houses leads to an oversupply, and prices might drop significantly.

3. The Economic Decision Whether to Buy a Home Might Be Affected by Local Rental Markets

When rents are very high compared to mortgage costs, home ownership is usually advantageous. In some markets, however, rents are very low compared to the costs of home ownership, thus making the rental option more attractive. You have to do some research, make some assumptions, and then do the math.

4. Generous Family Members Might Be Able to Help a Young Couple with a Down Payment on a House

If they can afford to do so, this could be blessing their children with an early inheritance (Prov. 19:14a) during a time of life when the money is more needed than it might be decades from now. Families should consult an accountant about the financial implications of such a large gift. Also, as attractive as such an offer might be, the young family must still evaluate whether the time is right and the house is right, based on the considerations above. Also, some of the relational risks that often accompany financial matters among family members should be considered (see chapter 29).

PAYING OFF
YOUR MORTGAGE

1. Make a plan to own your home free and clear as soon as possible, which will free up a great deal of money for spending, saving, and giving.

2. The most productive money you will spend on your house is the amount of each payment that reduces the principal you owe on your loan. Money spent on mortgage interest, like money spent on rent, is money spent and gone.

3. The benefits of owning a home free and clear almost always exceed whatever tax deductions one receives when paying mortgage interest.

4. Even when you have paid off your house, you will still have maintenance, utility, insurance, and tax expenses.

IS IT WISE TO USE YOUR HOME
EQUITY TO PAY OFF OTHER DEBTS?

Those who own a home often try to get out from underneath their credit-card (or other) debt by borrowing against the increased equity in their home. This can have the advantage of offering a lower interest rate because typically loans secured by a house have much lower interest rates than credit cards. It might also be simpler to make only one debt payment each month. This can be advantageous for those who will have the self-control to stick to their budget after the loans are consolidated. There are, however, significant risks.

For example, a family with $25,000 in credit-card debt owns a house that they purchased for $200,000 but is now worth $250,000. The bank might offer to lend them money to pay off the credit-card debt by either creating a new loan against the house or rolling the amount into their existing mortgage. Many families in this situation would then borrow $30,000 or more in order to have a cushion. This choice might create several problems.

1. This Approach Treats Only the Symptoms of the Debt Disease without Addressing the Cause

The undisciplined spending typically continues until the extra $5,000 is spent and more debt is incurred. The problem is compounded because now the family is making an additional monthly payment for their new home-equity debt. Then, assuming that the value of their home continues to increase, they will be back in a few years, seeking to borrow more money to pay off the newly incurred debt.

2. With the Higher Monthly House Payment, Such Homeowners Are at More Risk of Being Unable to Make Their Mortgage Payment(s) in the Future, Especially if They Experience a Financial Crisis Such as Loss of Employment Income

3. Home Values Can Drop in Times of Recession or Financial Crisis, in Which Case a Family Could Be "Upside Down," Meaning That They Would Owe More for Their House Than the Amount for Which They Could Sell It

This would make it very difficult for them to sell the house if they wanted to move for any reason.

4. This Postpones the Time When the Family Will Enjoy the Blessing of Owning Their Home Free and Clear

Debt consolidations using home-equity refinancing typically involve extending the length of the loan. After paying their old thirty-year mortgage for several years, a new thirty-year mortgage is created.

ARE REVERSE MORTGAGES EVER A GOOD IDEA?

Reverse mortgages are used by older people who have significant equity in their home and need income (ordinarily during retirement). The amount of money available in a reverse mortgage is dependent on the amount of equity (what a house is worth less what is currently owed). A reverse mortgage allows the homeowner to receive monthly payments from the bank, which will help the person with living expenses. Each payment increases the amount owed on the loan. The loan balance is also rising based on the interest owed on the loan each month. The potential benefit of a reverse mortgage is that an older person in need of retirement income could access the equity that is tied up in the home while still being allowed to live there until death (as opposed to having to sell the home). Ordinarily, upon the owner's passing, the loan would be paid off and any remaining equity would go to the owner's heirs. While reverse mortgages might help in certain situations, they tend to be complex and can be costly (typically higher interest rates and fees as compared to traditional mortgages). I recommend that every effort be made to avoid this financial product. If it is absolutely necessary to access the equity in one's home, refinancing the home while taking out equity or getting a home-equity line of credit (HELOC) could be less costly. Older people contemplating any of these options should seek financial advice from trusted friends and family members.

IS IT WISE TO TAKE EQUITY OUT OF YOUR HOME FOR THE PURPOSE OF INVESTING IT?

The short answer is that it is risky and unwise. We will cover this in more detail in chapter 35.

SUMMARY

Most people are eager to own a house. For many, home ownership can be a great blessing both personally and financially. There are some pitfalls, however, which potential home buyers must avoid as they seek to take care of their families and to be good stewards of the resources that God has entrusted to them.

— QUESTIONS FOR REFLECTION —

1. Why is home ownership so much a part of people's financial dreams?
2. What spiritual considerations might affect one's decision to buy or rent a home?
3. What financial considerations might affect the decision whether to rent or buy?
4. What are some of the pitfalls into which home buyers can fall?
5. What are the benefits of owning a home free and clear?

28

WHAT SHOULD WE THINK ABOUT THE USE OF DEBT IN BUSINESSES AND GOVERNMENT?

In the same way that individuals can be tempted to use debt to enjoy immediate benefits from money not yet earned, businesses and governments seek to gain advantages for themselves through using various forms of debt. While we cannot say that it is always wrong to use debt in this way, we can say that it is risky. Furthermore, most governments and businesses don't take the risk seriously enough. The lessons we learned about how a family should operate its finances—living within a reasonable budget, showing restraint in spending, and avoiding debt—apply to businesses and government.

HOW CAN BUSINESSES USE DEBT?

A 1910 Sears catalogue states that "buying on credit is folly."[1] In later years, Sears departed from that policy both by how it dealt with its customers in issuing credit cards and by how it used debt to finance its own business. Ironically, one of the reasons that Sears went

---

1. Quoted in Dave Ramsey, *The Total Money Makeover*, 3rd ed. (Nashville: Thomas Nelson, 2009), 23.

out of business was that it could no longer make the payments on its corporate debt.

Debt is a major part of the business world, from small family entities to major corporations. In order for businesses to operate, they need money to purchase income-producing assets, such as factories and equipment. They sometimes also require operating cash to pay for ongoing operational expenses that occur while they are waiting for income that will offset their expenses. These funds can come from one of two sources: capital or borrowing. Capital is the money that the business owners (or stockholders) put into the business from their own resources plus retained profits. The other source is borrowing. Most businesses borrow money from banks, which determine whether to lend and how much interest to charge based on the perceived loan risk. Risk is based on the borrower's perceived ability to pay off the loan and the collateral that the lender could seize in case of nonpayment. Interest rates also vary according to the length of the loan (more interest is usually charged for longer-term loans). Larger businesses, in addition to using banks, often borrow money by issuing interest-paying bonds to the public. Interest rates on bonds are also determined by the perceived risk that a business will not be able to repay, along with the length of the bond in years. The greater the risk, the higher the interest paid. For example, a U.S. government bond would pay the lowest interest because it is perceived to have the least risk. A financially healthy corporation (with steady income and significant assets) would pay a bit more interest than the government because the risk of default is somewhat higher. A small business or a corporation that is less healthy would pay much higher interest. I will talk about investing in bonds in chapter 36.

Borrowing can be alluring because debt can enable a successful business to make more money for owners/shareholders, as long as the return on the investment exceeds the cost of interest. The business that chooses to avoid debt has to either grow more slowly or raise more capital by inviting others to invest as owners/stockholders who will share in the profits and bear the risk of business failure.

Taking on debt always involves risk. A business must have sufficient current income to make payments. If that income stream is interrupted (for example, by a major economic downturn), the business might not be able to make its loan or bond payments. In this case, its creditors could force the company into bankruptcy, seizing its assets in order to get their money back. Even in good times, a company that relies heavily on debt might find that when the ratio of its debt to asset value increases, the interest rates that it is required to pay will go up, thus affecting income and profit.

Both large and small companies that rely heavily on debt often suffer or go out of business during hard economic times. It is like trying to swim in the ocean during a storm with a millstone around one's neck. These companies had unwisely assumed that the economy and their businesses would continue to prosper without interruption, so they were unprepared for financial challenges. Just like a family with major credit-card debt, they had been living on the financial edge before the downturn, which then led to their downfall.

HOW CAN A BUSINESS AVOID THE PERILS OF DEBT?

The more a business can rely on capital and the less it can rely on debt, the more financially healthy it will be. If the business does incur debt, it is wise to be sure that it has enough cash savings to weather a financial storm without having to liquidate assets.

A CASE STUDY WITH A SMALL BUSINESS

Joe and Sam both decide to open family restaurants at opposite ends of the same town. Each starts with $20,000 that he has saved, and each borrows $20,000 from the bank at 8 percent interest. The $40,000 is enough to enter into a lease, fix up the property, buy equipment, and cover two months' operation expenses. During the first two years of operation, each restaurant does well, so that both Joe and Sam are $10,000 ahead after paying all expenses, including their own salaries. Joe sees that business is good and decides to expand his business by leasing the space next door to his present restaurant at a cost of $2,000 per month, plus $20,000 in remodeling costs. Sam instead chooses to keep his $10,000 profit in savings. Now let us imagine two possible outcomes. In the first scenario, the economy continues to grow and their businesses boom. After two more years, Joe is $30,000 more ahead, but Sam after the expansion is $50,000 ahead. In the second scenario, however, the economy goes into a deep recession. Business plummets because people can't afford to eat out as often. Joe uses the $10,000 he's saved to get through the two years of downturn. Sam, on the other hand, can't afford the extra lease and loan expenses on his expanded restaurant and has to go out of business.

The bottom line is that businesses, like families, would be wise to do all that they can to avoid debt and to make it a goal to be debt-free. Even productive debt that has been invested in income-producing assets can be dangerous debt.

SHOULD WE BE CONCERNED ABOUT GOVERNMENT DEBT?

Governments, like businesses and families, often misuse debt. Governments pay for their expenses primarily through collecting taxes from citizens or through borrowing money. While government programs that provide various services tend to be popular with voters, taxes are very unpopular (Matt. 22:21). Therefore, just as families are tempted to use credit to enjoy present goods and services before the money has been earned, politicians are tempted to use debt in order to provide maximum government services to their constituents while minimizing taxes. This is true of government at every level—national, state, and local. Just as corporations borrow money for major capital projects and individuals borrow money for major purchases such as houses, local and state governments often borrow money (by issuing bonds) for large projects such as building schools or constructing roads or buildings. The federal government usually runs deficits in its ongoing expenses and borrows money to cover the deficits. Governments also tend to borrow large amounts of money in the midst of a crisis—war or major financial downturns. Some governments go from crisis to crisis while making little effort to control expenses or repay debts from the past.

Just as debt is costly and risky for individuals and businesses, it is costly and risky for governments. Just as a family's interest on credit cards must be paid for out of income, thus leaving less for ordinary expenses, interest on government debt/bonds must be paid for out of tax receipts, thus leaving less money available to provide ongoing services. Just as families in this situation are tempted to compound the problem by borrowing more money, governments tend to postpone reckoning with their lack of fiscal discipline by issuing more debt. Just as families can reach the point at which their income can no longer finance their debt payments, governments can also come to this point. Many national governments address their debt problems by simply creating (or printing) more money, thus devaluing their currencies (and stealing value from those holding their currencies in savings). There are many examples in recent history in which national governments have issued so much debt or created so much currency that their money became virtually worthless and the economy experienced a terrible crisis. Other governments have simply defaulted on their debt, which stole from borrowers and led to economic turmoil. When governments lose control of their economy, civil unrest often results. Many municipalities and state governments in the United States are on the verge of financial crisis because they have issued more debt and taken on more financial obligations than they can handle. Significant economic downturns, which bring down tax revenues, could bring some local governments to the point of default or bankruptcy. Rising interest payments also impede government's ability to continue to pay for and provide services, which can lead to both fiscal crisis and social upheaval. The politicians and government leaders who unwisely incurred excessive debt are often out of office when the seeds of financial destruction they planted bear their bitter fruit.[2]

---

2. See https://www.businessinsider.com/worst-hyperinflation-episodes-in-history -2013-9 for examples of currencies that have lost their value due to unsound government financial policies.

There are other concerns regarding government debt. While it is in the interest of the federal government, as a major borrower, to keep interest rates low, fiscal policies that manipulate interest rates hurt investors, including retirees, who want a safe return on their money. Another concern is that the federal government, as a huge borrower, stands to benefit from inflation, which allows them to repay past debt with less valuable dollars in the present and future. This also harms investors, whose money value is eroded by inflationary government policies.[3] In addition, if and when interest rates rise, government loan payments could rise dramatically, thus taking away an even larger percentage of revenue.

Just as we cannot say that it is always forbidden for individuals and businesses to borrow money, we cannot say that governments are forbidden by God to incur debt. But we should be concerned that the misuse of debt is irresponsible and destructive. Governments, like families and businesses, need to follow realistic budgets as they exercise fiscal discipline. They need to beware of taking on debt obligations that will be difficult to meet in the future, or for which the payments will hinder their ability to carry out their proper functions.

DEBT IS A CURSE

Under the old covenant, the nation of Israel was told that the blessing of covenant faithfulness would be that Israel would lend to other nations, while a curse of covenant disobedience would be that Israel would be a debtor nation. God told Israel that he would bless her "if only you listen obediently to the voice of the LORD your God, to observe carefully all this commandment which I am commanding you today. For the LORD your God will bless you as He has promised you, and you will lend to many nations, but you will not borrow; and you will rule over many nations, but they will not rule over you" (Deut. 15:5–6). While our nation is not, like Old Testament Israel, in covenant with God, the general principle remains. Debt is a curse.

3. Many would regard governmental inflationary policies as a kind of stealing.

Debtor nations become weak and subservient to nations that can lend. The lender is the master, and the borrower is like a slave (Prov. 22:7).

WHEN MIGHT THE DEBT BUBBLE BURST?

As of this writing, the national debt alone is over $26 trillion, which amounts to almost $70,000 per person or about $210,000 per taxpayer.[4] State and local debt amounts to another $10,000 per person. This does not include unfunded government obligations for retirement benefits, pensions, and the like, which some estimate could be as much as $100 trillion. I am not smart enough to know exactly how much government debt is excessive, or at what point (whether this year or twenty years from now) a government's debt bubble might burst, leading to financial collapse and the destruction of the economy. At present, it does seem that we are moving in that direction. The ratio of federal debt to gross domestic product has gone from 58 percent in 2000 to over 130 percent in 2020. Sooner or later, the ongoing irresponsible use of debt will have dire consequences. The leaders of other governments that misused debt, resulting in economic collapse, did not anticipate that it would happen on their watch. We as citizens should take this into account as we participate in government by voting and as we consider what we expect government to do for us. It can't give us something for nothing, at least not in the long term. We might also be wise to be prepared, as best we can, for the financial crises that could result from government financial profligacy.

WHAT ABOUT CHURCHES AND OTHER NONPROFIT MINISTRIES?

Many of the same principles that apply to families and businesses also apply to ministries. Debt may be reasonably and carefully used as a tool. For example, a church might owe for a mortgage on a building in the same way that a family might owe money for their home

4. www.usdebtclock.org/.

or a business might take out a loan for its facility. Some churches, instead of borrowing from a bank, seek to have their members lend them some of their savings (which would have otherwise been invested elsewhere). Ministries, like families and businesses, should be careful not to aggressively take on an amount of debt that would be difficult to repay, especially if hard times come. Like families, churches should strive to be debt-free.[5]

SUMMARY

It is almost impossible to imagine running a business or a government without the use of debt. But those who rely too heavily on debt are often irresponsible in the present and unprepared for a future when there could be financial crises during which obligations come due.

— QUESTIONS FOR REFLECTION —

1. What are the ways that a business is able to finance its capital costs and operations?
2. What are the different ways by which government can pay for things?
3. What are the possible benefits and risks of a business's borrowing money?
4. How can a business minimize risk if it chooses to borrow money?
5. When is it reasonable for a government to borrow money?
6. What harm can occur when governments borrow excessively?
7. When, if ever, should a church get into debt?
8. What are the risks when a church finances a building by borrowing from its own members?

5. Jeff Berg and Jim Burgess, *The Debt-Free Church: Experiencing Financial Freedom While Growing Your Ministry* (Chicago: Moody Press, 1996).

29

WHY IS IT UNWISE TO LEND, BORROW, OR COSIGN AMONG FAMILY AND CLOSE FRIENDS?

No aspect of personal finances poses greater risk to relationships than money matters among family and close friends. Family members who are in need often approach relatives who are better off, asking for a loan. A brother who can't get a car loan might ask you to be a cosigner so that he can upgrade his ride. Your sister and her husband have been told that they can get a much better interest rate on their home-equity loan if they can find a creditworthy cosigner, so they ask you to help them out. Family members are sometimes asked to take out loans for a relative who is in school. A more unusual way to make oneself liable for the debts of another is to put up that person's criminal bail. If the person doesn't show up in court, you will lose your money. If you express reluctance in any of these situations, your family member might assure you that there is no risk because he or she will make the payments. If you still refuse, the family member might become belligerent, calling you greedy and selfish because you won't help out. The person might even try to enlist other close relatives to pressure you to fulfill your family duty. Dave Ramsey warns that such financial matters among family members and friends "is the best way I know to lose a friendship or strain a relationship. The borrower feels awkward even being in the same room with the lender, and if something goes wrong, most friendships are destroyed."[1]

SCRIPTURE EXPLICITLY
WARNS AGAINST COSIGNING

Of all the foolish financial errors that one can make, including excessive personal debt, none is greater than making oneself liable for the debts of another person. "A man lacking in sense pledges and becomes guarantor in the presence of his neighbor" (Prov. 17:18). Ordinarily, lenders are willing (perhaps too willing) to lend money to people with good credit. A cosigner is required only if the lender is convinced that there is significant risk that the loan won't be repaid.[2] Your relative might have bad credit because of previous financial irresponsibility. Or the bank might realize that the person's income may not be enough to enable him or her to keep up with payments. The act of cosigning transfers the risk from the bank to you, the cosigner. You then receive none of the benefits from the loan, but you bear all the potential liabilities. Cosigning is by nature extremely risky.

COSIGNING MIGHT COST YOU

When the person who borrowed the money is unwilling or unable to pay, the lender will come after the cosigner. You will be expected to pay the loan in full. "He who is guarantor for a stranger will surely suffer for it, but he who hates being a guarantor is secure" (Prov. 11:15). The consequences can be dire: "Do not be among those who give pledges, among those who become guarantors for debts. If you have nothing with which to pay, why should he take your bed from under you?" (22:26–27). I have known of cosigners who, when their relative or friend

1. Dave Ramsey and Sharon Ramsey, *Financial Peace Revisited* (New York: Viking, 2003), 85.
2. The lender is probably more aware of the borrower's financial situation—income, other debts, payment records, and the like—than you are. Thus, the lender probably has a much clearer idea of the risk than you do.

stopped paying on a car loan and the bank came after them, became angry with the bank. They should have understood what they signed and the risk they took. You can also suffer significant financial loss when the person for whom you cosigned drops out of school, skips bail, or dies. Also, cosigning might affect your credit. For example, we knew of a case in which a single nurse cosigned for her parents' mortgage loan, but then when she married she and her husband had difficulty getting their own home loan because her credit was still tied up in her parents' house. About 40 percent of those who cosign wind up having to pay[3]—and in most of these situations, relationships are damaged.

COSIGNING MIGHT ALSO HURT THE RELATIVE FOR WHOM YOU COSIGN

You could also be harming your family member or friend by allowing the person to continue his or her own spiral of financial irresponsibility and covetousness by incurring debts for unnecessary and unaffordable purchases.

WHAT ABOUT LENDING MONEY TO RELATIVES?

If you have been financially wise and have accumulated savings, it is likely that a needy family member or friend will approach you, asking for a loan. The same principles we presented about cosigning apply here. If your relative or friend had good credit and his or her income could support the loan payments, the bank would be willing to lend the person money at a reasonable rate of interest. Thus, your relative or friend wouldn't need to be asking you. So this is a financially risky loan. For example, a family member might want a loan to start or expand a small business. The pitch to you might be that the bank wants to charge your relative a high rate of interest while the bank is paying you a low rate of interest on your savings; therefore, you can both win.

3. www.forbes.com/sites/laurengensler/2016/06/06/cosign-loan-credit-card-risk /#126b4d1760ad.

Your relative can pay you greater interest than you were receiving from the bank, but less than what he or she would pay the bank. But there is risk. The rate of interest charged by the bank is probably based on its evaluation of how risky the loan is. Another common situation arises when a close relative (e.g., your grown child) is in financial distress because of debt and asks you to bail him or her out. An additional aspect of the risk is that if you do help the person this time, he or she will probably be back in a few years, asking for another bailout.

MONEY MATTERS AMONG FAMILY AND FRIENDS OFTEN DAMAGE RELATIONSHIPS

The greatest harm that comes from financial matters among family members is often relational more than financial. I have observed many cases in which these arrangements have gone badly, resulting in bitterness and division. When money becomes tight, borrowers often feel much less pressure to repay family members than they would a bank. While the bank could put on pressure by coming after collateral, the borrower assumes that a relative wouldn't do that to a fellow family member. Furthermore, the borrower often thinks that the family member who lent the money has been lucky and is financially well off, so it won't hurt for that person to have to wait a bit longer. As is typical of those who are deeply in debt, such borrowers might have convinced themselves that someday they will repay, even though no plan or financial discipline is in place to actually make that happen. You, as the lender, will face temptation to anger and resentment when your family member not only doesn't pay you, but offers little or no explanation. You might be further tempted when you see the financial lifestyle choices that your family member is making while you are waiting for your money. "How can she afford a vacation to Disney World and new bikes for her children when she still owes us $16,000?"

Surprisingly, I have observed that often the borrower who is unable or unwilling to repay a loan begins to resent the lender, even when the lender is patient. You might ask yourself, "Why does my brother avoid me and seem upset with me when he is the one who has wronged me?" I believe that Proverbs 22:7 explains why: "The rich rules over the poor, and the borrower becomes the lender's slave." No one likes to feel like a slave or to be ruled over. Even if you are very patient, the relative who owes you money might feel shame and be tempted to resent it that you, as the lender, are above him.

WHAT SHOULD YOU SAY WHEN YOU'RE ASKED?

When a family member or friend approaches you, asking you to cosign or to lend money, you are probably under a lot of pressure. You need to make your decision based on what you believe would be most pleasing to the Lord in light of your stewardship of what he has given you (2 Cor. 5:9). If you decide that it would not be wise for you to agree, first pray that the Lord will help you to speak wisely and gently and that your words will be well received. "Sweetness of speech increases persuasiveness. . . . The heart of the wise instructs his mouth and adds persuasiveness to his lips" (Prov. 16:21b, 23; also see 25:11). You might briefly explain why you are unwilling in light of biblical warnings against debt and cosigning, your own stewardship of the resources that God has entrusted to you, and your concern that money matters among family members put relationships at risk. The person might not understand or might even be angry. He or she might accuse you of being greedy and shirking family responsibility, or claim that he or she would help you if you were in need or that you owe it to the person for some past kindness that he or she has shown you. You might sense that the person is being greedy, irresponsible, and envious, but don't argue or quarrel. "Keeping away from strife is an honor for a man, but any fool will quarrel" (20:3; also see 17:14). If you offer your lecture on the glories of living on a budget and the evils of debt, the person might not respond well. Remember that "a gentle answer turns away wrath" (15:1). When the pressure becomes intense, remember, "The fear of man brings a snare, but he who trusts in the LORD will be exalted" (29:25). If you go against biblical wisdom because you want to please men, you could wind up being caught in the snare of someone else's debt. You must do what you believe would please God (Gal. 1:10).

IS IT ALWAYS SINFUL TO COSIGN OR
TO LEND MONEY TO FAMILY AND FRIENDS?

While Scripture warns that making oneself liable for someone else's debt is extremely risky and usually very unwise, it is not necessarily sinful. If you want to lend your teenager money to buy his first car, or if you want to lend your daughter and her husband money for the down payment on their first house, or if you want to lend your grandson money for college, you are free to do so. I encourage you, however, to consider the following caveats:

1. Don't Lend or Cosign for Money That You Can't Afford to Lose
If the borrower's default would imperil your ability to take care of your family's needs (1 Tim. 5:8), it would be unwise for you to get involved.

2. Make Sure That the Detailed Terms of the Loan Are in Writing
This includes what will be done in case of default. Family members and friends often have conflicting expectations regarding financial matters, with each party expecting to be treated especially well by the other. It is far better and wiser to work these things out before there is a problem.

3. Be Sure That You and Your Spouse Are in Full Agreement about What You Are About to Do (If You Are Married)

4. Determine Now That If the Money Is Not Repaid, You Are Entrusting Your Resources to God and Will Not Be Angry, Bitter, or Vengeful (Rom. 12:19)

5. If There Is a Genuine Need and You Can Afford to Help, Consider Giving the Money as a Gift, Thus Avoiding the Potential Problems and Conflicts That a Loan Might Create

6. If There Is Not a Genuine Need, Don't Enable Your Family Member's Financial Irresponsibility and Endanger Relationships by Giving the Person the Money

NEITHER A BORROWER NOR A LENDER BE

I have been primarily addressing those who might be asked to lend money to relatives. Perhaps you are in the opposite situation and are considering asking a prosperous relative for a loan. Here are some things you should consider in light of what I have already written above. See the situation from your relative's side (Phil. 2:3–4). "In everything, therefore, treat people the same way you want them to treat you, for this is the Law and the Prophets" (Matt. 7:12).

1. You Might Be Putting Your Family Member in a Very Awkward Position by Asking for Help in This Way

2. You Might Not Fully Grasp the Amount of Financial and Relational Risk That You Are Asking Your Relative to Take on Your Behalf

3. Consider Whether Your Need Could Be Met by Exercising Greater Wisdom in Your Personal Finances

Is the need real and immediate? Or are you being unwise or impatient?

4. If Your Need Is Valid, for the Sake of Relationships, Consider Borrowing from a Bank Instead

The greater amount of interest you might have to pay could be worth it because you will avoid creating tension and risk in family relationships.

SUMMARY

Financial matters, especially loans, among family and close friends are very risky, both economically and relationally. Having the courage to say no in the short term can prevent many troubles in the long term.

— Questions for Reflection —

1. What are several reasons why it is unwise to cosign?
2. What are several reasons why it is almost always unwise to lend money to or borrow money from family members?
3. Is it always sinful to cosign or to lend money to family members?
4. When might it be right to lend money to relatives?
5. What is a wise way to answer a family member who wants you to cosign for him or her?

30

HOW CAN YOU GET OUT OF DEBT?

I hope that by now you see that debt is dangerous and potentially destructive to your personal finances and that becoming debt-free is an important financial goal. The road of freedom from debt is longer and harder for some than for others. The degree of the problem determines the severity of the measures that must be taken.

SOME ARE ON TRACK TO BEING DEBT-FREE

The only debt of people whose finances are relatively healthy might be their mortgage. They should continue to faithfully make their payments so that they can enter retirement completely debt-free, with no house payment. They will need to be careful to resist the temptation to increase their debt by borrowing against their growing equity. Ideally, they will pay more than the minimum on their monthly mortgage so that they can own their home free and clear even sooner.

SOME HAVE MANAGEABLE DEBT

In addition to owing on their homes, some people have car payments and perhaps use their credit cards to cover unexpected shortfalls. Their income, however, is sufficient to keep up with all their payments. They can usually pay more than the minimum credit-card payment and are well within their credit limit. They have a measure of financial discipline so that while the credit-card balances stubbornly linger, they are not increasing (much). These people would be wise to make the elimination of all nonmortgage debt a high financial priority and to create a detailed plan, including a budget, to achieve this.

SOME HAVE A MAJOR DEBT PROBLEM

The financial ship of these people is sinking. They aren't following a budget and don't really have a good grasp of where all their income is going. Their monthly debt payments are a major drain on their finances. During some months they barely break even, but when extra major expenses come along, such as car repairs, medical bills, or holidays, they use their credit cards, which are dangerously approaching their limit.

1. Identify and Repent of Any Sins That Contributed to Your Financial Crisis

Confess them to God and those people who have been affected (e.g., your spouse or those from whom you have borrowed, Matt. 5:23–24). Such sins might include laziness (Prov. 6:6–11), failure to plan (21:5), poor stewardship (Luke 12:48), lying by breaking promises to limit spending to budgeted amounts (Ex. 20:15), stealing by borrowing money that you can't pay back (Ps. 37:21; Eph. 4:28), rationalizing foolish expenditures, and covetousness/idolatry (Col. 3:5)—seeking ultimate satisfaction in earthly things (Prov. 21:17; Isa. 55:1–2). Repentance includes not merely feeling bad or saying that you are sorry, but acting to make things right: "He who steals must steal no longer; but rather he must labor, performing with his own hands what is good, so that he will have something to share with one who has need" (Eph. 4:28; also see Matt. 3:8; 2 Cor. 7:10–11).

2. Commit to Incurring No More Debt

3. Drastically Cut Expenses (See Part 3)

People in financial crisis can't merely get by with cutting some fat out of their budget. Sacrifices must be made. Lifestyles must be dramatically reduced until the financial situation has stabilized.

4. Increase Income by Working Harder and Smarter (See Part 2).

People in debt might need to take on second jobs, volunteer to work overtime, or even offer to perform paying work (such as yard-work, housecleaning, and babysitting) for family and friends.

5. Consider Whether a Nonworking Spouse Needs to Get a Job

Many have eliminated debt by living off the income of one spouse and devoting the entire income of the other spouse to debt reduction.

6. Sell Some of Your Possessions in Order to Bring Down Debt

Just as financially distressed corporations identify and sell assets, which will allow them to manage out-of-control debt, families who are deeply in debt need to look at their possessions to see what they might be able to liquidate in order to reduce what they owe. Some have sold jewelry, musical instruments, vehicles (getting by on one older car or a car and a bike instead of two late-model vehicles), tools, and so on.[1] This can be painful, but it might be necessary. When the ship is in grave danger of sinking, some of the cargo might have to be thrown overboard and sacrificed (Acts 27:18).

7. Cut Up Your Credit Cards (Plastic Surgery) If You Can't Restrain Yourself from Using Them

"If your right hand makes you stumble, cut it off and throw it from you; for it is better for you to lose one of the parts of your body, than for your whole body to go into hell" (Matt. 5:30).

8. Don't Get Deeper into Debt in Order to Pay Your Debts

People in debt often look for other ways to borrow money in order to pay the money that they owe. While this approach might provide some short-term relief, it addresses neither the cause nor the essence of the problem. Thus, it will usually make the financial situation much worse.

---

1. I do *not* recommend pawning your possessions because of the very high interest rates charged on these loans.

9. Seek Godly Counsel and Accountability

"Where there is no guidance the people fall, but in abundance of counselors there is victory" (Prov. 11:14). As you pursue victory over your debt, seek help from godly counselors who know Scripture well and are wise in financial matters. They will be able to help you to make a plan/budget, and they can keep you accountable to follow your plan (Heb. 3:13).

10. Pray Daily, Asking God for Help, Mercy, and Wisdom as You Face This Financial Trial (James 1:5)

Your plan will not succeed unless the Lord gives his help and adds his blessing: "Unless the LORD builds the house, they labor in vain who build it" (Ps. 127:1a; also see James 4:13–17).

SOME ARE DROWNING IN DEBT

You are so far behind on your house payments or rent that you are on the verge of foreclosure or eviction. Your car has been repossessed. Your credit cards are maxed out, and your debt is significantly increasing every month because of punitive interest and penalties. We have seen situations in which the crisis was exacerbated because one spouse had been hiding the extent of his or her financial woes from the other until the threatening letters and phone calls from creditors began to arrive. Some would call this financial infidelity.

1. Take All the Steps Listed Above for Those Who Have a Major Debt Problem

2. Try to Negotiate in Good Faith with Lenders, Expressing Your Desire to Meet Your Obligations

Banks will often prefer to offer more favorable terms (lower interest over a longer period) over having to write off a bad loan.

YOU MIGHT NEED TO APPEAL FOR MERCY

There is a biblical basis for pleading with a lender to show you mercy after you have ensnared yourself with financial obligations that you cannot afford to meet:

> My son, if you have become surety for your neighbor,
> Have given a pledge for a stranger,
> If you have been snared with the words of your mouth,
> Have been caught with the words of your mouth,
> Do this then, my son, and deliver yourself;
> Since you have come into the hand of your neighbor,
> Go, humble yourself, and importune your neighbor.
> Give no sleep to your eyes,
> Nor slumber to your eyelids;
> Deliver yourself like a gazelle from the hunter's hand
> And like a bird from the hand of the fowler. (Prov. 6:1–5)

MAY A CHRISTIAN EVER WALK AWAY FROM DEBT OR DECLARE BANKRUPTCY?

While centuries ago those who could not meet their financial obligations could be put into debtor's prison, modern bankruptcy laws shield debtors from the worst consequences of not being able to pay what they owe. While laws vary from state to state, bankruptcy generally allows a person to have certain debts discharged after liquidating his or her remaining financial assets, which are divided among the person's creditors. Some debts cannot be forgiven in bankruptcy (e.g., taxes owed), and some personal assets can't be seized by creditors in bankruptcy. Bankruptcy is a legal process, and those forced into bankruptcy almost always need the help of an attorney.

Scripture teaches that we should take our financial obligations very seriously. "The wicked borrows and does not pay back" (Ps. 37:21a; also see Prov. 3:27–28). Christians should never be among those who deliberately avoid paying their debts, manipulate bankruptcy laws ("strategic default"), or hide their assets from creditors. In some situations, however, a believer might be forced into bankruptcy or foreclosure because the person is hopelessly unable to meet his or her obligations. This could happen because of unwise past financial decisions, or it might be due to circumstances beyond the person's control, such as disability, job loss, or another calamity. Even in bankruptcy or foreclosure, a Christian should act with humble integrity and cooperate as far as possible with his or her creditors. If the person owes money to individuals or small businesses, it might be appropriate for him or her to personally seek forgiveness and to commit to paying them back in the future (Matt. 5:23–24). A believer who has gone through bankruptcy might also decide that even though he or she has been released from legal obligations, there is a moral obligation to repay the debts if the Lord again blesses the person financially. I have known of multiple cases in which Christians who had gone bankrupt later repaid merchants or friends to whom they owed money. In some cases, the merchants were speechless at this testimony of Christian integrity.

WHAT ABOUT SHORT-SELLING A HOUSE?

A short sale of real estate occurs when a seller gets the lender to agree to accept the net proceeds of the sale of the property, even if this amount falls short of the debt owed against the property. For example, a family purchased a house for $500,000 during a boom time that was followed by a deep recession. The house is now worth only $350,000. The "owners," who still owe $450,000, are no longer able to pay the mortgage because of loss of income. So they appeal to the bank to allow them to walk away from the house and the debt, including the extra $100,000 that they would still owe after the sale of the house.[2] From a biblical standpoint, this could be an application of Proverbs 6:1–5 (quoted above): the family who cannot meet a financial obligation can beg for mercy, that they might gain relief.

---

2. There could be significant negative tax implications for the former homeowner regarding the forgiven debt.

Short sales, however, should not be misused by homeowners who simply don't want to keep paying the mortgage on a house that has lost value (strategic default). If, for example, the couple who owed $450,000 on a home worth only $350,000 can still pay their mortgage, they should, even if they regret having purchased a home that has lost value. The righteous person "swears to his own hurt and does not change" (Ps. 15:4c). Perhaps God will bless them and the home will recover its value.[3]

WHAT IS THE BEST METHOD FOR GETTING RID OF DEBT?

Debt-reduction plans (and budgets) tend to work like diets for losing weight. They all work pretty well if you follow them. There are a few different ways that people have tackled their debt:

1. The Debt Snowball—Eliminate the Smallest Debt First

Dave Ramsey recommends that those who are serious about getting rid of their debt start with the smallest debt and then when that is paid off, pay off the next smallest debt, and then the next smallest after that, until all the debts have been eliminated.[4] Many people have found this method to be very helpful, probably because there is something psychologically reinforcing about having one debt completely paid off, which then spurs folks on to eliminate the next debt. This would be like the dieter's stepping on the scale daily and seeing immediate results.

2. Or Eliminate High-Interest Debt First

If you put the same amount each month toward eliminating the debt that charges the highest rate of interest, you should save money

3. In previous downturns in the housing market, many people engaged in "strategic default," simply walking away from houses that had lost value, even though they could afford the payments. In many cases, those who had originally purchased their homes when they were less expensive had borrowed against the houses' value, thus wiping out their equity and in many cases leaving them "upside down"—owing more than the homes were worth.
4. Dave Ramsey, *The Total Money Makeover*, 3rd ed. (Nashville: Thomas Nelson, 2009), 109.

in comparison to the debt-snowball approach. For example, if a family owes $3,000 on one credit card at 7 percent and $10,000 on another at 18 percent, they will save the most money in interest expenses by reducing the $10,000 debt first.

3. A Third Consideration in Eliminating Debt Is Relationships

If a friend or relative has lent you money and needs it (or if your failure to repay is causing tension), you might make repaying that person your first priority, even if he or she is charging you little or no interest.

SUMMARY

Debt is a weed that is extremely difficult to kill. The longer it grows, the deeper its roots. Many can get out of debt with God's help as they apply the wisdom of God's Word. Some have overwhelming debts that can be discharged only through bankruptcy. Those who have finally been given relief from debt should strive to honor God by managing their finances more wisely in the future.

— QUESTIONS FOR REFLECTION —

1. Should those who have manageable debt be concerned about becoming debt-free? Explain your answer.
2. What wise steps might a person who is deeply in debt take to get his or her financial house back in order?
3. What should a person who is drowning in debt do?
4. When might it be allowable for a Christian to walk away from a debt or declare bankruptcy?
5. How do some people sinfully avoid meeting their financial obligations?
6. How would a Christian who is in overwhelming financial distress act differently from an unbeliever?
7. What sins might lead to bankruptcy? Is bankruptcy always due to personal sin?

PART 5

PREPARING FOR THE FUTURE

31

WHAT ARE SOME COMMON MISUNDERSTANDINGS ABOUT PREPARING FOR YOUR FINANCIAL FUTURE?

IS THERE NO NEED TO SAVE IF YOU ARE CONSISTENTLY MAKING ENOUGH TO MEET YOUR EXPENSES?

Actually, the Bible commends the wisdom of thinking ahead (Prov. 21:5) in order to be prepared both for anticipated future expenses (such as retirement) and for those that you can't fully anticipate (such as a season of unemployment or a major home or auto repair). In chapter 32, we will explain why it is wise and biblical to have savings.

SHOULD THOSE WHO DON'T KNOW MUCH ABOUT INVESTING SIMPLY ENTRUST THEIR MONEY TO AN EXPERT?

Financial matters are very confusing for many people. Just as those who don't know much about cars want to find a trusted mechanic, many people search for a trusted financial adviser. The right adviser could be helpful. But no financial adviser can promise that you won't lose money or that he or she can outperform the market. Some financial advisers lose a lot of money for their clients. Also, many financial advisers make money based on the investment products they sell you, some of which are very costly to the buyer. Be careful. Just because an adviser goes to your church or is a friend or relative does not mean that the person is competent or will serve your best interests. I have known people who have lost a great deal of money by trusting an acquaintance from church who did not act in his clients' best interests. Some investment salespeople join a particular church largely for the purpose of cultivating potential clients in an environment where there is a great deal of trust. Unsuspecting clients have often been convinced to invest their money in costly schemes that pay high commissions to the salesperson, but gain poor returns for the investors. Even worse, some have been defrauded out of their savings. "A prudent man sees evil and hides himself, the naive proceed and pay the penalty" (Prov. 27:12). In chapters 34–35, we will offer some principles for wise investing along with qualities that you should look for (and others that you should avoid) in an investment adviser.

IF YOU JUST HAVE FAITH AND TRUST GOD, DO YOU STILL NEED INSURANCE?

It is true that we can't prove from the Bible that everyone must purchase insurance. Nor can we explicitly prove from the Bible that people must lock their doors. But biblical principles encourage us to take precautions in a dangerous world. Insurance, like savings, can be a wise way to be prepared for possible future financial calamities for which you couldn't otherwise afford to pay. In chapter 39, we will look at the kinds of insurance you should have and some that might be a waste of your money.

IS THE BEST INSURANCE THAT WHICH COVERS EVERYTHING WITH NO DEDUCTIBLES?

The purpose of insurance is to help you pay for expenses that you can't afford. Usually it is much cheaper to purchase insurance (e.g., auto, medical, and home) that covers the big claims while you pay for the smaller expenses out of your savings or income. This will also be covered in chapter 39.

CAN YOU FEEL SECURE ABOUT YOUR RETIREMENT BECAUSE YOU WILL RECEIVE SOCIAL SECURITY?

For most people, Social Security will not provide sufficient income to maintain their lifestyle;[1] therefore, they will need additional sources of income from savings or a pension.

IF YOU PLAN TO KEEP WORKING IN OLD AGE, DO YOU NEED TO BE CONCERNED ABOUT SAVING FOR RETIREMENT?

The Bible doesn't mandate that people must retire from work at a certain age. But as one gets older, his or her opportunity or ability to work might diminish; therefore, it is wise to be prepared by saving for the day when income from work could dwindle. In chapter 38, we will consider a biblical perspective on issues related to retirement.

DO THOSE WHO DON'T HAVE MANY ASSETS NOT NEED TO WORRY ABOUT MAKING A WILL?

A will can be a blessing to those you leave behind by making your wishes clear about how your possessions are to be distributed in the event of your death. One of the most important reasons to have a will is to give direction about who will take care of your minor children if something happens to you. Someone with significant assets might be wise to create a trust to go along with the will. In chapter 40, we will discuss making a will and considerations for seeking to care well for our loved ones after we are gone.

1. As of this writing, the typical Social Security payment is about $1,500 a month. money.usnews.com/money/retirement/social-security/articles/how-much-you-will

SUMMARY

A general theme in the book of Proverbs is that the foolish live only for the moment, while the wise think long term and are prepared for the future. The topics of investing, insurance, and making a will can be intimidating for some people. Biblical principles can help you to avoid making serious mistakes and to make wise choices.

— QUESTIONS FOR REFLECTION —

1. Why is it important to save for the future?
2. How would you answer someone who says that insurance isn't necessary if you have enough faith?
3. What should you look for when choosing an investment adviser?

-get-from-social-security.

32

WHY DO CHRISTIANS NEED TO SAVE?

There are many reasons why it is wise to save. It is good to save for known future expenses, such as upcoming bills, a major purchase, education, or retirement. Another reason to save is for possible unexpected expenses, such as major home or vehicle repairs or medical bills. A third reason to save is to build resources that will offer future benefit for one's family or various ministries. Saving, like budgeting, is a way of wisely planning for the future. "The plans of the diligent lead surely to advantage, but everyone who is hasty comes surely to poverty" (Prov. 21:5). Those who don't bother to save are at risk of poverty. Those who prepare for the future enjoy many advantages. One of the qualities of the diligent ant is that it gathers food for the future (6:8).

Saving is related to budgeting because you must include savings as part of your budget. But how much do you need to save? Careful planning will help you to make a wise estimate of what you will need. I will walk you through a practical way to determine how much you need to save.

CATEGORIES OF SAVINGS: FILE DRAWERS

You need to save money for various future expenses, some of which are likely to occur sooner than others. To illustrate, imagine three file drawers (or electronic file folders) that represent three broad categories of your savings:

1. The first drawer is for short-term savings that could be needed within the next year.
2. The second drawer is for midterm savings that could be needed within the next few years.
3. The third drawer is for long-term savings that could be needed several years, or even decades, from now.

Within each drawer there could be multiple files representing the various specific categories for which you need that type of savings.

YOU NEED SHORT-TERM SAVINGS FOR IMMEDIATE FINANCIAL NEEDS

1. Short-Term Emergency Fund

You need to be prepared with ready cash to cover unanticipated expenses that pop up. Budgeting systems won't work unless you start with some cash on hand that can serve as a cushion. Many people who get into debt were doing fine until a sudden unexpected bill came along. Because they had no savings cushion, they had to put the expense on a credit card, which was then hard to pay off. It is also important to define *emergency*. An emergency is an unavoidable expense, not the desire for a pair of shoes you had been looking at that went on sale after your clothing budget was already exhausted.

Recommendation: Start with at least $1,000 and budget at least $100 a month to refill this category.

2. Irregular Expenses

You need to save for irregular expenses and bills. Not all expenses occur on a regular monthly basis. Some bills are paid once a year or once a quarter. For example, many people pay for their car insurance or their life insurance only once or twice a year.[1] Other expenses vary from

---

1. While insurance companies will often allow you to make monthly instead of annual or semiannual payments, it is usually less expensive to pay the entire amount when the bill comes due.

month to month, such as medical and dental bills, car maintenance and repair, household maintenance and repair, certain fees and dues, vacation expenses, peak utility bills, and Christmas gifts.

Recommendation: Start with at least $2,000. Then make a detailed estimate of your annual irregular expenses and bills, divide by 12, and then budget that amount each month to refill this short-term savings. For example, a family might estimate that in the coming year they will have $1,200 in car repairs and maintenance (which will vary based on the age of the vehicles and how much they are driven), $2,400 in medical and dental bills not covered by insurance, $1,800 in household maintenance and repairs, $2,400 for the family vacation, and $1,200 for other irregular expenses. This total of $9,000 would require $750 per month to be added to short-term savings for irregular expenses. Because you might be hit with more expenses in the early months of the year, it would be wise to start with at least $2,000 in this category. In practical terms, you would allocate the unspent monthly amount from these variable budget categories to short-term savings and then withdraw from short-term savings when you incur expenses in these categories.

Because you might need short-term savings immediately, it is wisest and safest to keep it as safe and accessible (liquid) as possible. Checking, savings, or money market accounts can serve this purpose. Smaller amounts of savings could be kept at home in cash.

MIDTERM SAVINGS PREPARES YOU FOR MAJOR FINANCIAL OUTLAYS THAT MIGHT OCCUR WITHIN THE NEXT SEVERAL YEARS

1. Major Purchases

You should save for major future expenses, such as the purchase of a new vehicle, the down payment on a house, or a planned major household remodel. This amount could vary widely, depending on your situation. For example, if you already own your home, you don't need to save for a down payment. The savings for a vehicle is easier to estimate. If you anticipate buying a new car that costs $22,500 in three years, you need to save $625 a month. If you can wait five years, you need to save only $375 a month in your car savings folder. Or if you can make do with buying a vehicle that costs $15,000, you need to save $250 a month. If you plan to replace multiple cars, then multiple payments need to be paid to your car savings fund/folder. Another example is that if you are hoping to buy a house in two years for which you need an additional $24,000 for a down payment, you need to save $1,000 a month.

2. Emergency Savings for Income Disruption[2]

The reality of living in a fallen and unstable world means that financial recessions and other disruptions (such as a pandemic) will occur from time to time. "You do not know what misfortune may occur on the earth" (Eccl. 11:2b). In addition, individuals sometimes face periods of unemployment from various causes. During prosperous times, many people are totally unprepared for a major disruption to their income. In Genesis 41, Joseph interpreted Pharaoh's dream of seven healthy, fat cows that swallowed up seven gaunt cows as signifying that Egypt would have seven years of prosperity followed by seven years of famine. Joseph wisely helped the Egyptians to store up grain during the years of plenty so that they could survive the years of famine.[3] Unlike Joseph, we don't have a specific prophecy that we will experience poverty during a particular season in our lives. But as we consider the history of this fallen world, we know that seasons of economic hardship from various causes are inevitable, whether these be worldwide or individual. It is wise to be prepared for hard times by saving during the good times. In Joseph's day, those outside Egypt, including Joseph's family, were unprepared for famine. In the same way, both recent and distant history has shown that many individuals and corporations that seemed to be doing well during prosperous

2. For more biblical wisdom on preparing for and surviving a financial crisis, see Jim Newheiser, *Financial Crisis: What to Do When the Bottom Drops Out* (Greensboro, NC: New Growth Press, 2020).

3. Acts 11:27–30 offers another example of preparation for a crisis as the early church got ready for a worldwide famine.

times were unprepared for hard times and suffered great loss as a result. Those who have savings are usually able to weather the financial storms and then come out ready to enjoy financial success when the economic seas are calm again. *Recommendation: Seek to have a minimum of three months (ideally six months) of living expenses in emergency savings.*

Because midterm savings could be needed on short notice, this money, like the short-term savings, should be either kept in the bank or invested very conservatively (e.g., in short-term certificates of deposit).

YOU ALSO NEED TO SAVE FOR LONG-TERM NEEDS

1. Retirement

For most people, the most important long-term savings goal is retirement. Because of the way that investments and interest compound over time, the earlier in life you start saving and investing, the more likely it is that you will have sufficient resources available when you retire. The amount you need to save and invest each year can be estimated based on your current age, your expected investment returns, your current savings, other expected sources of income (e.g., Social Security and pensions), and the age at which you hope to retire. Websites and apps are available to help you calculate an estimate of how much you need to save each year in order to meet your retirement goals.[4] *Recommendation: Set aside a minimum of 10 percent of your income in retirement investments.* For those who are behind, this amount should be much greater.

2. Education

Many people save for their children's (or grandchildren's) future (often college) education. We want our offspring to have maximum opportunity to gain valuable skills and qualifications that will prepare them for a lifetime of productivity and success (Prov. 22:29). The government has set up tax-advantaged plans to encourage education

---

4. See retirementplans.vanguard.com/VGApp/pe/pubeducation/calculators /RetirementIncomeCalc.jsf; www.crown.org/resources/crown-calculators/.

savings.[5] Like saving for retirement, the earlier you start, the easier it is to meet your goals. One thing to consider when saving for your children's education is that the system does not always reward those who save. The amount of your assets/savings might adversely affect the financial aid offered by educational institutions. If this is a concern, you should investigate this, perhaps with the help of an accountant, years before your children are eligible for college.

Money that won't be needed for several years can be invested more aggressively than short-term or midterm savings, with the hope of obtaining a greater return. We will discuss various investment options in chapter 36. The closer one is to the time when the money will be needed (e.g., retirement or the first year of college), the more conservatively the money should be invested (e.g., bank deposits), because more aggressive investments bear the risk of a sharp decline that could put the goal at risk. If one has a longer time before the money is needed, it is very likely that the investments that temporarily lost value will recover.[6]

SUMMARY

Scripture teaches that those who are wise seek to prepare for the future—short term, midterm, and long term. Sadly, the great majority of Americans live from paycheck to paycheck[7] and are thus unprepared both for expenses that should have been anticipated and for those that are totally unexpected. Saving requires discipline—forgoing present consumption for the sake of future benefit. Thomas Stanley and William Danko point out that one of the distinguishing characteristics of high-wealth individuals ("millionaires") is that they choose to live well below their means, which enables them to accumulate savings.[8]

5. See www.savingforcollege.com.

6. Assuming that the investments were wise/sound ones and that there is not a long-term market downturn.

7. www.forbes.com/sites/zackfriedman/2019/01/11/live-paycheck-to-paycheck -government-shutdown/#33a151c24f10.

8. Thomas J. Stanley and William D. Danko, *The Millionaire Next Door: The Surprising Secrets of America's Wealthy* (Lanham, MD: Taylor Trade Publishing, 2010), 9.

— QUESTIONS FOR REFLECTION —

1. What is the importance of having short-term savings available?
2. What are some purposes for midterm savings?
3. For what reasons do most people need to put money aside for long-term needs?
4. How should each type of savings be invested?
5. Make an estimate of how much savings you need in each category.

33

IN PRACTICAL TERMS, HOW SHOULD SAVINGS BE ACCUMULATED?

Perhaps you were overwhelmed when you read the previous chapter. How can we save that much money? How do we keep track of how much we have saved? How much is enough?

WHAT IS THE CURRENT STATUS OF YOUR SAVINGS?

1. Make a List of All Your Liabilities/Debts and Financial Assets, Using the Balance Sheet in Appendix B

Here is the biblical basis for being aware of the condition of your economic resources: "Know well the condition of your flocks, and pay attention to your herds; for riches are not forever, nor does a crown endure to all generations" (Prov. 27:23–24).

2. Calculate How Much Money You Should Already Have in Each Savings Category

3. Compare the Amount You Already Have with the Amount You Should Have Saved

The difference is the additional amount of savings you need to accumulate in order to fill your savings "files." See the example in Appendix B.

HOW CAN YOU ACCUMULATE SAVINGS?

1. Make Savings in Each Category a Part of Your Budget, Just like Groceries and Utilities

Deposit or designate money into each "folder" each month.[1] These amounts should be reflected in your bank or brokerage accounts.

2. Resist the Temptation to Spend Money That Has Been Designated for Savings on Budget-Busting Lifestyle Choices

3. Keep Track of the Balances of Each Savings Category (Prov. 27:23)

This could be done by creating a separate bank or brokerage account for each category or by designating and keeping records of each within one account, using a program or a spreadsheet. For example, you could have a balance of $4,000 in short-term savings, of which $2,000 could be designated and ready for unexpected expenses and $2,000 for irregular expenses. In addition, you might have a balance of $25,000 in midterm savings, of which $20,000 could be designated as your emergency fund and $5,000 as your car fund. Each month, you would add the budgeted amount to each account so that the balances would grow. See Appendix B for an example of how to do this.

4. If You Receive a Windfall, Use It to Fund Your Savings

You might receive a financial gift from a family member, an inheritance, or a tax refund. Rather than running to the mall or going online to spend it (which is what most people do), after considering giving, use it to fill in the gaps in your savings (or pay your debt). Focus on the categories in which there is a shortfall, starting with short-term savings.

---

1. Many financial experts advocate regular monthly contributions to retirement accounts, as opposed to less frequent larger investments.

IS IT MORE IMPORTANT
TO SAVE OR TO GET RID OF DEBT?

1. Fund Your Short-Term Savings First, and Then Work toward Eliminating Debt

This is so that you will be able to pay ongoing expenses without having to resort to incurring debt (using credit cards) to pay your bills.

2. After Short-Term Savings Has Been Funded, It Is Usually Wise to Make Debt Elimination the Next Priority

Funding midterm and long-term savings might be reduced or even delayed while debt is being paid off.

3. Once the Monthly Loan Payments Have Been Eliminated, Much More Money Will Be Available for Savings

WHAT IF ONE SAVINGS CATEGORY
IS FULLY FUNDED OR EVEN AHEAD?

This would be a nice problem to have. My suggestion is to use the overflow in one category to fund any savings categories in which you have fallen behind. If your savings seem to be on schedule, then I encourage you to gratefully give more to the Lord's work.

MAY YOU MOVE MONEY AMONG
THE DIFFERENT SAVINGS CATEGORIES?

The short answer is: "Yes. It's your money! Just be careful." For example, if you are unemployed and have burned through your three to six months of emergency savings, you are free to use your car savings in order to pay the bills. We are also assuming that you are doing all you can to find work (Eccl. 11:6—see chapter 14). The greatest concern about moving money among funds is the situation in which a family raids other funds because they are not disciplined in their spending.

HOW MUCH SAVINGS IS ENOUGH?

I realize that many of us might never expect to face this question. John D. Rockefeller, one of the wealthiest men who ever lived, was once asked how much money is enough. His oft-quoted answer: "Just a little bit more." His words are a reminder of the truth that those who live for money will never be satisfied (Prov. 27:20; Eccl. 5:10). Ecclesiastes also observes the futility of accumulating wealth: "When good things increase, those who consume them increase. So what is the advantage to their owners except to look on?" (Eccl. 5:11). There are three things you can do when you have more money than you need. You can spend it on enhancing your lifestyle. You can accumulate it in savings. Or you can give more away for the Lord's work. There are no hard-and-fast rules about the lifestyle we should live or how much wealth is sinfully excessive. But we are warned against hoarding wealth (Eccl. 5:13; James 5:1–5). Jesus warns against selfishly hoarding wealth in the parable of the rich fool. It is foolish and wrong to store up earthly treasures while not being rich toward God (Luke 12:21). But more important than the exact amount of wealth saved or given away is the heart attitude, as Jesus explains as he introduces his parable: "Then He said to them, 'Beware, and be on your guard against every form of greed; for not even when one has an abundance does his life consist of his possessions'" (v. 15). Those of us who are blessed with resources might live in constant tension as we wrestle over how many of our resources may be enjoyed now, how much should be saved for a dangerous and uncertain future, and how much should be given away. As we make these decisions, we must first of all guard our hearts. As we learn from the parable of the rich fool, no amount of accumulated wealth will make us secure in the long run. "Riches do not profit in the day of wrath, but righteousness delivers from death" (Prov. 11:4; also see 23:3–4; Matt. 6:19–21). Nor will the pleasures that money can buy bring satisfaction (Eccl. 2:1ff.). Such considerations will help us to cling less tightly to our earthly wealth and should encourage us to put our faith into practice by being generous.

SUMMARY

Saving money for the future is wise, but it takes discipline and self-control. Having specific goals will help you to know how much to save for various anticipated needs. Those who are wise with the resources God gives them will be well prepared for the future and will be in a position to bless others by giving to God's work on earth.

— QUESTIONS FOR REFLECTION —

1. What are at least two ways in which you can accumulate savings?
2. How would you decide between eliminating debt and increasing savings?
3. Why is it important to keep track of your savings? In practical terms, how can you do this?
4. How should you decide how to divide your money between spending, saving, and giving?

34

WHAT ARE WISE GENERAL PRINCIPLES FOR INVESTING?

A few basic principles for investing will benefit people in all different kinds of financial situations.

1. Plan to Accumulate Wealth Gradually

"Wealth gained hastily will dwindle, but whoever gathers little by little will increase it" (Prov. 13:11 ESV). The wise accumulate wealth gradually. First, they earn a high income by working hard and working smart. Then they live at a reasonable standard of living and follow a budget that enables them to regularly put aside money for savings. Finally, they invest prudently, with the hopes of preserving their capital and gradually growing their assets.

2. Understand That Higher Returns Can Come Only at the Expense of Greater Risk

For example, the risk on short-term government bonds or savings accounts is minimal, but so is the return (at this writing about 1 percent). Stocks offer much higher potential returns, but at a greater risk. There are years when the stock market might go up as much as 25 percent—but stock markets are volatile, are sometimes stagnant, often drop, and occasionally crash, causing the investors' assets to decline, often significantly. This does not mean that taking risk is always wrong. It might be fine to take reasonable risk in the long term in order to produce higher long-term returns. If you invest only in extremely low-risk investments, you will be limited to very low returns. You can't beat the risk-reward chart by getting higher returns with no risk (going below the line), but you can go above the line by getting lower return with greater risk. It is important to ensure that expected returns are sufficient in proportion to the risk taken. One of the worst-case scenarios is to take very high risks for investments whose potential returns are low (e.g., lending to family members—see chapter 29).

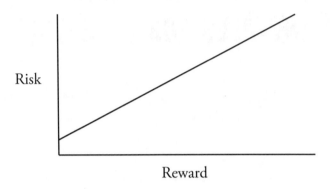

Fig. 34.1. Risk-Reward Chart

This chart illustrates the principle that it is generally impossible to go below the line (more reward with less risk) but possible to go above the line (more risk with less reward).

3. Be Sure That You Understand That in Which You Are Investing[1]

"The mind of the prudent acquires knowledge, and the ear of the wise seeks knowledge" (Prov. 18:15). One way to reduce investment risk is by researching investment options. Putting money in the bank at interest might be the simplest kind of investment to understand. Some investment products, however, are very complex and are suitable only for sophisticated investors (if anyone). It can be very dangerous

---

1. For a detailed explanation of different kinds of investments, I recommend Austin Pryor, *The Sound Mind Investing Handbook: A Step-by-Step Guide to Managing Your Money from a Biblical Perspective* (Chicago: Moody Publishers, 2014).

to simply rely on the supposed expertise of your investment adviser, especially if he or she is pressuring you to risk your money in a venture that you don't understand. Do your research. Ask lots of questions. If you aren't confident that you fully grasp the nature of the investment product, take your money elsewhere. I have had investments pitched to me that sounded great on the surface, but I was never able to fully comprehend how they planned to succeed. I have never regretted walking away from such opportunities (27:12).

4. **Understand the Various Risks of Different Investments**
   A. There is no completely risk-free investment. If you stuff all your cash into a mattress, you won't lose it when the stock market crashes. But your house could catch on fire or thieves could find it. If you put all your dollars into a government-insured bank, inflation, like rust, could eat away at the purchasing power of your savings. Or hyperinflation could wipe out most of the value of your money. There is no ultimate security in this fallen world, "where moth and rust destroy, and where thieves break in and steal" (Matt. 6:19b).
   B. Each category of investment has its own risks. For example, if you invest in stocks, the entire market could sharply decline or crash. If you invest in real estate or precious metals, a bubble could burst and your investment could lose value. If you commit to a long-term corporate bond, market interest rates could rise, thus giving you substandard returns on your investment and lowering the value of your bond if you wish to sell it.
   C. Particular investments have particular risks. During a rising stock market, you could invest in a company whose products are shown to cause cancer, thus leading to lawsuits and corporate bankruptcy. Or you could invest in a rental property that requires major unexpected repairs shortly after you purchase it, or for which it's difficult to find a renter over a long period, or you could get a bad tenant who doesn't pay rent and then trashes your property.

5. Know That If It Sounds Too Good to Be True, It Is Almost Certainly Too Good to Be True

Just as it is foolish to think that you can earn lots of money without work and skill, it is foolish to think that you can earn significant returns without taking significant risk. For example, several years ago when the banks were paying 3 percent on savings, someone approached me, promising that he could get me a 12 percent risk-free return on my money. I concluded that either he was trying to deceive me by hiding the risks or he was self-deceived and ignorant of the risks. If at that time there was a surefire way to get a 12 percent return risk-free, the banks would stop issuing mortgages at 3 percent and business loans at 6 percent and would go all in with this wonderful opportunity. "The prudent sees the evil and hides himself, but the naive go on, and are punished for it" (Prov. 22:3).

6. Understand the Costs Associated with Your Investments

Insist on knowing how your investment adviser or broker is being paid and what the ongoing investment-related expenses will be. See the next chapter for more detailed warnings about the cost of investing.

7. Realize That Diversification Can Reduce Risk

"Divide your portion to seven, or even to eight, for you do not know what misfortune may occur on the earth. . . . Sow your seed in the morning and do not be idle in the evening, for you do not know whether morning or evening sowing will succeed, or whether both of them alike will be good" (Eccl. 11:2, 6). Another way of saying this is: "Don't put all your eggs into one basket." Diversification might keep you from participating in spectacular returns in one particular type of investment, but it should help protect you from major losses.

A. Diversify your stock and bond investments. For example, if you put all your savings into one stock and then that particular company experiences major troubles (e.g., lawsuits, product failures, new powerful competitors), its stock could drop and you could lose most or all of your investment. Investing in a variety of individual stocks enables you to spread out your risk among many companies. Further diversification can take place as you invest in companies in a variety of industries. For example, you would achieve little diversification if you invested only in technology companies, as opposed to spreading your risk by also investing in energy, retail, and transportation companies.

B. Many investors use mutual funds in order to diversify risk. These funds pool money from many investors to buy many different stocks or bonds, thus spreading risk among many different corporations. One can also choose diverse kinds of mutual funds (e.g., some that invest in bonds, some in stock indexes, some in foreign stocks, and some in particular industries or sectors of the economy).

C. Spread your financial risk among different types of investments, such as bonds, CDs, real estate, precious metals, and so forth. The idea is that if one declines, the others might go up or at least remain stable.

8. Invest Money That You Might Need in the Short Term Very Conservatively

For example, if you have $25,000 saved to buy a car next year, you wouldn't want to invest it in the stock market, which might decline, thus leaving you without enough money to buy your vehicle. The safest place to put money is in a government-insured bank deposit or savings account.

9. Realize That Money That Won't Be Needed for Many Years Can Be More Aggressively Invested

For example, if you don't need your $25,000 until you retire twenty-five years from now, you can invest it in the stock market, knowing that even if it declines in the short term, it will probably recover in the midterm and offer higher returns in the long term. Because very low-risk returns are so small, most people have to take some risk (e.g., buying stocks as opposed to leaving the money in the bank) in order to make a decent return on their investment.

10. Pursue High-Quality Investments

If you invest in stocks or bonds, choose companies that are well managed, are financially strong (not too much debt), and have strong prospects for long-term growth. If you purchase a rental property, make sure that it is well constructed and in a neighborhood where values are rising and homes are well cared for.

11. Be Careful in Your Selection of a Professional Investment Adviser

An investment adviser should have appropriate training and experience with a verifiable track record of success with his or her clients. You also want someone whose philosophy of investing is compatible with your goals. If you see an investment adviser violating the other principles listed above, flee.

12. Seek Wise Financial Counsel from Wise People Who Don't Stand to Gain from the Advice They Offer You

"Without consultation, plans are frustrated, but with many counselors they succeed" (Prov. 15:22). Many investment consultants might want to steer you into investments on which they make the highest commissions, which makes it hard for them to offer objective advice. Find trusted, wise friends with whom you can talk over your approach to finances and investing. When you are considering an investment that you are not absolutely sure about, have someone who is both objective and financially savvy look it over with you. I have had friends come to me with an investment opportunity or a money-making scheme that at first seemed potentially lucrative until we looked more closely to discover the high costs and risks associated with such opportunities. I believe that tens of thousands of dollars have been saved as a result.

SUMMARY

While our ultimate security is in heavenly treasure, we are called to be good stewards of the earthly resources that God has entrusted to us. We can do this by understanding our investment options, including potential risks and rewards, which enables us to make wise choices. These wise choices can lead to greater opportunities to do spiritual good with our wealth (Luke 16:10).

— QUESTIONS FOR REFLECTION —

1. Why does investment risk typically increase with potential investment rewards? Why can't this principle be successfully circumvented?
2. What kinds of risks are associated with investing?
3. What is a wise strategy for short-term versus long-term investments?
4. Is it wrong to take risk with investments? If not, when is it wise to take on some risks?
5. Why shouldn't you invest in something you don't understand?

35

WHAT ARE THE BIGGEST MISTAKES PEOPLE MAKE WHEN INVESTING?

Scripture acknowledges the reality that riches are sometimes "lost through a bad investment" (Eccl. 5:14). When I was a boy, my father encouraged me to invest my savings from mowing grass in a few individual shares in the stock market. Sadly for me, I bought at the end of a stock-market rally, which was followed by many years of flat or down markets. Every day I would eagerly turn in the newspaper to see whether my two stocks, in which I had one share each, had finally gone up. During my twenties, I worked for an oil company in the Middle East, where I made a lot of money (my fat-cow years before going into ministry) and was around many people who were earning even more. As a young investor, I made some mistakes and narrowly avoided making some more. I also observed other people lose small fortunes through foolish investing. Some of the smartest and wealthiest people I have known have been total failures at investing. I have wondered why. Is this simply the Lord's way of redistributing wealth (Prov. 23:4–5)? Or are they the target of the charlatans who have little interest in small fish like me?

WHAT ARE SOME OF THE DEADLIEST INVESTMENT ERRORS?

1. Falling for "Get-Rich-Quick" Schemes

"A faithful man will abound with blessings, but he who makes haste to be rich will not go unpunished" (Prov. 28:20). Just as the baseball players who always try to hit home runs tend also to be those who strike out most often, investors who go for the big score often strike out. Big risks accompany the prospect of big returns. Many get-rich-quick schemes are promoted by unscrupulous advisers who take advantage of investors' greed. People rarely become wealthy through investing. Investing helps you to preserve and gradually grow your wealth. People become wealthy by earning money through hard work and entrepreneurial skills and then spending less than they make, thus enabling savings. People lose their wealth by making risky investment decisions. For every story of the investor who got in early on the hot tech stock, there are thousands who lost significant sums on speculative investments.

2. Failing to Understand the Risks of That in Which They Are Investing

Investment promoters often entice people by emphasizing the large upside possibilities while burying the downside risks in the fine print. I have known many people who bet big on "surefire" high-return investment schemes, only to lose their money. Remember the general rule that greater investment returns can be pursued only at proportionately greater risk. Your risk will be significantly compounded by your ignorance: "The prudent sees the evil and hides himself, but the naive go on, and are punished for it" (Prov. 22:3). John Temple warns, "The financial industry thrives on mystery in order to make unjustified profit. Beware!"[1]

---

1. John Temple, *Family Money Matters: How to Run Your Family Finances to God's Glory* (Leominster, UK: Day One Publications, 2010), 74.

3. Engaging in Short-Term Speculative Investing as Opposed to Long-Term Value Investing

This is the domain of day traders in stocks and options who attempt to time the market, trying to get in before the stock goes up and to get out before it goes down, with little consideration of the long-term prospects of an investment. This approach resembles gambling more than investing.

4. Tying Up Money You Need Soon in Long-Term Investments

Certain investments, including many annuities, either have restrictions on when you can make withdrawals or force you to pay significant penalties to access your money. Another example is a long-term bank CD in which you commit your money for several years.

5. Investing Merely to Avoid Taxes

People with high incomes are often highly motivated by investments, such as municipal bonds (which can be a good investment), which can help keep their tax bills down. In addition, some are encouraged to invest in complicated investments such as certain forms of partnerships designed as tax shelters. While the impact of taxes is a legitimate factor to consider, it is unwise to invest in a venture that is extremely risky or a scheme that you don't fully understand. It is also important not to merely trust the pitch of the investment salesperson, but to have an accountant verify the tax benefits. I have known situations in which people who purchased tax-sheltered investments either lost a great deal of money or experienced costly complications with their own tax situations.

6. Failing to Understand the Costs Associated with an Investment

A. Commissions paid to investment advisers plus ongoing fees related to the investment can eat into investment returns or even your capital. For example, an investment that returns 12 percent but has annual costs and fees of 2 percent will net you only 10 percent, which might not seem to be a great problem if it keeps going up 12 percent. But if your investment

236

goes up 4 percent, the 2 percent fee cuts your returns in half. Another example is that if you invest $10,000 in a fund that gives your investment adviser a 5 percent commission, your investment is worth only $9,500, which means that you are behind from the start. Sometimes the commissions and fees are much higher than in the examples listed above.

B. Some costs are hidden. For example, many years ago an investment adviser (from church) convinced me to buy into a mutual fund he was selling, saying that there was no load (initial charge for buying into the fund). I learned later, however, that the annual fees and expenses for this fund were much higher than the industry average (which is how the adviser gets paid) and that I would be charged a sizable exit fee if I were to take my money out of that fund.

7. Overpaying Your Adviser

Investment advisers are typically paid in a few different ways.

A. Some advisers make money from commissions they receive when you buy investment products from them. These commissions can be very high on certain investments, such as annuity and insurance products. Another potential problem with this method of payment is that it might create a conflict of interest if the adviser is predisposed to sell you products that give him or her the greatest amount of commission (like the waiter in the restaurant who is told by the manager to push the salmon tonight), rather than what is best for your long-term financial future. The professional standard for such advisers is typically that they offer you suitable options, but not necessarily the best possible option (e.g., you might be able to buy a very similar product elsewhere without having to pay a commission or load).

B. Some advisers will manage your investments for a flat percentage of your assets, typically around 1 percent (but this varies according to the size of your account). Such advisers are expected to act in your best interests. The worst of both worlds could be an adviser who charges you to manage your investments while also steering you into investments that pay him or her a sizable commission.

C. Some advisers charge a flat fee (which could be several hundred dollars or more) to go through your finances and to help you draw up an investment plan to potentially meet your goals. You would then be responsible to manage your own investments based on the advice you received.

8. Trusting Incompetent Investment Advisers

Just as some plumbers and house painters are more skilled than others, some investment advisers are more capable than others. Unfortunately, I have seen cases in which huge sums of money have been lost by incompetent or inexperienced advisers who had attracted investors among their network of friends and fellow church members. In one sad case, Sam, who lost his corporate job in 2006, decided to try his hand as an investment adviser. He took some classes and started to work under the supervision of a mentor. The mentor became convinced that great opportunities were available through investing in distressed mortgages for homes in the Detroit area. Sam then persuaded various family members, friends, and fellow church members to invest their savings in these distressed mortgages (for which Sam and his mentor received high commissions). Within several months, the housing market crashed, and these investments became almost worthless. While Sam had not deliberately defrauded his friends, he was guilty of gaining their trust by misrepresenting himself as an investment expert.

9. Trusting Unscrupulous Investment Advisers

While some advisers are incompetent, others are out-and-out frauds. They exploit people's greed by claiming secret or inside information while promising unrealistic returns. They pressure potential clients by claiming that they must act quickly before a unique opportunity goes away.

10. Not Being United with Your Spouse

I have seen cases in which one spouse is better than the other at sensing financial danger. Both spouses should agree when making major investment decisions.

IS IT EVER WISE TO BORROW MONEY IN ORDER TO MAKE MONEY?

It is very risky to borrow money for the sake of investing it because you are relying on the assumption that the return on the investment will significantly exceed the cost of the interest on the money borrowed. Given that greater returns can come only with greater risk, it is very possible that the investment will not pay off as much as had been expected and that your loss will be compounded by the interest you pay on what you borrowed.

1. Buying on Margin

Borrowing money to invest in stocks is called buying on margin. Bill receives a hot stock tip. He has enough cash to buy fifty shares, or he can purchase a hundred shares on margin, which involves borrowing money (at a moderate interest rate) for the second fifty shares, using all the shares as collateral. If the stock doubles, then Bill's gain will be nearly doubled. If the stock declines, however, he will lose twice as much (plus interest). If the stock goes down by half, then Bill is upside down, owing more than the stock is worth.

2. Borrowing against Your Home Equity in Order to Invest at a Potentially Higher Return

During the housing boom in the early 2000s, people who had purchased homes in Southern California for less than $200,000 suddenly realized that their houses were now worth over $500,000. During that time, many homeowners were convinced by investment advisers to borrow against the equity in their homes and invest it in the stock market or annuities. The pitch was that the homeowner would come out far ahead by receiving more than 10 percent return on the investment while paying less than 7 percent interest on the money borrowed against home equity. The homeowner might then borrow an additional $250,000 against his or her home equity and entrust it to the adviser. For many families, this strategy proved to be disastrous. When the housing market crashed in 2008, the home that had been worth $500,000 was now worth only $300,000. The homeowner was now upside down by $150,000 or more, owing much more on the mortgage(s) than the house was worth. In addition, the return on the investment was often significantly below what had been promised. Furthermore, the money invested was tied up and could not be withdrawn without significant penalties. Many homeowners wound up losing their homes to foreclosure, along with a significant portion of the money they had invested. The only ones who came out ahead were the investment advisers. The moral of the story is that it is a great blessing to have equity and a greater blessing to own your home free and clear. Don't be greedy! Those who promise greater returns are putting your money at greater risk.

WHY DO PEOPLE MAKE FOOLISH INVESTMENT DECISIONS?

1. Greed

Greed can make some people an easy target for unscrupulous investment advisers (confidence men) who prey on their fear of missing out on big potential gains (Luke 12:15; 1 Tim. 6:10). Others are lured in by advertisements offering secret information that will enable someone with a small amount of capital to make a fortune by day trading, investing in precious metals, or flipping in real estate with little or no money down.

2. Pride

Some investors believe that they can outsmart the system. I have known several people who, after reading a book or following some Internet posts, have become convinced that if they follow a certain investing system (often involving day trading), they can achieve spectacular returns. I have known people who were very successful in their vocations who have lost their life savings this way. Perhaps they assumed that because they were smart and successful in their field, this would carry over to their investment decisions. Why would you think that you could come to the day-trading poker table with your $200,000 and a book you read about stocks, expecting to out-wit people with Harvard MBAs who have been managing billions of dollars for decades? "He who trusts in his own heart is a fool" (Prov. 28:26a).

3. Impatience

Rather than building wealth gradually, some are in a hurry to get rich (Prov. 28:20).

4. Laziness

Some who are diligent at making money are sluggardly when it comes to taking the time to understand and manage their investments.

SUMMARY

Many people exercise poor stewardship of the resources that the Lord has entrusted to them by investing foolishly. Sometimes this is due to ignorance of costs and risks of various investments. Often it is due to pride and greed. When we hear of others who make a killing in the market, we can be tempted to be afraid of missing out. We need to be wise, careful, and patient.

— QUESTIONS FOR REFLECTION —

1. What heart sins make us vulnerable to making foolish investment decisions?
2. What should an investor know before entrusting his or her financial resources to an adviser?
3. What are the risks of borrowing money for the purpose of investing it?

4. What can go wrong if you borrow against your home equity for the purpose of investing?
5. How would you counsel someone who says that he plans to quit his job in order to be a day trader in stocks?

36

WHAT KINDS OF INVESTMENTS ARE AVAILABLE, AND WHAT ARE THE RISKS? (BANKS, BONDS, AND STOCKS)[1]

Many different investment options are available. Each has potential risks and rewards. Generally speaking, the closer you are to needing to access the money, the fewer risks you should take.

MANY INVESTMENTS INVOLVE LENDING YOUR MONEY AND RECEIVING INTEREST

In most of these investments, you give your money to an entity that will give it back to you with interest after a set time. Sometimes it pays the interest periodically during the term of the loan, while repaying the principal at the end of the loan. In other situations, the interest is compounded into the loan amount, with interest and principal being paid at the end of the loan period.

DOES THE BIBLE FORBID TAKING INTEREST FROM THOSE TO WHOM WE LEND MONEY (USURY)?

Under the old covenant, it was forbidden for one Israelite to charge interest on a loan to his fellow Israelite: "You shall not charge

1. One of the best resources from which to learn more about various investment

interest to your countrymen: interest on money, food, or anything that may be loaned at interest" (Deut. 23:19). The purpose was to keep those with resources from taking advantage of the desperate need of other people by charging high interest on a loan. For example, if your neighbor was out of food and his family was hungry, and you had plenty, it would be wrong to offer to lend him five pounds of grain under the condition that he pay you back ten pounds within a week. A modern example might be that your neighbors are on the verge of being evicted from their home, so you lend them $1,000, with the expectation that they pay you back $1,500 in two months. In spite of what the law taught, sometimes the Israelites had to be rebuked for exploiting one another by acting like loan sharks (Neh. 5:4, 7). The law encouraged those whom God had blessed with wealth to either freely give resources to a needy brother or lend to him at no interest (Ex. 22:25; Deut. 15:7–8). An application under the new covenant is that we should be ready to show mercy to brothers and sisters who are in major financial trouble, without demanding that they pay us back with high interest. This reflects God's generosity to us. Speaking of the righteous man, the psalmist says, "All day long he is gracious and lends" (Ps. 37:26a).

Not all interest was forbidden, however, even under the old covenant: "You may charge interest to a foreigner" (Deut. 23:20). There is also a difference between sinfully taking advantage of desperate individuals by charging high interest (usury) and receiving interest for the use of your resources in a business venture (Luke 19:23). Another argument for charging interest is that inflation eats away at the purchasing power of your money (see below). In contrast, if someone borrowed five ounces of gold or a hundred pounds of grain and then repaid you after a period of time, the person could give you back exactly what you had lent him or her.[2]

---

options is Austin Pryor, *The Sound Mind Investing Handbook: A Step-by-Step Guide to Managing Your Money from a Biblical Perspective* (Chicago: Moody Publishers, 2014).

2. Of course, if the cost of grain or gold fluctuated, then the value in dollars would differ.

WHAT ARE THE RISKS OF
INTEREST-PAYING INVESTMENTS?

1. Default Risk

Whether you lend money to an individual or a large corporation, there is a possibility that the person or entity will fall on hard times and thus be unable to repay you. Default risk can be minimized by lending money to the federal government or a government-insured bank. Default risk tends to be much greater when you lend to individuals, smaller business ventures, and large companies that are financially unhealthy. Such bonds are referred to as *junk bonds*. There can also be some default risk when lending to local governments that have been fiscally irresponsible and are at risk of not being able to repay their debts. There can be significant risk in lending to certain foreign governments that have pursued reckless fiscal policies and have a track record of defaulting on their debt. There is also currency risk (loss of value in dollars) when investing in foreign bonds.

2. Risk of Inflation

Inflation eats away at the buying power of money. For example, if you lent someone $10,000 twenty years ago and you were repaid $10,000 today, the purchasing power of your money would have declined by about one-third. Thus, it would take almost $15,000 to buy the same goods and services that you could have purchased for $10,000 when you lent the money twenty years ago. This example assumes low inflation. If inflation had been higher, your purchasing power would have eroded much more. The interest paid on a loan should be sufficient to pay the lender for the value lost due to inflation plus some additional return. Sadly, government policies often harm savers both by keeping interest rates artificially low (thus robbing them of a fair return on their savings) and by promoting inflation (which eats away at the buying power of their assets).[3]

3. See https://www.businessinsider.com/worst-hyperinflation-episodes-in-history -2013-9 for examples of inflated currency.

3. Risk of Rising Interest Rates (or Getting Locked into a Low Rate)

For example, let's imagine that you purchased a bond by which you lent a company $10,000 for ten years at 3 percent. The company would give you 3 percent ($300) each year for ten years and then give you back your $10,000 at the end of the term. What would happen if, a year after you purchased the bond, market interest rates rose to 8 percent? First, you would regret it because you would be getting only 3 percent while others were receiving 8 percent ($800) a year. Furthermore, if you wished to sell your bond, it would be worth less than $10,000 because of the rise in interest rates. The longer the term of the loan, the greater the interest-rate risk, because if interest rates rose you would miss out for a longer period.

WHAT TYPES OF INTEREST-BEARING INVESTMENTS ARE AVAILABLE?

From lowest to highest risk:

1. U.S. Government Debt, Including Savings Bonds and Treasury Bills, Is Very Low Risk because the Default Risk Is Almost Zero

The government has the power to tax or print money in order to meet its obligation. Interest rates on government debt tend to be low. Generally speaking, the longer the term of the debt, the higher the interest rate (because of the risk of rising rates over time). Government debt can be for as little as three months and for as long as thirty years.[4] Government bonds can generally be resold on the open market, but they can go down in market value when interest rates rise. You may buy these bonds directly from the government, or you may choose to invest in government securities through a mutual fund.

2. Insured Bank Accounts

Banks offer savings and money market accounts, which are insured by the government (FDIC) up to a certain amount (currently

---

4. There is talk of the government's issuing fifty-year bonds.

$250,000). These pay relatively low interest. They are very "liquid" in that you can get your money whenever you wish. Interest rates rise and fall with market rates.

3. Certificates of Deposit (CDs)

Banks offer CDs, by which you lend your money for a fixed time (from a few months to ten years). These offer higher interest than savings accounts because of the time value of money. Typically, the longer the term, the higher the interest rate paid (and the greater risk of regret on your part if interest rates rise). Normally, you can't access your money until the term of the CD is over, but many banks allow you to access your money after paying an early-withdrawal penalty.

4. Mutual Fund Money Market Funds

These function like the bank money market funds, but they are not government-insured, so there is slightly more risk. The mutual fund invests the money in very safe short-term debt from many companies or government entities. These funds are often used for the convenience of investors who want to have liquid assets (cash) available to use to purchase other investments (stocks, bonds, and other mutual funds) at a later time.

5. Local and State Government Bonds

Other government entities sell bonds, including municipal bonds. These can be relatively safe from default risk when the full credit of the governmental entity stands behind them. Bonds of fiscally unsound government entities (at risk of default) or bonds that are tied to the revenue from a particular project are riskier. Municipal bonds typically have the advantage that they are not taxed at the federal, state, or local level, which enables local governments to pay less interest to lenders. These bonds tend to be longer term, and like most other bonds, they can be bought and sold on the open market. Their value goes up and down based on fluctuations in interest rates and perception of risk. Investors typically buy these bonds through a broker or investment adviser. Or one can invest in a wide pool of municipal bonds through a mutual fund.

6. Corporate Bonds

Large corporations borrow money from the public by using bonds or similar financial instruments. These function much like government bonds. The amount of interest received depends on the length of the bond and perceived risk.[5] Some bonds are classified as junk bonds, which means that default risk is high. Such bonds pay more interest than higher-grade bonds. Most people invest in corporate bonds through mutual funds. An advantage of purchasing bonds through a mutual fund is that default risk is spread out among many companies.

7. Loans to Individuals and Small Businesses

These carry the most default risk. If you choose to invest in this way, it is important to put everything in writing so that mutual expectations will be clear in case of future troubles.

INVESTING IN STOCKS

Another major investment category involves partial ownership of a business, ordinarily through purchasing stocks. Investing in stocks enables you to own a fraction of a company. For example, as of this writing, there are approximately half a billion shares of Amazon outstanding, which means that if you were to buy one share, you would own 1/500,000,000 of Amazon. On the other hand, you could invest in a smaller company and own a larger percentage of the business.

HOW DO YOU MAKE MONEY INVESTING IN STOCKS?

1. Rising Stock Value

If the business prospers, the company might become more valuable on the market, and thus the stock price will rise. Sometimes these

---

5. Corporate bonds are evaluated by ratings agencies, which give them grades according to perceived risks that are based on the financial health of the issuing company.

increases can be dramatic—for example, if a company introduces a successful product or service (such as the first iPhone).

2. Dividends

Many stocks often pay periodic dividends (cash payments) to shareholders out of their earnings. Most companies also give shareholders the option of taking dividends in cash or reinvesting their dividends in more shares of stock. While dividends are often calculated as a percentage of the stock's value, they are not like interest because they are not guaranteed. A company has to be profitable in order to keep paying dividends. Also, some profitable companies choose not to pay dividends because they want to use their earnings to expand their businesses.

WHAT ARE THE RISKS OF STOCKS?

1. Market Risk

The entire stock market might drop or crash, broadly affecting the price of shares. Some types of stock are affected more than others by a market crash. For example, a company selling luxury goods might be affected more greatly by a deep recession than a company that sells food or medicine (which people still need even in economically hard times).

2. Risks Associated with Particular Stocks

The stock of a specific company might drop in value if it suffers losses due to reasons such as product liability (people using their product are harmed and sue the company), mismanagement, or being surpassed by competitors (e.g., local retailers' being supplanted by online businesses).

3. Failure to Diversify—Putting Too Many Eggs into One Basket

This can happen when an investor puts money into only one particular company or industry, thus putting a large percentage of his or her assets at risk if that company or industry faces a crisis. This risk can be compounded when one's employment income and investments are concentrated in the same company. Large corporations often encourage their employees to invest in their stock, which will be attractive to loyal workers who are convinced that their company is well run. The problem is that if the company has major problems, the employees might simultaneously lose both their jobs and the value of their savings.

WHAT OPTIONS ARE AVAILABLE FOR INVESTING IN STOCKS?

1. Individual Stocks

Some people invest in individual stocks. You might have heard a hot stock tip from a friend or an investment adviser. Or you might be optimistic about the future of a particular company or be impressed with how a particular business is run. For example, on our frequent travels, my wife and I have had excellent experiences with one airline and one restaurant chain. So several years ago she put part of her retirement savings into stocks from these companies, which have continued to do very well. I only wish we had invested more. If you choose to invest in stocks, it is generally wise to reduce risk by spreading your savings among different companies so that if one has financial trouble, the others can offset your losses. It can also be wise to reduce risk by investing in different industries. For example, buying shares in ten different oil companies would still leave you vulnerable to a downturn in that industry. You could diversify by purchasing shares in companies representing a variety of industries—retail, manufacturing, utilities, healthcare, and so on.

2. Mutual Funds and ETFs

Many invest in stocks through mutual funds or exchange-traded funds (ETFs).[6] Instead of diversifying by buying shares in several dif-

---

6. ETFs typically operate like mutual funds. The difference is that ETFs can be sold, like stocks, on the market throughout the day, whereas mutual funds are typically sold or exchanged on only a daily basis.

ferent corporations on your own, you could invest in mutual funds, which pool money from many investors to buy shares in many different companies, thus spreading risk. Mutual funds are offered by various investment companies, such as Fidelity and Vanguard. Each fund is run by professional managers. A great variety of mutual fund options are available.

A. Many invest in mutual funds that seek to follow a particular market index, such as the S&P 500. The value of these investments rises and falls with that index.

B. Many mutual funds are professionally managed by experts who try to pick stocks that they anticipate will surpass broad market returns. These managed funds operate according to a stated strategy. Some pursue stocks that pay high dividends, others invest in stocks that they believe are poised for growth, and still others invest in a particular industry (such as energy, healthcare, or real estate).

C. Some mutual funds diversify and seek to balance risk and return by investing in a mixture of stocks and bonds.

D. It is important to understand the costs of owning a mutual fund. Some funds charge a percentage load/fee when you buy them, which typically goes to the investment adviser. Other funds charge back-end load, which means that you are charged a percentage of the value of your investment when you sell your shares. Ordinarily, it is wisest to invest instead in the many mutual funds that charge no load. The other cost of owning a mutual fund is its annual fees and expenses, which are typically stated as a percentage of the value of your assets. This is how the mutual fund company covers its expenses (including paying fund managers) and makes money. These expenses can be as high as 2 percent a year and as low as less than one-tenth of 1 percent. Lower expense ratios are better for the investor.

SUMMARY

Lending your money at interest to banks or investing in bonds can be a safe and profitable way of investing your money. Returns can be limited, however, and there are still risks when you invest in this way.

Investing in stocks (equities) offers the opportunity for significant returns, but the risks can also be great. Stock purchases should be carefully researched and are most suitable for longer-term investments.

— QUESTIONS FOR REFLECTION —

1. When, if ever, is it wrong to receive interest for money you lend out?
2. When, if ever, is it right to receive interest for money you lend out?
3. What determines how much interest a given investment pays?
4. What risks are associated with investments that involve lending your money out at interest?
5. What are two ways in which you can make money from investing in stocks?
6. Why is it usually best not to put money that you might need soon into the stock market?
7. What risks are associated with investing in stocks?
8. How do mutual funds work?

37

WHAT OTHER INVESTMENTS ARE AVAILABLE, AND WHAT ARE THE RISKS? (RENTAL PROPERTIES, PRECIOUS METALS, ETC.)

While investing in banks, bonds, and stocks is the most common way in which people allocate their savings, some put their money into rental property, precious metals, and other less conventional investments. Often these alternative investments provide the benefit of diversification. If stocks and bonds decline, real estate and precious metals might appreciate in value.

REAL ESTATE AND RENTALS

Some people invest some (or much) of their savings in rental houses or multiunit dwellings. Some people, when they move, choose to keep their former house as an investment and rent it out. Most rentals are long term with annual leases. Many rentals are utilized as short-term vacation rentals. Some people own a second home that they rent out when they aren't using it. Owning rentals can be attractive because it is a business that most of us can understand and it can be a "hands-on" investment. But rental ownership involves risk, will take

253

time and effort, and can become surprisingly complicated (especially because of tax issues).

HOW DO YOU MAKE MONEY IN RENTAL PROPERTIES?

1. You Might Have a Positive Cash Flow When Rental Income Exceeds Expenses

Owning rental properties will also affect your taxes, which might be reduced by losses[1] or increased by gains.

2. The Value of the Rental Property Might Go Up over Time

For example, a rental house purchased in 2005 for $150,000 might be worth over $250,000 in 2020. Warning: selling a rental property might create a significant tax bill.[2] Consult your tax adviser.[3]

WHAT ARE THE RISKS OF OWNING RENTAL PROPERTIES?

1. Not All Rental Properties Produce a Positive Cash Flow

Rental income does not always exceed expenses, which include mortgage, insurance, maintenance, repairs (Eccl. 10:18), insurance, and homeowner's association fees. This creates a regular drain on the owner's finances. This is why you want to do your research before you buy a rental. Owning a rental free and clear is the best way to improve

---

1. Because the U.S. tax code currently requires that owners of rental properties depreciate their property for tax purposes, owners often save money on taxes if the rental business shows a loss, even though cash flow might be positive.

2. The taxable gain on a sale of a rental property is calculated by subtracting the basis of the property from the sales price. The basis is the purchase price less any depreciation taken. For example, if depreciation of $100,000 had been taken on the house purchased for $150,000, the basis would be $50,000 and the taxable gain from the sales price of $250,000 would be $200,000. Unlike the sale of a personal residence, the gain on the sale of a rental is taxable. Taking depreciation is not optional.

3. Current tax law allows an investor to sell a rental and to reinvest the proceeds in another rental property without having to pay tax on the gain.

cash flow. An expensive mortgage might make it almost impossible to have a positive cash flow.

2. Vacancy Might Interrupt Cash Flow

If the rental property remains vacant for a significant time, you continue to have most of your expenses with no income. People who own rental properties, whether they are intended for short-term or long-term tenants, need to have sufficient cash on hand to cover expenses for gaps in rental income.

3. Bad Tenants Can Be Costly

If tenants stop paying rent, evicting them can be expensive and time-consuming.[4] While few people treat a rental as well as they would their own home, some tenants do extensive damage, leading to expensive fix-up costs.

4. Rental Properties Can Be Very Time-Consuming

If you choose to manage your rental yourself, you might get calls in the middle of the night when the water heater goes out, and then you might spend much of the next day solving the problem. If the property is vacant, you must find a qualified tenant and check references. You can hire someone to manage your rental(s), but then you will have to pay the manager 10 percent or more of your rental income.

5. The Value of the Rental Property Might Remain Stagnant or Decline during Down Markets or in Certain Less Desirable Neighborhoods

6. Flipping Houses Is Very Risky

Purchasing and renting property long term is an investment. Buying and flipping houses with the hope of making a quick short-term gain is speculative and very risky (perhaps resembling day trading).

4. The laws in some jurisdictions strongly favor the tenants, which makes it even more difficult to evict those who won't pay. It is usually extremely difficult to recover

SOME INVEST IN COMMODITIES
(USUALLY PRECIOUS METALS)

Commodities are attractive to some investors. While one could invest in oil or pork bellies through commodity futures, precious metals are the most common way for ordinary investors to invest in commodities. Gold and silver are traditional stores of value and are easier to store than thousands of barrels of oil. People can buy coins made of gold or silver or they can buy bars of bullion. Some choose to invest in gold-mining stock, which rises and falls with the value of the commodity. It is also possible to invest in certain commodities through mutual funds.

WHY DO PEOPLE INVEST IN COMMODITIES?

1. Commodities Are a Way of Diversifying Investments

Some advisers have suggested that it is prudent to have from 5 to 15 percent of your savings in precious metals. When stock markets sharply decline, commodity prices tend to rise as people seek alternative investments that appear to offer more protection against further stock-market drops.

2. Owning Hard Assets Can Be a Form of Protection against Inflation

As a currency loses purchasing power due to inflation, it takes more money to buy the same goods and services. Gold and silver can be seen as a more stable way of storing value than a currency that might be mismanaged and inflated by the government. When countries have experienced hyperinflation, which made their currencies virtually worthless, those who owned hard assets sometimes avoided losing their fortunes.

3. Some Own Gold and Silver as Protection against a Major Breakdown in Financial or Civil Order

---

costs to repair damages that tenants cause.

4. Some Find Greater Financial Security in Commodities

For example, in some cultures, people's wealth is traditionally stored in gold, which is regarded as the safest investment, as opposed to banks, stocks, or other investments.

WHAT ARE THE DOWNSIDES OF INVESTING IN COMMODITIES?

1. Commodities Don't Pay a Return

Unlike bonds, which pay interest, and stocks, which can appreciate and pay dividends, gold and silver are unproductive assets. Ten ounces of gold today will be ten ounces of gold in fifty years.

2. It Is Hard to Protect These Assets from Theft (Matt. 6:19)

If you store your gold in your home, thieves could steal it. If you store it in a bank safe-deposit box, you might not be able to access it in an emergency.

3. Governments Might Interfere with Your Right to Buy, Sell, and Own Gold

Many are unaware that in 1933 President Franklin Roosevelt signed Executive Order 6102, which made private ownership of gold as an investment illegal in the United States.[5] Owners of gold were forced to sell it to the government at an artificially low price. This rule was not repealed until 1974. A government might confiscate gold if it regards private gold ownership as a threat to its economic policies (and its control of the economy). Such seizures amount to a form of theft. While it might not be likely that our government would do this again, many do not regard this scenario as impossible.

4. Commodities Can Also Go Down in Value

Gold and silver prices are affected by supply and demand, can be driven up by speculation, and can crash after a bubble. For example,

5. en.wikipedia.org/wiki/Executive_Order_6102.

the price of silver reached almost $50 an ounce in 1980 and then dropped to less than $4 an ounce a few years later. Just as financially unstable times with high inflation can drive up the price of precious metals, stable seasons with low inflation can diminish both demand and the price of gold and silver.

5. Commodities Are Less Liquid, and Transaction Costs for Commodities Can Be Expensive

If you have some gold coins and want to make a purchase, you can't just walk into the store and pay for your groceries with them. You have to find someone who can turn your gold coins into cash. Those with a market in commodities make their money by selling them at a higher price than they paid for them. For example, a dealer might offer to sell a one-ounce gold coin for $1,850 and be willing to buy such a coin for only $1,750.

6. Precious Metals Might Not Be of Much Help in a Worst-Case Financial Scenario

Some hold gold and silver because they fear that the economy will collapse, that credit cards won't work, and that cash will be worthless. I am not sure, however, that in such a situation it would be practical and safe to spend your gold and silver. It seems that the risk of theft in such a situation would increase dramatically. While precious metals might provide help in certain financial-crisis scenarios, our ultimate trust must be in the Lord.

THERE ARE MANY OTHER INVESTMENT OPTIONS

Space does not allow me to treat every other possible investment choice, such as cryptocurrency (e.g., bitcoin), stock options, limited partnerships, commodity futures, or collectibles. Most of these are very risky and are suitable only for very sophisticated investors, if anyone. Many wealthy people who thought of themselves as sophisticated have lost their savings in such schemes.

SUMMARY

It is good stewardship to put long-term savings into investments that are likely to increase in value over time. Prudent research and diversification can reduce risk. But there is no ultimate security in any earthly investment (Matt. 6:19). Ultimately, what is valued on earth will burn up (2 Peter 3:10–11) and what will matter most is the treasure we have stored up in heaven (Matt. 6:20–21).

— QUESTIONS FOR REFLECTION —

1. How can people make money through purchasing rental properties?
2. What are the significant financial risks of investing in real estate?
3. What amount of time and effort should you expect to spend when investing in rental properties?
4. What can you do to reduce your investment risk when investing in real estate?
5. What are some of the possible tax consequences of owning real estate?
6. What are some of the possible benefits of investing in hard assets such as gold and silver?
7. What are the possible downsides of investing in gold and silver?

38

HOW CAN YOU WISELY PREPARE FOR RETIREMENT?

We have already seen how important it can be to plan for possible future events (Prov. 21:5). Few events are more likely than getting old. It is also very possible that you will have some unique financial needs in your later years for which you need to be prepared.

IS IT BIBLICAL TO RETIRE?

For many, the American dream is to retire at a young age so that as many years as possible can be spent playing golf and traveling. As we have already observed, however, God made humankind to work (Gen. 2:15; Ex. 20:9; Prov. 10:4). Much of our earthly fulfillment comes from being productive. Some people who retire young find that relaxing and living the "good life" isn't all that it was cracked up to be. I have counseled people who retired young and became depressed. Their depression lifted when they focused on pleasing God, rather than themselves (2 Cor. 5:9), and became productive again—whether in paid work or by volunteering in service to Christ. J. C. Ryle observes: "The most miserable creature on earth is the man who has nothing to do. Work for the hands or work for the head is absolutely essential to human happiness."[1]

1. J. C. Ryle, *Practical Religion: Being Plain Papers on the Daily Duties, Experience,*

There can be good reasons to retire. Some people retire young so that they can be productive by serving the Lord in missions, their local church, or a parachurch ministry. Many such organizations are richly blessed to have an experienced productive worker at little or no cost. Some can no longer work for reasons beyond their control, such as health issues. Interestingly, the Old Testament law required Levites to retire from their work in the Tent of Meeting at age fifty (Num. 8:25–26). This does not, however, mean that they did no work whatsoever for the rest of their lives.

SHOULDN'T OUR KIDS TAKE CARE OF US?

As we have already seen, Jesus explicitly teaches that provision for needy parents is part of the duty required in the fifth commandment (Matt. 15:4–6). Likewise, Paul commands children and grandchildren to support needy widows (1 Tim. 5:3–8).[2] Many of us probably have godly children who would gladly help us if we were in financial trouble. But it would be much better for us to wisely save during our working years so that we will not be a burden[3] on them while they are raising their own families.

WHAT ARE SOME WISE INVESTMENT PRINCIPLES FOR PREPARING FOR RETIREMENT?

1. The Earlier You Start, the More Prepared You Will Be

Money invested when you are in your twenties might have forty years to grow until you need it. For example, an investment of $10,000 in a NASDAQ stock-market index fund made in 1980 would have

---

Dangers, and Privileges of Professing Christians, ed. J. I. Packer (Cambridge: James Clarke & Co., 1977), 154.

2. Financially needy women who have been abandoned by faithless husbands also fall into this category.

3. Perhaps an analogy is the apostle Paul's having the right to expect support from the churches he served, but choosing to work hard so that he would not be a burden to them (1 Thess. 2:9; 2 Thess. 3:8).

been worth over $750,000 in 2018.[4] While such returns might not be equaled in the future, the principle that wisely invested money grows over time stands true.

2. Tax-Deferred Retirement Accounts Offer Significant Advantages

The government encourages people to save for retirement by giving them significant tax benefits for money invested in retirement savings (such as IRAs, 401(k)s, and 403(b)s). The income that a person invests in these retirement accounts is excluded from taxable income each year, and annual tax debt is thus reduced. When the taxpayer reaches retirement age, he or she withdraws[5] money from these retirement accounts in order to cover his or her expenses. Income taxes are then collected on the money withdrawn.

3. Do All That You Can to Take Advantage of Your Employer's Contribution to Your Retirement Account

Many employers offer to match employees' contributions up to a certain percentage of their income. This match provides an immediate 100 percent return on your money. For example, if your employer offers to match up to 5 percent of your income of $50,000 in your 401(k), you could contribute $2,500, to which the employer would add another $2,500. Sadly, some employees lose out because they don't think they can live without using the $2,500 for current expenses.

4. Roth IRAs (as Well as Roth 401(k)s and Roth 403(b)s) Allow the Taxpayer to Invest in Retirement Accounts That Will Not Be Taxed upon Withdrawal

This is because a Roth account is funded with money on which the taxpayer has already paid taxes. The money in a Roth, like a regular

4. www.nasdaq.com/articles/heres-what-10000-investment-sp-500-index-fund-1980-would-be-worth-today-2018–02–08.

5. The government sets a certain minimum withdrawal percentage once taxpayers reach a certain age. This is so that the government can collect tax on the money in tax-deferred accounts. The expectation is that the rate of income tax will be lower because the retired person is no longer receiving his or her income from employment.

IRA, continues to grow tax-free. A Roth IRA could be preferable if an investor anticipates that his or her tax rate during retirement will be high.

5. Avoid Taking Money Out of Your Retirement Accounts before Retirement Age

Some people see their retirement account balances and become tempted to spend the money on lifestyle enhancement. Others are forced by unemployment or other financial crises to raid their retirement funds. The government usually makes it costly to prematurely withdraw money from your tax-advantaged retirement accounts. Not only must you usually pay taxes on the money withdrawn, but there is usually an additional penalty (currently 10 percent). A corollary to this principle is that you shouldn't put money that you might need soon into a retirement account. Another downside of taking early withdrawals from your retirement accounts is that you thereby make it much less likely that you will have enough money when you retire.

6. Avoid Borrowing against Your Account Balance

Some retirement accounts allow you to borrow against your balance. What you borrow must be repaid. Furthermore, such a financial move will usually have a very negative impact on the needed growth of your retirement savings.

7. Retirement Accounts Might Be Held in a Bank, But Are Most Often Invested in Mutual Funds, Which Typically Offer Greater Prospects for Growth (See Chapter 36)

8. The Closer You Are to Retirement, the More Conservatively You Should Invest Your Money

The person who is in his or her twenties can invest aggressively in stocks because in case of a crash there is plenty of time for the market to recover before the money is needed. The plans of a person who is close to retirement could be severely disrupted by a market crash. See chapter 36 for a description of how to reduce risk. Generally, this involves moving from stocks, which are volatile, to shorter-term bonds and bank investments, which tend to be more stable. Most mutual fund companies offer target-date funds, which automatically adjust the allocation of your assets as your retirement date approaches. These target-date funds operate according to the conventional wisdom of financial experts.[6] For example, as of this writing a retirement fund with a target date five years out might be 50 percent stocks and 50 percent bonds, while a fund with a target date twenty-five years out might be invested 90 percent in stocks and only 10 percent in bonds.

9. Annuities and Other Insurance Investment Products Might Benefit Certain People

Some annuities allow an investment to accumulate earnings tax-free (without the benefit of tax deferrals on the amount initially invested). Some annuities provide a guaranteed[7] stream of income for the life of the beneficiary.[8] Annuities can be complex and are often expensive to purchase and own because of fees and commissions. Generally, it is wisest to maximize your investment in IRAs and 401(k)s before considering these insurance products. If you are considering investing in any of these, be sure that you understand all costs, risks, and limitations. I strongly advise that you seek outside objective advice (not just from the salesperson!).

10. Estimate Your Retirement Needs So That You Can Plan to Save Enough Money

Take into consideration possible income from Social Security and pensions and increased medical costs. The closer you get to retirement, the more carefully you need to make such calculations.

---

6. Of course, conventional wisdom and experts can be mistaken.

7. The guarantee is only as good as the financial strength of the insurance company issuing the annuity.

8. This could be good if the beneficiary lives for a long time, but if the beneficiary dies young, the payments stop. The amount paid per period is based on actuarial calculations performed by the insurance company, which are based on your expected life span, the amount invested, and the like.

11. Social Security Almost Certainly Will Not Provide You with Enough Money on Which to Live

You can go to the Social Security website online to estimate your retirement benefits.

12. Those (Including Many Ministers) Who Do Not Participate in Social Security Need to Save More in Order to Make Up for What They Will Not Receive

If they are not eligible for Medicare, they will need to save even more to cover medical expenses during retirement. Part of planning for retirement is to ensure that one has sufficient work history to qualify for these programs. A nonworking spouse is qualified through his or her employed spouse.

13. Pensions Can Be a Tremendous Benefit to Those Who Are Eligible for Them

In contrast to self-directed retirement plans such as 401(k)s and IRAs on which returns are uncertain, pension plans offer a guaranteed lifetime stream of income to an employee and possibly his or her spouse (after the employee's death) upon retirement. Pensions, however, have become rare among private corporations, which expect employees to rely instead on tax-deferred retirement plans such as 401(k)s. But many government employees (including military, police, fire, and teachers) are eligible for pensions, some of which can provide as much as 90 percent of their previous income upon retirement. Such pensions can significantly reduce the amount of savings needed for retirement. Some private-sector unions also provide pensions for their members. The greatest risk to pension income is the insolvency of the fund from which pensions are to be paid.[9] Another risk could be

9. Some pension funds haven't accumulated sufficient funds to meet future obligations. Apparently healthy pension funds might be put into a precarious situation when their assets are reduced by downturns in financial markets. Some pension funds that are behind invest aggressively in order to catch up, only to fall further behind when their gambles don't pay off. When a government pension fund fails, the government might choose to keep it solvent through taxation or issuing debt.

inflation, which would reduce the value of the periodic pension check over time. Some pensions avoid this risk by increasing payments at the rate of inflation.

14. If Possible, Avoid Reverse Mortgages

See chapter 27 for a discussion of reverse mortgages.

SUMMARY

Most people anticipate being retired one day. Even during retirement, our focus should be on using our time and our money to the glory of God. Careful planning can remove financial pressure so that our later years can be joyful and productive.

— QUESTIONS FOR REFLECTION —

1. How would you answer someone who said that he or she has no plans to retire?
2. When should you start planning for retirement?
3. What are the best things a younger person can do to prepare for retirement?
4. What are the advantages and disadvantages of tax-deferred retirement accounts?
5. What are the advantages of pension plans?

39

WHAT INSURANCE DO YOU NEED?

Purchasing insurance can be both wise and beneficial as a means of being prepared for possible future financial calamities.

GENERAL PRINCIPLES ABOUT INSURANCE

1. Insurance Spreads Risk for Various Risks (Calamities) among Many Policyholders

For example, if the statistics show that in a given year 1 in 2,000 healthy thirty-year-old American men dies, an insurance company could charge $550 per year to each of 200,000 healthy thirty-year-old men with the anticipation that approximately a hundred of them would die, each of whose heirs could be paid a million dollars. The actual realities of the insurance industry are similar, but more complex. Similar examples could be given for spreading risk among many people with auto (accident), health (surgery), disability, and homeowner's claims. Everyone pays premiums so that the one whose house catches on fire (or whose car is stolen) won't suffer catastrophic financial loss.

2. Insurance Companies Are Not Charities

They must charge sufficient premiums to cover the expected cost of paying losses, plus their overhead and profits. They calculate premiums based on their estimate of the risk that they will have to pay out. For example, an uninsured person who has recently been diagnosed with terminal cancer cannot expect an insurer to offer a million-dollar life insurance policy with a low premium. Because of risk, the premiums for young drivers with bad driving records will be much higher than the premiums for experienced, safe drivers.

3. You Don't Want to Collect on Your Insurance

From the standpoint of the buyer, insurance is a bet that the insurance company wins if there is no claim (death, injury, auto accident, theft, property damage) and that you win when there is a claim. This is a bet that you should want to lose.

4. You Need to Insure Only Expenses That You Can't Afford to Pay from Your Income and Savings

For example, medical insurance that covers major expenses, but expects you to pay for smaller expenses such as normal doctors' visits, might be much less expensive than medical insurance that covers every possible expense. While you might not enjoy paying $75 every time you go to see the doctor, what you need insurance for is the hospital bill that can run into the tens or even hundreds of thousands of dollars. If you self-insure for minor losses, you will save a lot of money on premiums and will probably come out ahead financially in the long term.

5. You Can Usually Save Money by Buying Insurance with the Largest Deductibles You Can Afford

For example, if you are given a choice between spending $1,500 a year for automobile collision insurance that requires you to pay $500 toward the cost of a repair after an accident, or a deductible of $100 that costs $1,750 a year, you are probably better off spending less for insurance while being ready to pay the extra money out of pocket for the deductible in case of an accident. Even if you had a claim every three years, you would be better off with the higher deductible. Insurance is most needed for any major damage to people and property for which it would be difficult for you to pay from your own resources.

6. Shop Around

There can be a wide price difference among different reputable companies for virtually the same insurance products.

7. Buy Insurance Only from a Financially Healthy Company

Insurance is useful only if the insurance company has sufficient assets to pay claims. You can refer to agencies that rate the financial strength of insurance companies.

8. Beware of Insurance Policies for Which the Insurer Only Pays Claims for a Small Percentage of Premiums Collected.

DO PEOPLE WHO TRUST GOD NEED INSURANCE?

Given that we live in a fallen world in which there are many physical and financial dangers, insurance can be a way to ensure that you can fulfill your responsibility to provide for your family (1 Tim. 5:8), even in case of calamity.

WHAT KINDS OF INSURANCE DO YOU NEED?

1. Auto Insurance That Covers Damage to People and Property

Most states require that you have auto insurance that covers your liability in case you are found at fault in an accident, which could include property damage (usually to vehicles) plus liability for injuries. Auto insurance can also cover harm you suffer when the other party is at fault but does not have insurance. The most important aspect of auto insurance is coverage of liability and personal injuries, which can run into the hundreds of thousands of dollars in the worst case. Your assets could be seized in order to pay for what is not covered by your insurance, which is why I recommend that you maximize your liability limits (typically $500,000). On the other hand, you can save money on auto insurance by maximizing the deductibles for damage to your vehicle (see the example above).

2. Homeowner's Insurance for Your Property

If you have a mortgage, your lender will require that the property be insured for major losses such as fire and weather damage. Even if your home is paid off, you need this insurance to cover losses that you could not afford to pay out of pocket. In some regions, flood or earthquake insurance might be advisable or even necessary. Your homeowner's insurance should also cover liability in case someone is injured on your property. Homeowner's insurance also covers your personal property, such as furniture and clothing, from losses due to theft, fire, or other risks. Valuables such as jewelry, valuable coins, and art can be added on to a homeowner's policy at extra cost.

3. Renter's Insurance

Even if you don't own your home, it is usually advisable to have renter's insurance that would cover your personal property in case of theft or fire.

4. Health Insurance for Major Medical Bills

Because medical bills can run into the hundreds of thousands of dollars (think heart transplant), it is wise to be prepared for this risk with health insurance (Prov. 27:12). Some people have experienced financial ruin because of medical expenses and debt. Furthermore, if your spouse or child has a medical emergency, you want to be able to access the best medical care without having to worry about whether you can afford it. Because medical costs are so high, medical insurance is expensive. As you age, anticipated medical costs tend to rise, which leads to increases in premiums. As is the case with auto insurance, you will usually save money on premiums by paying for the smaller bills yourself (or accepting higher copays for doctors' visits and prescriptions) while relying on insurance for very large medical bills. Many people get subsidized medical insurance through their employers, which will usually save money compared to individual policies. As of this writing, those who can't get insurance through an employer can obtain it through a government insurance exchange. The premiums for such policies can be very expensive but are often subsidized for those with lower income. Medical insurance is highly regulated by the government, which could determine what insurance companies must cover, affecting the price of insurance. An additional advantage of having medical insurance is that insurers often have negotiated fees for various medical services, prescriptions, and products that are lower than the ordinary costs. Even if the insured has to pay, the person can get the lower negotiated price.

5. What about Christian Medical-Expense-Sharing Plans?

Many use privately run programs that allow people to spread risk by sharing each other's medical expenses, instead of buying medical insurance. Those participating pay a monthly amount to help pay one another's medical bills. Often money is sent directly to a family with medical bills. This is *not* insurance, but can take the place of insurance for some. These programs are typically less expensive than insurance. Christians are attracted to these programs because they might reflect some biblical values of conduct and because members are encouraged to pray for one another. One possible downside is that they often have conditions of who may participate according to lifestyle, and they may exclude certain preexisting medical conditions from coverage (which could leave you with a very large medical bill). Another concern is whether these medical-expense cooperatives will always have the capacity to pay massive medical expenses.

6. Disability Insurance

Statistics show that it is more likely that you will face disability than death during your working life. Disability insurance replaces a portion of your salary (typically 60–80 percent) for a period during which you are unable to work. A disability insurance policy might cover short-term or long-term disability (which could become permanent). Social Security offers some disability benefits for covered workers, but for most people this will not be sufficient. Most disability insurance requires a waiting period before benefits begin (which is another reason to have emergency savings). Different policies cover different types of disability, so it is important to research them carefully before committing. Some injuries or conditions might prevent someone from engaging in his or her current occupation, but the person might still be able to do a different job. Many companies offer disability coverage to employees as a benefit.

7. Dental and Optical Insurance

Many companies provide dental and optical benefits to employees. Dental insurance can be useful because some dental procedures can be very expensive. Many dental and optical plans offer limited coverage with high copays, so you should carefully research any coverage offered to see whether it is likely to be worth the money.

8. Life Insurance

A. The most common purpose of life insurance is to provide resources for those left behind in case of the death of the insured. The most common reason to have life insurance is to replace the income of a breadwinner. For example, a married man with children whose wife is a stay-at-home mom would want to have enough life insurance for his family to have sufficient resources to meet their ongoing needs (household expenses, education, etc.) in case of his death.[1] It might also be wise for them to have some life insurance on the wife, because if she were to pass away the husband would have extra expenses, such as child care. For most families, at least $1 million in life insurance is appropriate. Ordinarily, payout of life insurance upon the death of the insured party is not taxed.

B. Some take out life insurance related to their businesses. For example, two business partners might each take out an insurance policy on the other so that if one dies, the other can pay off his or her heirs and maintain control of the business.

C. As with other types of insurance, the premiums for life insurance are based on the risk to the insurance company of a claim. Younger, healthier clients will pay less. Premiums rise for those with health problems and for older clients. Those applying for life insurance will usually be required to answer

---

1. While Scripture encourages younger widows to remarry (1 Cor. 7:39; 1 Tim. 5:14), it cannot be assumed that this will happen or known when it might happen. Therefore, it is safer for a younger widow to have sufficient insurance so that she does not have to worry about finances.

many questions about their health and to submit to a medical exam so that the insurance company can evaluate its risk.

D. There are basically two kinds of life insurance, with some variations. With term insurance, your premiums pay only for the insurance. Other insurance (often called permanent or whole life insurance) functions both as insurance and as an investment or savings vehicle. The premiums are much higher than for term insurance, but the policy builds cash value over time in addition to providing insurance. Insurance salespeople often encourage clients to purchase "permanent" insurance because of the investment benefit. My advice is to buy the less expensive term life insurance with your insurance money,[2] and then to put the money that you wish to save into a separate investment account, such as a mutual fund. Money invested in the mutual fund will most likely grow faster than money entrusted to the insurance company. One reason for this is that the "permanent" insurance typically pays a large commission to the salesperson, which then leaves less of your money to grow. For example, a healthy thirty-year-old male might be able to purchase a $1 million term life insurance policy for $500 a year, while a policy with an investment element could cost thousands of dollars a year.[3] He would probably do better financially by buying term insurance and investing the difference.[4] Also, permanent insurance typically offers less flexible investment options than investing in mutual funds.

E. I recommend purchasing guaranteed renewable level-premium term life insurance,[5] ideally for a period of years as long as

---

2. The lower premium would also be less strain on your budget.

3. Some "permanent" insurance allows for some flexibility in payments.

4. Insurance salespeople often argue that most would spend rather than invest the difference; therefore, the built-in enforced discipline of putting money away in the whole life insurance would leave the person better off in the long term.

5. Some term insurance has premiums that start very low and then go up each year. Level-premium term insurance has a higher initial premium, but it remains the same for the number of years specified in the policy.

you expect to need the insurance. Such policies guarantee that you will remain insured and your premiums will not go up as long as you make your annual payments. A significant advantage of a longer-term policy is that once one is qualified, the person can keep the policy even if he or she develops a significant health problem, which would make a new policy either expensive or impossible to buy. For example, a man who is starting a family might consider purchasing a thirty-year level-premium insurance policy, which would keep his family insured for most or all of the years that the children are growing up.

F. The amount of life insurance for which one can qualify will be based on the person's current financial situation, including the income that the insurance is meant to replace. For example, someone making $30,000 a year probably wouldn't qualify for a $10 million life insurance policy. Life insurance companies don't want those who are left behind to be better off financially after the insured dies than they would be if the insured were alive.

G. As you get older (and likely less healthy), life insurance will probably become very expensive and should no longer be necessary if you have saved enough money for retirement.

9. For Some, Umbrella Insurance Coverage

Umbrella insurance covers you for liability claims in excess of what your homeowner's or auto insurance might cover and for claims that might not be covered by other kinds of insurance. People with significant personal assets that could be lost through a major liability claim often obtain this kind of insurance.

WHAT KINDS OF INSURANCE DO YOU PROBABLY NOT NEED?

Unnecessary insurance covers risks that you could afford without insurance, or risks that you could afford to pay out of your own income and savings. These types of insurance tend to collect far more in premiums than they pay out in claims, thus making them a poor value.

1. Specific Disease Insurance

Some insurance companies sell separate policies for diseases such as cancer. These are an unnecessary expense if you have medical insurance as described above.

2. Burial Insurance

This is a form of life insurance, usually for a relatively low amount, such as $10,000. While the loss of any loved one is a tragedy, it is wiser economically to have an emergency fund from which such unlikely expenses could be covered for family members who don't have ordinary life insurance.

3. Car-Repair Insurance

Because the insurance company has to pay claims for repairs plus paying for its corporate expenses (including the salesperson's commission), you are usually better off in the long run paying for your own repairs. Such policies might also limit the options of when and from whom you can get your car repaired.

4. Home Warranties

In reality, they are a kind of insurance against home-repair costs. While these might be a way of leveling out repair expenses, it is usually financially advantageous to save and pay directly for your own household repairs rather than paying a warranty company, which must make a profit in addition to arranging for any repairs that your home might need.[6] Warranties for specific possible home-related losses are usually not worth it. For example, my natural gas company writes to me almost every month, asking me to spend $7 per month to insure

---

6. Home-warranty policies, like other forms of insurance, typically have exclusions and deductibles that must be paid. In addition, the warranty company, rather than the homeowner, will usually choose the contractor or the repair person.

against the possibility of the gas line from the street to my house breaking. While I am sure that this has happened to someone, I don't know of anyone to whom it has happened. I also believe that it is a very unlikely event for which I could afford to pay. I am also suspicious that my gas company (or the insurer with which it is working) is spending money to send me (deceptively) official-looking solicitations ("Open immediately. Urgent communication from your gas company") each month that seek to motivate me with fear to give it money.

5. Insurance on Phones and Appliances

As in the case of car and home-repair insurance, you can usually afford to pay for these repairs yourself. The policies typically take in far more money than they pay out. Much of the money you pay for such insurance goes to commissions for the salespeople who push these products.

6. Life Insurance for Your Mortgage

This is a form of life insurance that would pay off your mortgage in case of your death.[7] These policies are often promoted in connection with your mortgage lender. Usually you would do better to buy ordinary term life insurance to ensure that your family's housing needs would be met in case of your death.

DO OLDER PEOPLE NEED LONG-TERM-CARE INSURANCE?

Many people will no longer be able to live at home in their old age due to illness or incapacity. Because nursing-care facilities can be very expensive, some people purchase long-term-care insurance to pay for some of those costs. Medicare sometimes covers the costs for people with limited resources. Those with more significant resources buy long-term-care insurance for the purpose of protecting their assets. A

---

7. The expression "He bought the farm" comes from times when a farmer bought life insurance that would pay off the loans on his farm in case of his death.

possible downside of long-term-care insurance is that payouts are often limited to a certain dollar amount per day, which could be less than the actual costs of nursing-home care. Also, premiums might rise sharply. Ideally, one would have sufficient retirement savings to cover this risk.

SUMMARY

Insurance can be a way of protecting yourself from major risks (Prov. 22:3). But it is possible to be "insurance-poor"—spending too much on insurance premiums, which then leaves too little for other expenses. Keep insurance costs down by insuring only for major expenses that you could not afford to cover out of savings.

— QUESTIONS FOR REFLECTION —

1. What is the purpose of insurance?
2. How can you wisely save money on insurance?
3. What kinds of insurance do you need?
4. How do some people waste money on insurance?
5. What is the best kind of life insurance to buy?

40

HOW CAN YOU PREPARE FOR THE END OF YOUR LIFE? (MAKING A WILL AND LEAVING A LEGACY)

Perhaps one of the most common ways in which people fail to be prepared for their financial future is their failure to prepare for what will happen after their death. Since you can't take it with you ("As he had come naked from his mother's womb, so will he return as he came. He will take nothing from the fruit of his labor that he can carry in his hand," Eccl. 5:15), you can plan for how your resources can be wisely used after you are gone by making a will. Making your wishes clear will also help those you leave behind. While Jesus did not have a legal will in the sense that we do today, he did make provision for those he left behind. He sent the Holy Spirit to meet our needs (John 14:18), and he ensured that his (most likely widowed) mother would be cared for by John when he could no longer do so in person (19:26–27). We do not know when we will die, but we can do our best to ensure that those we leave behind know our wishes and are well cared for. Even after we are gone, we also want to be good stewards of what happens to the resources that God has given to us. "When there is a man who has labored with wisdom, knowledge and skill, then he gives his legacy to one who has not labored with them. This too is vanity and a great evil" (Eccl. 2:21).

WHY DO YOU NEED A WILL?

1. Your Will Designates Who Will Care for Your Children in Case of Your Death

For example, if a husband and wife both died in an auto accident, their wills would state who would assume guardianship of their surviving children. If you die without a will, those left behind will not know your wishes, and the state will determine who will care for your children. Conflict could arise among family members over what your intentions were or what is best for the children. When we do premarital counseling, one reason that we usually encourage a couple to make their wills is the possibility of their having children. When choosing a potential guardian for your children, you should select someone (normally a married couple) whom you trust to raise your children according to your wishes and beliefs. Ordinarily, it is better if the guardians are family members, but some parents might choose close friends instead. You should ask whomever you choose whether they are willing before putting them into your will. It is also wise to designate at least one backup couple in case there is some reason that your first choice becomes unavailable. As your children get older, you should tell them who would take care of them in case something happens to you. One other consideration is that you want those who would be taking care of your children to have sufficient resources to bear the extra financial burden of an enlarged family. One way in which this can be done is by making your children the secondary (after your spouse) beneficiaries of your life insurance proceeds, with their guardians managing those funds until your children become adults.

2. Your Will Designates How Your Assets Should Be Disposed Of upon Your Death

If you do not make a will, the state will dispose of your assets to family members in ways that you might not have wished. Dying without a will also makes conflict among your potential heirs more likely. Ordinarily, a married person will designate his or her spouse to receive all the assets. But it is wise to designate backup beneficiaries in case your spouse also passes away. Normally, this would be your

279

children (2 Cor. 12:14). If they are still minors, their guardians would need to manage their inheritance until they reach a certain age. Many believe it wise to wait until a child is at least twenty-five before giving the child full control of his or her inheritance because there is a risk of an immature person's squandering the parents' resources: "An inheritance gained hurriedly at the beginning will not be blessed in the end" (Prov. 20:21). As you get older, you might also want to designate some inheritance for your grandchildren: "A good man leaves an inheritance to his children's children" (13:22). You might also choose to leave some of your wealth to your church or favorite faithful charities. Randy Alcorn points out that our money belongs to God, not our children. Sometimes children can be presumptuous about their right to inherit, and some who inherit a significant sum never mature by learning to provide for themselves.[1] You might also choose to designate particular assets or family heirlooms that should go to particular people who would appreciate them. Your clear instructions will be of great help to those left behind. As your children reach adulthood, the question might arise whether you must treat them all equally in your estate planning. An irresponsible child might not benefit from a large inheritance. For example, I knew a man who struggled with drug addiction and squandered his entire $50,000 inheritance in less than a year. He would have been better off either not receiving it or having a trustee designated to wisely manage and distribute his inheritance. You might also wish to consider the different needs of your children in their adulthood. For example, one child might be extremely wealthy, while the other is a missionary abroad; thus, you might choose to designate more for the needier child. If you choose to treat your children differently in your will, or choose to leave a substantial portion of your assets to charity or non-family members, I strongly urge you to explain your plans to your children before you die in order to avoid conflict after your death (Luke 12:13).[2] Those who are single or who

1. Randy Alcorn, *Managing God's Money* (Carol Stream, IL: Tyndale House, 2011), 211.
2. This passage might illustrate the fact that if your children are of a mind to fight over your inheritance, they might not be worthy of an inheritance.

don't have children should still create a will in order to designate how they would want their assets distributed among relatives, friends, and various charities and ministries.[3]

SOME PEOPLE MIGHT BE WISE TO CREATE A LEGAL TRUST FOR THEIR ASSETS

A person with significant assets might choose to put them into a trust. The trust document would, along with the person's will, set forth how his or her assets would be distributed in case of death. To be clear, if you have a trust, you still need a will. Trusts are sometimes structured in a way to avoid taxation of the estate. Another advantage of a trust is that it can enable the heirs to avoid the time and expense of having to go through the legal process of probate. You should consult with a lawyer, an accountant, or both for more information about trusts.

KEEP YOUR FINANCIAL AFFAIRS IN ORDER FOR THE SAKE OF YOUR HEIRS: A LEGACY DRAWER (OR SAFE)

Ahithophel (who had great foresight in spite of bad character), when he knew that he was about to die (in his case by suicide), "set his house in order" (2 Sam. 17:23; also see 2 Kings 20:1). Sometimes grieving families' troubles are compounded when they have difficulty knowing what assets the deceased owned and how to access them. This problem can be further compounded when the spouse who was handling the finances passes away.[4] You can keep your affairs in order by keeping good records of your various accounts (including bills) and by making them accessible, along with your will, to your heirs when the time comes. It would also help them to have sign-on and

---

3. An excellent book for working through all these decisions and communicating them to your family is Ron Blue's *Splitting Heirs: Giving Your Money and Things to Your Children without Ruining Their Lives* (Chicago: Northfield Publishing, 2008).

4. Other concerns might be how bills are paid (including autopay) and concerns over the closing of accounts (and credit cards) in the name of the deceased.

password information for your key personal and financial accounts. Or you might want to write individual letters to family members in which you could pass on biblical wisdom. Some suggest that you keep these crucial documents in one (secure) place, such as in a locked desk drawer or a safe, to which those left behind could have access.

LEAVE A LEGACY OF WISDOM

You can offer your children something even better than a financial inheritance: "How blessed is the man who finds wisdom and the man who gains understanding. For her profit is better than the profit of silver and her gain better than fine gold. She is more precious than jewels; and nothing you desire compares with her" (Prov. 3:13–15). Proverbs reminds us that wisdom begins with honoring or fearing the Lord (1:7). In the New Testament, we learn that Jesus is the embodiment of God's wisdom: "In [Him] are hidden all the treasures of wisdom and knowledge" (Col. 2:3; also see 1 Cor. 1:24). As we train our children to treasure Christ above all, we can then teach them to be good stewards of that which he has entrusted to us, including our vocational skills and any financial resources he gives us (including an earthly inheritance). We should train our children from an early age to recognize God's ownership of all things, the importance of working hard and working smart, the priority of generously giving to the Lord's work, the benefits of carefully planning (budgeting) our finances,[5] the folly of debt, and the wisdom of planning for the future. As a result, we may hope that our children will be good stewards of the wealth they inherit (Prov. 20:21). You might also want to leave a legacy of wisdom

---

5. We taught our children to manage their money by giving them a certain amount each month for their regular expenses, such as clothing and entertainment. If they wanted something expensive, they had to save up over a period of months. On one occasion, our twelve-year-old son spent all his money on an expensive pair of shoes, which he then wore in the mud and ruined after just a few weeks. Rather than giving him money for new shoes, I let him borrow an old pair of my running shoes (which were about two sizes too large for him) until he could save up enough to buy a more reasonably priced pair of everyday shoes.

for your family members with a written testimony of your faith and God's faithfulness, to be read upon your death.

SUMMARY

Death is inevitable: "it is appointed for men to die once and after this comes judgment" (Heb. 9:27). The time of your death is uncertain. It is most important for your soul to be prepared for death (Luke 12:20) by knowing that your sins are forgiven through the substitutionary sacrifice of Christ. Thus, you can be confident of going to be with him (2 Cor. 5:8). But it is also important that your financial affairs be prepared for your death. Making your wishes known shows love to those who are left behind. Your will also gives you opportunity to be a good steward of that which God has entrusted to you in this life.

— QUESTIONS FOR REFLECTION —

1. What is the purpose of a will?
2. Who needs a will?
3. What should be included in your will?
4. What else can you do to get your affairs in order before death?

41

HOW DOES MONEY POINT US TO THE GOSPEL?

For you know the grace of our Lord Jesus Christ, that though He was rich, yet for your sake He became poor, so that you through His poverty might become rich. (2 Cor. 8:9)

We have seen from God's Word that it is foolish to take on irresponsible debt (Prov. 22:7) and that it is most foolish to make oneself liable for the debts of others, which can lead to your own financial ruin (6:1–4; 22:26–27). Yet Scripture proclaims that we owed a debt of sin that we could not pay. In the parable of the unmerciful servant, our debt is portrayed as ten thousand talents, which would be billions of dollars in today's money. But even that amount does not adequately portray the extent of our guilt. The enormous debt we owe could be paid only through a costly death (Rom. 6:23).

Jesus, who is sinless, willingly left heavenly glory and took on our impoverished human nature. He then took all the guilt of our debt of sin upon himself and died in our place (1 Peter 3:18), willingly paying the infinite price to satisfy God's justice, thus enabling us to escape the eternity in hell that we deserve to incur. What amazing love that God the Son should allow our sin to be imputed to him and then to bear the penalty for us.

But his kindness does not end there. In the parable of the unmerciful servant, the master forgave what the servant owed, thus making

284

the servant debt-free, which was incredibly gracious. But Christ has done more for us. He not only paid off our debt, but also makes us rich (2 Cor. 8:9). Not only was our guilt imputed to him, but his perfect righteousness has been imputed to us, so that we may be "found in Him, not having a righteousness of [our] own derived from the law, but that which is through faith in Christ, the righteousness which comes from God on the basis of faith" (Phil. 3:9). Christ has enriched us so that when God looks upon us, he sees us not merely as innocent or debt-free, but as rich with the perfect righteousness of Christ. As a result, God treats us as though we had perfectly kept his law. In the terms of the parable of the unmerciful servant, it would be as though the master had not only forgiven the servant's great debt, but also adopted him as a son and made him an heir.

The gospel should change how we live. Paul's conclusion in 2 Corinthians 8 is that those of us who have received such grace should imitate Christ by being compassionate and generous toward those in need. Because he willingly gave up his life for us, we should gladly use our earthly resources to bless our brothers and sisters who are in need.

God's Word, which was written thousands of years ago, contains timeless wisdom for all people at all times. It's a sure and certain guide as you face your financial difficulties. We have seen how Scripture teaches us how to be financially successful through working hard in our carefully chosen vocation, avoiding the debt trap, seeking wise counsel, avoiding get-rich-quick schemes or gambling, careful budgeting, thoughtful saving, and so forth.

The Bible teaches us principles that are far more important than mere keys to earthly financial success. We are taught to live for what matters most so that our lives will count in eternity. We are reminded to put God first in our affections above material things. We are encouraged that we can put our trust in him to take care of us when we are in financial trouble. We are exhorted to live not merely for ourselves, but for his glory as we spend our resources not only to build our own kingdom, but to invest in his heavenly kingdom as we help those in need and promote the spread of the gospel.

— Questions for Reflection —

1. In what sense did Jesus become surety (cosigner) for our debt?
2. In what way has Jesus made us not merely debt-free, but rich?
3. How does Paul use Christ's generosity toward us to motivate us to generosity?

Appendix A

BUDGETS

The following budgets are examples. Guideline % will vary according to a family's situation (debt, education expenses, number of children, etc.). Some of these budget examples demonstrate what can go wrong with overspending and debt. You can download budget templates at https://jimnewheiser.com/financial-resources/.

INCOME

Earned income (salary, commission)	$ _____		
Unearned (interest, div., capital gains)	$ _____		
Other (Fam. support, Soc.Sec., pension)	$ _____		
Total income	$ _____		

ANNUALIZED INCOME $ _____

ANNUALIZED EXPENSES $ _____

EXPENSES		%	Guide%
Lord's work	$ _____	0.0%	10%
Income Tax (Fed., State, FICA)	$ _____	0.0%	10%
Housing	$ _____	0.0%	34%
- mortgages (rent, insurance, tax)	$ _____		
- utilities (gas, electric, water, sewage)	$ _____		
- services (TV, internet, phones)	$ _____		
- maintenance* (~1% of home value/yr)	$ _____		
- furnishings* (appliances, computer)	$ _____		
- misc.* (Fees, lawn, storage, cleaning)	$ _____		
Groceries (incl. grocery and drug stores)	$ _____	0.0%	7%
Automobile / transportation	$ _____	0.0%	8%
- car payments	$ _____		
- gas, tolls, fares	$ _____		
- insurance, license, club*	$ _____		
- maintenance, repairs*	$ _____		
- replacement	$ _____		
Insurance	$ _____	0.0%	4%
- life	$ _____		
- medical	$ _____		
- dental, vision, disability	$ _____		

* indicates an irregular expense (varies month to month).

Debt payments		$ _____	0.0% 0%
- credit cards	$ _____		
- student loans	$ _____		
- other	$ _____		
Entertainment / recreation		$ _____	0.0% 4%
- eating out (perhaps by person)	$ _____		
- events (movies, sports, sitters)	$ _____		
- vacation*	$ _____		
Personal Care* (by person)		$ _____	0.0% 3%
- clothing	$ _____		
- hair, nails	$ _____		
Medical, Dental, Optical		$ _____	0.0% 3%
Education / Child Care		$ _____	0.0% 2%
- tuition, books, supplies	$ _____		
- day care, child support	$ _____		
Miscellaneous*		$ _____	0.0% 3%
- subscriptions, supplies	$ _____		
- mad money (per person)	$ _____		
- gifts* (incl. Christmas)	$ _____		
Savings / Investments		$ _____	0.0% 12%
- short (incl. $2,000 liquidity)	$ _____		
- mid (incl. 6-month emergency)	$ _____		
- long (education, retirement)	$ _____		
TOTAL EXPENSES		$ _____	0% 100%
NET SURPLUS		$ _____	

* indicates an irregular expense (varies month to month).

This next example budget is based on the approximate average family income at the time of this writing. For some, this would be a very tight budget. This budget assumes no automobile or credit-card debt. When such debt exists, adjustments would need to be made to income and/or expenses in order to account for this debt.

INCOME

Earned income (salary, commission)	$$5,000	
Unearned (interest, div., capital gains)	$ -	
Other (Fam. support, Soc.Sec., pension)	$ -	
Total income	**$ 5,000**	

ANNUALIZED INCOME	$60,000
ANNUALIZED EXPENSES	$60,000

EXPENSES			%	Guide%
Lord's work		**$500**	10.0%	10%
Income Tax (Fed., State, FICA)		**$500**	10.0%	10%
Housing		**$1,700**	34.0%	34%
- mortgages (rent, insurance, tax)	$1,200			
- utilities (gas, electric, water, sewage)	$200			
- services (TV, internet, phones)	$50			
- maintenance* (~1% of home value/yr)	$100			
- furnishings* (appliances, computer)	$100			
- misc.* (Fees, lawn, storage, cleaning)	$50			
Groceries (incl. grocery and drug stores)		**$350**	7.0%	7%
Automobile / transportation		**$400**	8.0%	8%
- car payments	$ -			
- gas, tolls, fares	$100			
- insurance, license, club*	$100			
- maintenance, repairs*	$100			
- replacement	$100			

* indicates an irregular expense (varies month to month).

Insurance		**$200**	4.0%	4%
- life	$40		
- medical	$130		
- dental, vision, disability	$30		
Debt payments		**$ -**	0.0%	0%
- credit cards	$ -		
- student loans	$ -		
- other	$ -		
Entertainment / recreation		**$200**	4.0%	4%
- eating out (perhaps by person)	$100		
- events (movies, sports, sitters)	$50		
- vacation*	$50		
Personal Care* (by person)		**$150**	3.0%	3%
- clothing	$100		
- hair, nails	$50		
Medical, Dental, Optical		**$150**	3.0%	3%
Education / Child Care		**$100**	2.0%	2%
- tuition, books, supplies	$50		
- day care, child support	$50		
Miscellaneous*		**$150**	3.0%	3%
- subscriptions, supplies	$50		
- mad money (per person)	$50		
- gifts* (incl. Christmas)	$50		
Savings / Investments		**$600**	12.0%	12%
- short (incl. $2,000 liquidity)	$150		
- mid (incl. 6-month emergency)	$150		
- long (education, retirement)	$300		
TOTAL EXPENSES		**$5,000**	100%	100%
NET SURPLUS		**$ -**		

* indicates an irregular expense (varies month to month).

The next budget is for a family with a modest amount of debt. Note that savings for future expenses is significantly reduced even with a below-average amount of credit-card and student-loan debt.

INCOME

Earned income (salary, commission)	$5,000
Unearned (interest, div., capital gains)	$ -
Other (Fam. support, Soc.Sec., pension)	$ -
Total income	**$5,000**

ANNUALIZED INCOME	**$60,000**
ANNUALIZED EXPENSES	**$60,000**

EXPENSES			%	Guide%
Lord's work		**$500**	10.0%	10%
Income Tax (Fed., State, FICA)		**$500**	10.0%	10%
Housing		**$1,700**	34.0%	34%
- mortgages (rent, insurance, tax)	$1,200			
- utilities (gas, electric, water, sewage)	$200			
- services (TV, internet, phones)	$50			
- maintenance* (~1% of home value/yr)	$100			
- furnishings* (appliances, computer)	$100			
- misc.* (Fees, lawn, storage, cleaning)	$50			
Groceries (incl. grocery and drug stores)		**$350**	7.0%	7%
Automobile / transportation		**$400**	8.0%	8%
- car payments	$ -			
- gas, tolls, fares	$100			
- insurance, license, club*	$100			
- maintenance, repairs*	$100			
- replacement	$100			

* indicates an irregular expense (varies month to month).

Insurance		$200	4.0%	4%
- life	$40			
- medical	$130			
- dental, vision, disability	$30			
Debt payments		$200	4.0%	0%
- credit cards	$100			
- student loans	$100			
- other	$ -			
Entertainment / recreation		$200	4.0%	4%
- eating out (perhaps by person)	$100			
- events (movies, sports, sitters)	$50			
- vacation*	$50			
Personal Care* (by person)		$150	3.0%	3%
- clothing	$100			
- hair, nails	$50			
Medical, Dental, Optical		$150	3.0%	3%
Education / Child Care		$100	2.0%	2%
- tuition, books, supplies	$50			
- day care, child support	$50			
Miscellaneous*		$150	3.0%	3%
- subscriptions, supplies	$50			
- mad money (per person)	$50			
- gifts* (incl. Christmas)	$50			
Savings / Investments		$400	8.0%	12%
- short (incl. $2,000 liquidity)	$150			
- mid (incl. 6-month emergency)	$150			
- long (education, retirement)	$100			
TOTAL EXPENSES		**$5,000**	100%	100%
NET SURPLUS		$ -		

* indicates an irregular expense (varies month to month).

This family has moderate debt. Notice how most families with this burden of debt believe they are unable to give even 10% to the Lord's work. Also, savings for future expenses is almost completely eliminated. They need to increase income or decrease discretionary expenses in order to get their finances under control.

INCOME

Earned income (salary, commission)	$5,000	
Unearned (interest, div., capital gains)	$ -	
Other (Fam. support, Soc.Sec., pension)	$ -	
Total income	**$5,000**	

ANNUALIZED INCOME	**$60,000**
ANNUALIZED EXPENSES	**$62,700**

EXPENSES		%	Guide%
Lord's work	**$350**	7.0%	10%
Income Tax (Fed., State, FICA)	**$500**	10.0%	10%
Housing	**$1,700**	34.0%	34%
- mortgages (rent, insurance, tax)	$1,200		
- utilities (gas, electric, water, sewage)	$200		
- services (TV, internet, phones)	$50		
- maintenance* (~1% of home value/yr)	$100		
- furnishings* (appliances, computer)	$100		
- misc.* (Fees, lawn, storage, cleaning)	$50		
Groceries (incl. grocery and drug stores)	**$375**	7.5%	7%
Automobile / transportation	**$750**	15.0%	8%
- car payments	$450		
- gas, tolls, fares	$100		
- insurance, license, club*	$100		
- maintenance, repairs*	$100		
- replacement	$ -		

* indicates an irregular expense (varies month to month).

Insurance	**$200**	4.0%	4%
- life	$40		
- medical	$130		
- dental, vision, disability	$30		
Debt payments	**$600**	12.0%	0%
- credit cards	$300		
- student loans	$300		
- other	$ -		
Entertainment / recreation	**$200**	4.0%	4%
- eating out (perhaps by person)	$100		
- events (movies, sports, sitters)	$50		
- vacation*	$50		
Personal Care* (by person)	**$150**	3.0%	3%
- clothing	$100		
- hair, nails	$50		
Medical, Dental, Optical	**$150**	3.0%	3%
Education / Child Care	**$100**	2.0%	2%
- tuition, books, supplies	$50		
- day care, child support	$50		
Miscellaneous*	**$150**	3.0%	3%
- subscriptions, supplies	$50		
- mad money (per person)	$50		
- gifts* (incl. Christmas)	$50		
Savings / Investments	**$ -**	0.0%	12%
- short (incl. $2,000 liquidity)	$ -		
- mid (incl. 6-month emergency)	$ -		
- long (education, retirement)	$ -		
TOTAL EXPENSES	**$5,225**	105%	100%
NET SURPLUS	**$(225)**		

* indicates an irregular expense (varies month to month).

This family is deeply in debt. Their financial ship is sinking. Radical short-term steps need to be taken to reduce expenditures and to increase income. Possessions should probably be sold to pay off debt. Long-term plans need to be made in order to decrease and retire debt.

INCOME

Earned income (salary, commission)	$5,000	
Unearned (interest, div., capital gains)	$ -	
Other (Fam. support, Soc.Sec., pension)	$ -	
Total income	**$5,000**	

ANNUALIZED INCOME	**$60,000**
ANNUALIZED EXPENSES	**$65,100**

EXPENSES			%	Guide%
Lord's work		**$100**	2.0%	10%
Income Tax (Fed., State, FICA)		**$500**	10.0%	10%
Housing		**$1,800**	36.0%	34%
- mortgages (rent, insurance, tax)	$1,300			
- utilities (gas, electric, water, sewage)	$200			
- services (TV, internet, phones)	$50			
- maintenance* (~1% of home value/yr)	$100			
- furnishings* (appliances, computer)	$100			
- misc.* (Fees, lawn, storage, cleaning)	$50			
Groceries (incl. grocery and drug stores)		**$375**	7.5%	7%
Automobile / transportation		**$750**	15.0%	8%
- car payments	$450			
- gas, tolls, fares	$100			
- insurance, license, club*	$100			
- maintenance, repairs*	$100			
- replacement	$ -			

* indicates an irregular expense (varies month to month).

Insurance		**$200**	4.0%	4%
- life	$40			
- medical	$130			
- dental, vision, disability	$30			
Debt payments		**$1,000**	20.0%	0%
- credit cards	$500			
- student loans	$300			
- other	$200			
Entertainment / recreation		**$150**	3.0%	4%
- eating out (perhaps by person)	$50			
- events (movies, sports, sitters)	$50			
- vacation*	$50			
Personal Care* (by person)		**$150**	3.0%	3%
- clothing	$100			
- hair, nails	$50			
Medical, Dental, Optical		**$150**	3.0%	3%
Education / Child Care		**$100**	2.0%	2%
- tuition, books, supplies	$50			
- day care, child support	$50			
Miscellaneous*		**$150**	3.0%	3%
- subscriptions, supplies	$50			
- mad money (per person)	$50			
- gifts* (incl. Christmas)	$50			
Savings / Investments		**$ -**	0.0%	12%
- short (incl. $2,000 liquidity)	$ -			
- mid (incl. 6-month emergency)	$ -			
- long (education, retirement)	$ -			
TOTAL EXPENSES		**$5,425**	109%	100%
NET SURPLUS		**$(425)**		

* indicates an irregular expense (varies month to month).

Appendix B

BALANCE SHEETS

You can download balance-sheet templates at https://jimnewheiser .com/financial-resources/.

ASSETS	Amount	Short-term Savings	Midterm Savings	Long-Term Savings
Liquid				
Bank accounts	$ -			
Savings accounts	$ -			
Money market	$ -			
Cash on hand	$ -			
Total	$ -			
Non-retirement				
Fixed-income	$ -			
Stocks / Funds	$ -			
Real estate	$ -			
Precious metals	$ -			
Misc.	$ -			
Total	$ -			
Retirement				
CDs	$ -			
Stocks / funds	$ -			
Real estate	$ -			
Precious metals	$ -			
Misc.	$ -			
Total	$ -			
Use Assets				
House	$ -			
Verhicle 1	$ -			
Vehicle 2	$ -			
Other	$ -			
Total	$ -			
Total Assets	$ -			

LIABILITIES	Amount	Interest Rate	Term Remaining	Monthly Payment
Mortgage(s)	$ -			$ -
Student loan(s)	$ -			$ -
Credit card(s)	$ -			$ -
Auto loan(s)	$ -			$ -
Personal loan(s)	$ -			$ -
Other loan(s)	$ -			$ -
Total Liabilities	$ -			$ -
Net Worth	$ -	-	$ - =	$ -

	Assets		Liabilities	Net Worth
Emergency fund	$ -			
Irregular expenses	$ -			
Other	$ -			
Short Term Total	$ -			
Income-disruption fund	$ -			
Car savings	$ -			
Other	$ -			
Midterm Total	$ -			
Retirement	$ -			
Education	$ -			
Other	$ -			
Long Term Total	$ -			
Total Investments	$ -			

The following is an example balance sheet.

ASSETS	Amount	Short-term Savings	Midterm Savings	Long-Term Savings
Liquid				
Bank accounts	$3,000	X		
Savings accounts	$5,000		X	
Money market	$ -			
Cash on hand	$1,000	X		
Total	$9,000			
Non-Retirement				
Fixed-income	$10,000			X
Stocks / funds	$20,000		X	
Real estate	$ -			
Precious metals	$5,000			X
Misc.	$ -			
Total	$35,000			
Retirement				
CDs	$ -			
Stocks / funds	$130,000			X
Real estate	$ -			
Precious metals	$ -			
Misc.	$ -			
Total	$130,000			

Use Assets	
House	$275,000
Verhicle 1	$30,000
Vehicle 2	$15,000
Other	$25,000
Total	$345,000
Total Assets	$494,000

Liabilities	Amount	Interest Rate	Term Remaining	Monthly Payment
Mortgage(s)	$225,000	3.5%	300.0	$1,126.40
Student loan(s)	$30,000	8.0%	144.0	$324.70
Credit card(s)	$6,400	18.0%	61.5	$160.00
Auto loan(s)	$15,000	5.0%	38.0	$427.59
Personal loan(s)	$ -			$ -
Other loan(s)	$ -			$ -
Total	**$276,400**			$2,039
Net Worth	$494,600	-	$276,400 =	**$217,600**

| | Assets | | Liabilities | Net Worth |

	Assets
Emergency fund	$2,000
Irregular expenses	$2,000
Other	$ -
Short Term Total	**$4,000**
Income-disruption fund	$20,000
Car savings	$5,000
Other	$ -
Midterm Total	**$25,000**
Retirement	$130,000
Education	$15,000
Other	$ -
Long Term Total	**$145,000**
Total Investments	**$174,000**

Appendix C

RANDY ALCORN'S TREASURE PRINCIPLES

Randy Alcorn's Treasure Principles:[1] "You can't take it with you—but you *can* send it on ahead."

1. "God owns everything. I'm his money manager."
2. "My heart always goes where I put God's money."
3. "Heaven, not earth, is my home [Heb. 11:16]."
4. "I should live not for the dot [present earthly life] but for the line [eternity]."
5. "Giving is the only antidote to materialism."
6. "God prospers me not to raise my standard of living, but to raise my standard of giving."

1. Randy Alcorn, *The Treasure Principle: Discovering the Secret of Joyful Giving* (Colorado Springs: Multnomah, 2001), 95.

RECOMMENDED RESOURCES

BOOKS

Alcorn, Randy. *Managing God's Money.* Carol Stream, IL: Tyndale House, 2011.

———. *Money, Possessions, and Eternity.* 2nd ed. Wheaton, IL: Tyndale House, 2003.

———. *The Treasure Principle: Discovering the Secret of Joyful Giving.* Colorado Springs: Multnomah, 2001.

Bentley, Chuck. *The Root of Riches: What If Everything You Think about Money Is Wrong?* N.p.: FORIAM Publishers, 2011.

Berg, Jeff, and Jim Burgess. *The Debt-Free Church: Experiencing Financial Freedom While Growing Your Ministry.* Chicago: Moody Press, 1996.

Blue, Ron, with Michael Blue. *Master Your Money: A Step-by-Step Plan for Experiencing Financial Contentment.* 5th ed. Chicago: Moody Publishers, 2016.

Blue, Ron, with Jeremy White. *Splitting Heirs: Giving Your Money and Things to Your Children without Ruining Their Lives.* Chicago: Northfield Publishing, 2008.

Burkett, Larry. *The Complete Guide to Managing Your Money.* New York: Inspirational Press, 1996.

Coleman, Ken. *The Proximity Principle: The Proven Strategy That Will Lead to the Career You Love.* Brentwood, TN: Ramsey Press, 2019.

Cortines, John, and Gregory Baumer. *God and Money: How We Discovered True Riches at Harvard Business School*. Carson, CA: Rose Publishing, 2016.

Crosson, Russ. *Your Money Made Simple*. Eugene, OR: Harvest House, 2019.

Dayton, Howard. *Your Money Counts: The Biblical Guide to Earning, Spending, Saving, Investing, Giving, and Getting Out of Debt*. Carol Stream, IL: Tyndale House, 2011.

———. *Your Money Map: A Proven 7-Step Guide to True Financial Freedom*. Chicago: Moody Publishers, 2006.

Ferguson, Niall. *The Ascent of Money: A Financial History of the World*. New York: Penguin Books, 2008.

The Financial Stewardship Bible. Philadelphia: American Bible Society, 2011.

Grudem, Wayne A. *Business for the Glory of God: The Bible's Teaching on the Moral Goodness of Business*. Wheaton, IL: Crossway, 2003.

Newheiser, Jim. *Financial Crisis: What to Do When the Bottom Drops Out*. Greensboro, NC: New Growth Press, 2020.

———. *Money: Seeking God's Wisdom*. 31-Day Devotionals for Life's Problems. Phillipsburg, NJ: P&R Publishing, 2019.

Petty, James C. *Act of Grace: The Power of Generosity to Change Your Life, the Church, and the World*. Phillipsburg, NJ: P&R Publishing, 2019.

Pryor, Austin. *The Sound Mind Investing Handbook: A Step-by-Step Guide to Managing Your Money from a Biblical Perspective*. Chicago: Moody Publishers, 2014.

Ramsey, Dave. *The Total Money Makeover*. 3rd ed. Nashville: Thomas Nelson, 2009.

Ramsey, Dave, and Sharon Ramsey. *Financial Peace Revisited*. New York: Viking, 2003.

Ryle, J. C. *Practical Religion: Being Plain Papers on the Daily Duties, Experience, Dangers, and Privileges of Professing Christians*. Edited by J. I. Packer. Cambridge: James Clarke & Co., 1977.

Swanson, Gerald J. *The Hyperinflation Survival Guide: Strategies for American Businesses*. Lake Oswego, OR: Eric Englund, 2004.

Temple, John. *Family Money Matters: How to Run Your Family Finances to God's Glory.* Leominster, UK: Day One Publications, 2010.

Tripp, Paul David. *Redeeming Money: How God Reveals and Reorients Our Hearts.* Wheaton, IL: Crossway, 2018.

WEBSITES

bankrate.com. Up-to-date interest rates on savings vehicles, mortgages, credit cards, car insurance, and so forth.

christiancreditcounselors.org. Christian credit counseling 501(c)(3) agency that helps clients with debt management.

Compass, Finances God's Way. Founded by Howard Dayton. Includes calculators for mortgages, retirement savings, savings, loans, and other free resources. compass1.org.

Crown Financial Ministries. Founded by Larry Burkett. www.crown.org.

———. Debt Repayment Schedule: www.crown.org/wp-content /uploads/2017/05/financial-planning-workbook.pdf.

———. Personal Financial Statement: www.crown.org/wp-content /uploads/2017/05/financial-planning-workbook.pdf.

Dave Ramsey. www.daveramsey.com.

Eternal Perspective Ministries. Founded by Randy Alcorn. www.epm .org; http://store.epm.org/category/money-giving.

The Gospel Coalition. www.thegospelcoalition.org.

kingdomadvisors.com. Certified Christian financial planners, investment and insurance professionals, estate and tax lawyers, and accountants.

Moneywise. Live call-in radio program founded by Larry Burkett. www.moneywise.org.

ronblueinstitute.com. Delivers biblically based financial wisdom to the body of Christ by providing content through church, professional, consumer, and academic channels.

Saving for College. www.savingforcollege.com.

soundmindinvesting.com. Information about subscribing to the SMI newsletter; many free articles on biblical investing.

usa.gov. One stop for all U.S. federal government webpages.

INDEX OF SCRIPTURE

Genesis
1:26—52
1:28—68
1:31—51
2:3—43
2:15—25, 43,
  52, 68,
  260
2:15–16—9
2:18—126
3:17–18—10
3:17–19—24
3:17b–19—53
4:20–22—53n3
11:1–9—54
13:6–7—10
14:17–20—117
26:18–22—10
28:20–22—117
41—130, 218
41:33–36—5

Exodus
16:17–18—15
20:8–11—15,
  43, 76

20:9—260
20:9–11—54
20:15—4, 11,
  46, 75,
  202
20:17—4
22:25—244

Leviticus
19:9–10—72,
  115
25:13—15
25:23—110
25:23–28—15
27:30—116

Numbers
8:25–26—261
18:24—116
32:23—13

Deuteronomy
8:18—24, 109
10:18—15
14:22—116
15:4—30

15:4–5—15
15:5–6—190
15:7–8—244
15:10—114
23:19—244
23:20—244
24:14–15—11,
  15
24:15—76
24:19–21—15
28—54, 119
28:1–14—14
28:15–68—12
28:44—154

Joshua
7—78n1

Ruth
2—72, 115

1 Samuel
2:7—33

2 Samuel
17:23—281

1 Kings
17—14
17:1—12
21—4, 15

2 Kings
5—78
6–7—24
6:25—24
7:16—24
20:1—281

1 Chronicles
29:11–12—24
29:12—33

Nehemiah
5:3–5—154
5:4—6, 244
5:7—244

Psalms
9:18—30
15:4c—207
24:1—24, 110
34:8—36
37:12–15—12

37:21—8, 155–56, 202
37:21a—205
37:25—14, 38, 120
37:26a—244
50:10—24, 110
62:10—83
73:3—28
73:16–17—78
90—56
90:1–2—56
90:3–6—56
90:10—56
90:12—56
90:17—56
112:9—30
127:1a—204

Proverbs
1:7—282
3:9—6, 113
3:9a—113
3:10—119
3:11–12—12
3:13–15—282
3:27–28—156, 205
6:1–4—284
6:1–5—5, 205, 206
6:6–11—4, 55, 65, 202
6:7—66
6:8—5, 215
6:9–10—69
6:9–11—12

6:11—71
8:24–31—51
9:8—69
10:2—74, 83–84
10:3—33
10:4—4, 30, 46, 55, 59, 71, 74, 99, 260
10:4a—135
10:15—29, 31
10:22—30
10:26—70
11:4—32, 225
11:14—204
11:15—194
11:25—119
11:26—48, 76
11:28—32
12:11—74, 89
12:24—59, 71
12:27—69, 69n4
13:4—71
13:11—5, 30, 67, 74, 84, 227
13:11a—78
13:22—43, 280
13:25—34
14:15—141
14:20—31
14:23—70
14:24—30
14:30—134
15:1—197
15:6—5
15:16–17—33
15:19—55, 71

15:22—232
15:27—78
16:8—33
16:9—121, 152, 176
16:16—32
16:21b—197
16:26—71
17:14—197
17:18—5, 194
18:9—70
18:15—228
18:16—43
19:4—29
19:7—29
19:14a—180
19:17—6, 30, 114, 119
19:24—69
20:3—197
20:4—70–71
20:14—76
20:17—78
20:21—30, 280, 282
20:23—11, 75
21:5—7, 10, 121–22, 124, 155, 202, 211, 215, 260
21:5b—122
21:6—75
21:14—43
21:17—5, 139, 165, 202
22:1—33

22:3—141, 230, 235, 277
22:7—5, 29, 153–54, 163, 171, 191, 197, 284
22:9—119
22:13—70
22:16—49, 76, 78
22:26–27—5, 194, 284
22:27—154, 176
22:29—4, 60, 74, 99, 219
23:3–4—225
23:4–5—32, 84, 234
23:20–21—139
24:27—174
24:30–32—55
24:30–34—59, 67
25:11—197
26:12—6
26:13—70
26:14—69
26:15—69n4
26:16—69
27:12—142, 162, 212, 229, 270
27:20—225
27:23—223
27:23–24—67, 222

28:8—78
28:19—12, 67, 74, 100
28:19–20—5
28:20—235, 241
28:20b—74
28:22—5, 74, 84
28:26a—241
29:25—111, 197
30:8–9—27, 83
30:9—29, 32
30:9a—110
31:10—56
31:12–27—72
31:16—49
31:16–18—88
31:18—49
31:24—88, 99

Ecclesiastes
2:1ff.—225
2:17–23—53
2:21—278
2:24—52
4:8—77
5:10—17, 105, 225
5:11—225
5:13—225
5:14—234
5:15—278
5:18—31
9:7—52
9:9—77
10:18—177, 254
11:2—230
11:2b—218

11:6—95, 97, 224, 230

Isaiah
10:5–6—12
15:6–7—12
19:5–10—12
40:8—3
55:1–2—36, 78, 105, 134, 202
55:6–7—12

Jeremiah
22:13—5
29:7—68

Daniel
4—109
4–5—12
4:30—54, 110

Habakkuk
2:6–8—12
3:17—12

Joel
1–2—12

Haggai
1:6—12
2:8—24

Matthew
3:8—202
5:23–24—202, 206
5:29—85, 161
5:30—203

6:1–4—118
6:2b—119
6:11—37
6:19—11, 170, 257, 259
6:19b—229
6:19–20—19
6:19–21—6, 39, 57, 78, 114, 120, 174, 225
6:20—14, 49
6:20–21—259
6:24—77
6:25ff.—154
6:33—33, 120
7:12—199
7:24–27—10
15:4–6—261
22:21—188
25:14–23—110
25:14–29—25
25:14–30—43
26:15—78n1

Mark
2:27—77
7:20–23—78
10:25—110
12:17—29
12:28–30—34
12:31—34

Luke
3:14—67
9:58—49, 174
10:7—49, 76
10:30—11

12:13—280
12:13–21—12, 32
12:15—81, 134, 225, 240
12:16–21—109
12:20—283
12:21—6, 225
12:48—202
14:28–30—121
16:10—233
16:10–11—25
16:11—25
16:19–31—32
18:18–30—32
19:8—75
19:8–9—15
19:23—244
20:22—6
21:1–4—108

John
4:14—36
5:17—51
6:48—36
13:35—91
14:1–3—40, 49
14:2–3—174
14:18—278
16:33—49
17:4—43
18:36—15
19:26–27—278

Acts
2:44–45—15, 48, 100
2:45—114

4:32—48
4:34–35—48
5:1–11—78n1
5:3–4—48
5:4—48
6—48
6:1—15, 114
8:20—78n1
11:27–30—
   218n3
17:24–25—114
18:3—98n3
19:19—15
20:35—118
27:18—203

Romans
6:23—284
8:18—39
8:18–25—13
11:35—114
12:19—198
13:1–7—14
13:6—29
13:6–7—6
13:8a—156
15:22–33—14

1 Corinthians
1:24—282
4:2—25
5:11—7
7:23—153
7:39—272n1
9:13–14—115
10:10—67
10:12—84
10:31—8, 25,

34, 85,
  110
16—14
16:1–2—117

2 Corinthians
5:8—174, 283
5:9—8, 25, 34,
  197, 260
7:10–11—202
8—285
8–9—14, 48,
  114
8:1–5—39
8:2–3—108
8:3—117
8:3b–4—118
8:9—118, 284
8:12–15—15
9:7—48, 118
9:10–11—119
11:27—49
12:14—43, 280

Galatians
1:10—197
2:10—15, 114
5:15—136
5:23—125
6:1—135
6:7—12
6:10—116

Ephesians
4:25—90, 136
4:28—15, 56,
  72, 75,
  114, 202

4:31–32—135
5:11—85
6:5–8—15, 44,
  55
6:6–7—66
6:9—15, 55

Philippians
1:4—38
1:5—118
1:18—38
1:25—38
1:29—38
2:3–4—136, 199
2:14—67
2:17–18—38
3:1—38
3:9—285
3:20–21—39
4:1—38
4:4—38
4:10—39
4:11—63
4:11–13—38,
  134
4:12—49
4:14–17—39
4:15–17—43,
  118
4:15–18—38
4:19—38, 119

Colossians
1:17—51
2:3—282
3:5—32, 78, 90,
  105, 134,
  202

3:23—68
4:1—15

1 Thessalonians
2:9—98n3,
  261n3
5:18—39

2 Thessalonians
3:6–12—71
3:7–9—45, 56
3:7–12—31
3:8—261n3
3:10–12—56,
  116
3:11–12—46

1 Timothy
4:3–4—31, 139
4:3–5—106
5:3–8—114, 261
5:8—18, 30, 46,
  56, 63, 97,
  153, 198,
  269
5:14—272n1
5:17–18—115
5:18—11
5:38—114
6:2—100
6:5—18
6:6–8—39
6:8—63
6:9—18
6:9–10—33
6:9–11—90
6:10—18, 78,
  240

6:17—31, 106,
    111, 118
6:17–19—48,
    117
6:18–19—31

2 Timothy
2:6—49
3:16–17—3

Titus
2:4–5—99

Hebrews
3:13—204

4:1–11—57
9:27—283
11:16—305
12:5–11—37
13:5—90, 134
13:14—174

James
1:2–4—13, 37
1:5—204
1:27—15
2:6—11
2:6–7—29
4:6—54, 109

4:11–12—111
4:13–17—54,
    121, 176,
    204
5:1–5—225
5:1–6—11, 49,
    53
5:1–7—5
5:4—12, 29, 76

1 Peter
1:4—15
2:14—14
2:18–20—53

3:7—136
3:18—284

2 Peter
3:10—174
3:10–11—259

Revelation
7:16—13
14:13—57
21:3–4—13
22:2—13
22:3—44, 57
22:4—57

INDEX OF SUBJECTS AND NAMES

Abraham, 30, 32, 55
Adam and Eve, 9, 24–25, 51
Ahab, 4
Ahithophel, 281
Alcorn, Randy, 3, 20, 32, 36, 92, 117, 140, 280, 305
Amazon, 88, 248

Bible
  commands vs. principles, 7, 126, 131
  legalism, 7
  revelation, 6
Boaz, 96
borrowing money
  against home equity, 181, 201, 239
  cosigning, 149, 193–94
  credit rating, 148, 194–95
  dangers of, 169
  discerning whether to lend, 197
  for a house, 155
  for assets (or capital), 186
  from a retirement account, 263
  from family and friends, 208
  to increase earning, 166, 239
  to increase spending, 147
  lending to family and friends, 149, 193, 195, 228
  ministries, 191
  mistakes when, 162
  mortgage terms, 178
  not repaying, 155, 194, 196, 198, 202, 205–6
  principles of, 155–56, 199
  principles of lending, 199
  variable-rate mortgages vs. fixed-rate mortgages, 178
  whether it is sinful, 155
  whether it is sinful to lend, 198
budget
  balancing of, 82, 84, 123, 128, 141, 202, 207
  benefits of, 132, 207
  and credit cards, 160
  and debt consolidation, 181
  a definition, 121
  envelope system, 125
  estimating, 123
  helps saving money, 129, 137

the need for trust, 136

no budget is laziness, 122

no budget leads to financial suffering, 122, 207

prioritizing giving, 113, 123

refining, 123

relational problems, 135

spiritual problems, 133

tracking, 124, 207, 223

using a shopping list, 140

who decides, 136

wisdom of having a, 107, 165, 197, 207, 215

with irregular income, 131

Burroughs, Jeremiah, 39

business

bad business partners, 11

borrowing money, 151

freelance, 98

gig economy, 98

going out of, 152, 187

investing in, 186

labor relations, 53, 96

loans, 5

management, 31, 60, 66

micromanaging, 66

and networking, 95

profit sharing, 63

purchasing assets (or capital), 186

self-employment, 45, 88

the trades, 44–45, 62

work as a solution to poverty, 116

capitalism, 47, 164, 268

private property, 4, 11, 15, 46, 48

Christian liberty, 84, 111, 126, 212

church

building campaigns, 114–15

discipline of, 7, 56, 84

the early church, 67

and hiring other Christians, 96, 100, 115

and networking, 88, 91, 96

the New Testament Church, 14, 47, 71, 106, 114, 118

the offices of, deacon, 122

the offices of, paying elders, 115

Cohen, Jonathan, 81

covenants

financial promises and curses, 12, 14, 54, 190

new covenant, 15, 55, 244

old covenant, 12, 54, 154, 190, 243–44

old vs. new, 15, 116

the people of, 14

Crosson, Russ, 124

Daniel, 55

Danko, William, 142, 220

David, 30

debt

abuse of, 191

as addiction, 147

bailing others out, 196

as borrowing, 147

caused by failure to plan, 122, 165

caused by sin, 11

consolidation, 150, 181

cost of, 153

creates a biblical obligation, 8, 194, 204–5

credit cards, 107, 147–48, 154, 157, 159, 181, 203, 216
dangers of, 5, 99, 187
economics of, 151
education, 45, 149, 162, 165
forgiveness of, 15, 205
and lifestyle, 153
medical, 10, 29, 31
paying for college, 164
paying interest, 142
ruins a budget, 131, 202
as slavery, 153–54, 163, 171, 190, 197
the solution, 40
and stress of, 154
symptoms vs. cause, 182
through giving, 108
through insurance, 277
time-shares, 141
usually accrued gradually, 152, 171
vs. debt-free, 60, 154, 156, 177–79, 182, 201, 207–8, 224
as a weed, 208
whether it is sinful, 7
Dickens, Charles, 156
disability, 10, 53, 206, 267, 271
Disney, 17, 129, 196

earning money
dividends, 249
dual income, 99, 176, 203
duty of, 46, 97, 153
get-rich-quick schemes, 5, 14, 29, 44, 51, 67, 74, 79, 81, 85, 100, 235, 285
getting hired, 62
higher education, 44–45, 60, 62–63, 83, 97, 149, 163, 165–66
homemaking, 63, 203
how to increase, 60, 68
interest, 78, 243, 246, 248, 257
investments, 243, 252
legal vs. biblical, 76
legitimate sources, 43, 83
in moderation, 77
pensions, 64, 191, 219, 265
planning ahead, 66, 70, 152
raises, 61, 64, 67, 96
rentals, 98, 254
retirement, 64, 183, 191, 219, 262, 264
rewards for work, 4, 49, 63
selling assets, 98, 203
supplementary income, 98, 203
switching jobs, 46, 60, 95
whether it is sinful, 49, 88
economic justice
abuse of power, 76
and business, 53, 55, 75
and earning, 5, 11, 15, 48, 59–60, 63–64, 67, 76, 96, 137
God's care for, 12
and income disparity, 60
and law, 9, 11, 13–14, 54, 76, 92–93, 96, 111, 116, 119, 185, 190, 199, 205–6, 244–45, 254–55, 257, 261, 267, 270–76, 285
and profit, 48, 74, 83, 88, 235
and sin, 54
and slavery, 11, 18, 29, 55, 63, 153–54, 156–57, 163, 191, 197

economics
  class mobility, 81
  cold market, 179
  and credit, 148
  and debt, 151
  history of, 4, 6, 21–22, 47
  job creation, 23, 62
  and laziness, 70
  supply and demand, 5, 76, 180
Elijah, 14
England, 47
epistemology
  irrationalism, 83
ethics

fulfilling duties, 30, 62
false teachers
  giving to bad organizations or
    unsound theology, 115
  the place of giving, 114, 120
  prosperity gospel, 18, 49, 108
Ferguson, Niall, 4, 6
Fidelity, 251
financial advisors, 122, 180, 204,
    211, 229–30, 232, 236–38,
    240, 264, 273
financial suffering
  bankruptcy, 159, 187, 205, 208,
    229
  bubbles and crashes, 180, 191,
    229, 263
  COVID-19 pandemic of 2020,
    152, 218
  and debt, 151, 156
  the end of, 13, 16
  exposes sin, 35
  and gambling, 82

God's judgment, 12, 154, 190
government, 10
  its source, 9, 24, 53, 161
  leads to godliness, 13
  leads to temptation, 35
  living in, 13
  mitigating, 10, 12, 31, 67, 140,
    160, 187, 269
  natural disasters, 10, 29, 53
  not always caused by sin, 13
  personal sins, 11, 67, 202
  poverty, 28–29, 33, 67, 71,
    83–84, 99, 106–7, 122
  predicting, 12
  recession, 5, 24, 31, 63
  sins of others, 11, 53
  as trial, 37, 39
  types of, 9
  uncertainty in a fallen world, 152
  unemployment, 94, 250
fruit of the Spirit
  ambition, 56
  compassion, 107, 118, 285
  contentment, 38–39, 67, 134,
    152
  endurance, 39
  faith, 79, 113, 118
  faithfulness, 55, 118
  forgiveness, 135
  generosity, 15, 30, 47, 56, 76,
    100, 111, 114, 117, 119, 180,
    193, 285
  godliness, 55, 76, 97
  good reputation, 83
  hard work, 4–5, 30, 44, 56,
    66–67, 72, 74, 77, 81, 109,
    115, 282

hard work vs. workaholism, 77
holiness, 37
honoring parents, 261
humility, 95, 137, 204–5
joy, 5, 106, 118
kindness, 15
love, 68, 76
mercy, 244
patience, 67, 74, 152
self-control, 5, 122, 132, 153,
    160, 201, 220, 226
spiritual maturity, 25, 30, 35,
    65–66
thankfulness, 31, 38–39, 100,
    106, 109, 119
usefulness, 66
wisdom, 6, 12–13, 30, 49, 55,
    62, 65, 119, 121, 150, 208,
    214, 228, 282

gambling, 29, 31, 44, 51
    and addiction, 82, 84
    as dangerous, 85
    costs society, 82
    squandering earnings, 84
    as stealing, 83
Garden of Eden, 51, 57
Germany, Weimar Republic, 22
giving money
    as blessing, 118
    compulsion vs. cheerfully, 48
    the difficulty, 32
    discerning, 115
    and God's provision, 119
    and hope, 119
    inheritance, 180
    instead of lending, 198

as an obligation, 107, 114
    in the Old Testament, 72
    to the poor, 6, 15, 18, 48, 72,
        75, 111, 114
    prioritizing believers, 114
    proper recipients of, 56
    supporting the church and para-
        churches, 6, 18, 31, 39, 107,
        111, 113–15, 118, 127, 167,
        224–26, 282, 285
    in secret, 118
    tithing, 110, 113, 115–16, 119
    tithing, whether it is obligated,
        116
    when poor, 107
God
    answers prayer, 37, 96
    cares for the poor, 29
    confirms or establishes human
        works, 56
    the covenant maker, 16, 54
    the Creator, 16, 18, 24, 43, 51,
        54, 61, 77
    the deliverer, 12, 37
    designer of economics, 4, 44
    designer of human labor, 4
    designer of work, 43, 51, 260
    does not show favoritism, 32
    faithfulness, 13
    giver of joys, 31
    gracious and merciful, 12
    his aseity, 114
    his care, 36
    his eternity, 56
    his faithfulness, 37
    his forgiveness, 283
    his generosity, 244

the glory of, 4, 8, 12–13, 16, 24–25, 34, 44, 49, 52, 54, 55–58, 63, 66, 85, 109–11, 119, 197, 260, 266, 285

and his gospel, 15, 18, 38, 43, 45, 75, 118–19, 284–85

his grace, 207, 284

the judge, 12, 14, 32, 71, 76, 78, 284

his kindness, 109, 284

his kingdom, 14–16, 21, 49, 55, 114, 120, 285

his love, 284

his love for his people, 14, 37–38, 54

his mercy, 204, 284

his presence, 57

his promises, 15–16, 49, 54

his providence, 51, 109

his provision, 14, 38–39, 77, 109, 111, 113, 119, 198, 204, 285

his sovereignty, 33, 38, 78, 121, 152

his use of means, 114, 118–19

his wisdom, 4, 14, 30, 32, 56, 74, 78, 108, 111, 204

honoring with wealth, 6, 113, 117, 208, 233, 278, 285

imitation of, 12–13, 37, 118, 244, 285

owner and source of all wealth, 24, 106, 109–10, 113, 282

the worship of, 76–77, 113, 118

godly repentance vs. worldly sorrow, 202

God's law

first use, 13, 54

general equity, 15

loving others, 34

third use, 54

government

borrowing money for, 151, 188

corruption of, 11, 189, 191

education, 163, 167

education incentives, 219

financial aid, 71–72, 75

from God, 13

funding public education, 82

home-ownership incentives, 177

issuing currency, 21, 23

loans, 163, 167

punishes financial sins, 13

spending, 5

theocracy, 12, 15, 55, 190

welfare (including Social Security), 213, 219, 265, 276

Grudem, Wayne, 20–21, 116

happiness

found in Jesus, 36, 38, 78, 134, 282

sin destroys, 56

through work, 45, 52–53, 57

whether money brings, 17, 33, 36, 38, 78, 81–82, 105, 133, 155–56, 202, 225

Hitler, Adolf, 22

Holy Spirit, 278

human nature

brevity of life, 56, 77

contingence, 121

discerning God's plan for your life, 61–62

the heart, 18, 40, 74, 78–79, 225

image of God, 52–54, 58
is sinful (total depravity), 10, 16, 46, 118
is unchanging, 4, 79
life perspective, 68
men's and women's roles, 99, 126, 272
self-deception, 83
vs. animal nature, 20, 53

IBM (business), 63
imputation of righteousness, 284
inflation, 11, 22–23, 163, 175, 179, 190, 229, 244–45, 256, 258, 266
deflation, 22–23
hyperinflation, 22, 229, 256
risk of, 245–46
Zimbabwe, 22
insurance, 107
auto insurance, 269
disability, 271
health, 270, 272
life, 272
life, term vs. whole life (or permanent), 273
medical-expense-sharing plans (or medical-expense cooperatives), 271
other assorted types, 274
purpose of, 212
umbrella, 274
whether it is sinful, 212, 269
Internet, 3, 62, 80, 85, 89, 95, 131, 140, 157–58, 165, 223, 240, 249, 265
cryptocurrency, 258

online statements, 158
password management, 282
social media, 92
investments
accumulating gradually, 227, 235
annuities, 236, 264
bonds, 230–31, 264
buying on margin, 239
certificates of deposit (CDs), 231, 247
commodities, 19, 23, 229, 231, 253, 256–57
corporate bonds, 248
cryptocurrency, 258
day trading, 85, 236, 240
diversification, 230, 249, 253
exchange-traded funds (ETFs), 250
flipping houses, 240, 255, 258
government bonds, 19, 186, 188, 227, 246
government bonds, municipal, 247
and inflation, 245
insured bank accounts, 231, 245–46
junk bonds, 245
limited partnerships, 258
mutual funds, 231, 247, 250, 263–64, 273
no risk-free, 229–30
owning a house, 179
personal loans, 248
researching, 228, 232, 235
risks of, 212, 220, 227, 245, 249, 252, 254–55, 257–58, 266
small business loans, 248

stocks (or equities), 227, 229–30,
248, 250, 263
Israel, 12, 15, 55, 68, 77, 116, 119,
190, 243

Jesus
cared for his family, 278
did not own a house, 173
embodiment of God s wisdom,
282
example of giving, 118
his great exchange, 284
his humiliation, 284
his obedience, 43, 285
his perfection, 284
his Second Coming, 38
his substitutionary sacrifice, 283
his willing sacrifice, 285
sent the Holy Spirit, 278
source of happiness, 36
teaching on prayer, 37
Job, 30
John the Baptist, 67
Joseph, 55, 131, 218

Keller, Tim, 68
Keynes, John Maynard, 23

last will
benefits of, 279
blessing of having a, 213
Las Vegas, NV, 83
Lazarus, the poor man, 32
lifestyle
and debt, 153, 196
downsizing, 130

extravagant, 5, 11, 17, 140
impoverished, 5
minimalism and asceticism, 31,
33, 39, 63, 77, 106, 128, 139,
142, 220, 223
moderation, 33
thriving, 77, 142, 225
Lloyd-Jones, D. Martyn, 118–19

marriage and family
balancing priorities, 77, 99
complementarianism, 126
and debt, 153
and divorce, 77
and home ownership, 176
generational sin, 83
husband and wife should work
together, 239
and laziness, 56, 71
providing, 62, 64, 67, 72, 87–88,
97, 153, 272, 275, 279
raising children, 63, 180
temptations, 134–35, 193, 196
whether wealth or purchases can
fix marriage problems, 105
Marx, Karl, 46
materialism and consumerism, 133,
305
instant gratification, 6, 152, 155,
214, 220
money
cash vs. credit cards, 157,
160–61
currency risk, 245
exchange of, 20
fiat currency, 21, 23

its value, 21, 23, 25, 33
nature of, 21
and power, 29
types of, 21
multilevel-marketing
  risks of, 88–89
  sins of, 90–92

Naboth, 4
Naomi, 96
NASDAQ, 261
Nebuchadnezzar, 54, 109–10
Nehemiah, 55

owning a car
  cost of, 170, 172
  insurance, 269, 275
  leasing, 171
  principles of purchasing, 170
  purchasing, 148, 169
  repairs, 31, 171, 275
owning a house
  benefits of, 173, 177–78
  blessing of, 173
  closing costs, 174
  costs of, 176, 179
  down payment, 173, 175, 180
  foreclosure, 180
  a home vs. an investment, 179
  how big, 38
  insurance, 270, 275
  looking to heaven, 173
  mortgage payments, 178, 180–
    82, 201, 207, 276
  principles of purchasing, 177
  purchasing, 150, 155, 173
  purchasing vs. renting, 173–75

repairs, 31, 107, 176, 181, 275
reverse mortgages, 182, 266
short sale, 180, 206
upside down, 175, 182, 206, 240

penal substitutionary atonement,
  284
Popeye, 152
  Wimpy, 152
prayer, 37, 100, 197, 204, 271
prosperity of the wicked, 12–13,
  30, 77
Pryor, Austin, 228, 244

Ramsey, Dave, 8, 87, 95, 149, 152,
  185, 193–94, 207
  debt snowball, 207
risk
  of cosigning, 194
  of debt, 186, 189
  foreclosure, 176
  impossibility of removing,
    228–29
  of lending to family and friends,
    195, 198
  its source, 53
  reducing, 230, 259, 267
  reinvesting home equity, 183
  variable-rate mortgages, 178
  whether it is sinful, 227
Rockefeller, John D., 36, 225
Ruth, 96
Ryle, J. C., 28, 32, 39, 46–47, 120,
  260

Samaria, 24
San Clemente, California, 71

Satan, the devil, 13

saving
wisdom of, 5

saving money
accumulating gradually, 227, 241
benefits of, 6, 30, 132
earthly vs. heavenly possessions,
6, 14–15, 19, 32, 40, 49, 57,
77, 106, 113, 174, 225, 232,
259, 282, 285
in education, 164-65
for education, 164, 219
emergency savings, 174, 211,
216, 224
frugality, 142
for a house, 177
for income disruption, 218
inheritance, 15, 43, 77, 180,
183, 223, 279, 282
insurance, 268–70
interest payments, 142
IRAs, 401(k)s, 403(b)s, 262, 265
for irregular expenses, 216
with an irregular income, 131
for major purchases, 217
a method, 215
as obligation, 111
planning ahead, 106, 211
reasons for, 215
retirement, 107, 211, 213, 219,
261, 263–64
retirement, whether it is sinful,
260
risk of not, 215
trusts, 213, 281
wisdom of, 214

Scripture
its principles for financial wisdom,
14, 25, 30, 156
promises vs. maxims, 30

Sears (business), 185

sin
anger, 134–35, 195, 198
apathy, 66, 70
approving of and enabling, 71,
84, 116, 195, 198
bitterness, 136, 196, 198
bribery, 7
circumstances of, 35
coveting (or envy), 11, 28, 78,
81, 90, 94, 105, 111, 133–35,
139, 155, 196, 202
the debt of (or the guilt of), 284
discontent, 155
dishonoring parents, 33, 261
division, 196
drunkenness, 70
the forgiveness of, 283
gluttony, 134
greed, 15, 17–18, 32–33, 74,
78–79, 90, 105, 133, 172,
193, 202, 225, 240
grumbling (or complaining), 61,
64, 67
idolatry, 32–33, 53, 77–79, 105,
133, 202
impatience, 74, 134, 155, 241
its effects on finances, 10
judging others, 111
laziness, 15, 46, 53, 55, 59,
67–68, 70–71, 75–76, 94,
100, 115, 122, 135, 202, 241

legalism, 106

lying, 33, 48, 75, 82, 90, 115, 136, 193, 202, 238

misleading business practices, 11

murder, 18, 33, 54

neglecting to meet together, 92

negligence, 135

not caring for family, 97

offenses often are grouped together, 83

people-pleasing, 66, 134, 197

poor stewardship, 12, 202, 241

presumption, 152

pride, 46, 54, 69, 74, 78, 83, 85, 100, 106, 109, 118, 240

repentance of, 12, 33, 67, 69, 71, 75, 79, 94, 202

revenge, 135, 198

robbing God, 113

selfishness, 135, 193

sex trafficking, 18

sexual immorality, 33

spending money wrongly, 105

stealing, 7, 11, 15, 28–29, 33, 67, 72, 75, 83, 90, 155, 202, 257

unbelief, 74

usury, 78, 244

usury, whether it is sinful, 243

violating contracts, 11

violating the Sabbath, 76

wasting resources, 11, 18, 55, 67, 81, 94, 100, 115, 158

workaholism, 76

worldliness, 81

socialism (or communism), 46–47, 50, 234

Solomon, 30, 35

S&P 500, 251

spending money

analyzing expenses, 129, 140, 174

autopay, 158, 160

big purchases, 5, 107, 141

coupons, 142

credit card incentives, 160

daycare, 99

do research, 141

education, 107

on hobbies and passions, 135

interest, 148, 153–54, 158, 170–71, 177–78, 181, 186, 189

overspending, 128, 133, 135, 139, 150, 153, 159, 165, 169, 224

time-shares, 141

with borrowed money, 147

with credit cards, 147

zero percent interest, 149, 171

Spurgeon, Charles, 56, 70

Stanley, Thomas, 142, 220

stewardship, 6, 9, 18, 25, 67, 83, 108, 110, 112, 115, 121–22, 135, 183, 197, 202, 232, 259, 278, 282–83

student loan, 3, 159, 162, 167

tax, 5–6, 23, 29, 75, 99, 140, 171, 176–77, 181, 188–89, 205–6, 219, 223, 236, 246, 254, 259, 262–66, 281

fairness, 6

is not theft, 6

paying, 7

Temple, John, 235
Tennessee, Ernie Ford, 154
the cultural mandate, 43, 52–54, 58
Tripp, Paul, 133

United States, 21–23, 62, 80, 82,
    162, 189, 246, 254, 257
    American dream, 17, 173
    Americans live paycheck to pay-
        check, 220
    average American debt, 151
    Executive Order 6102, 257
    Federal Reserve, 23

Vanguard, 251
vocation
    and desire, 63
    difficulties, 24
    high earning, 60
    homemaking, 63, 87, 94, 99, 203
    modern complexities of, 3, 46
    purpose of man, 56
    secular vs. sacred, 15, 68, 166
    skills, 45, 60–62, 64, 74, 81,
        96–97, 100, 109, 219, 230,
        282
    success in, 4, 62, 67, 74, 240

wealth
    abuse of, 29, 48
    benefits of, 31
    comes from God, 30
    commodities, 19
    dangers of, 27
    differences between poor and
        rich, 6, 27, 31, 33, 70
    its moral status, 18, 31, 48–49
    Jesus, teaching, 3
    lies of, 33, 36
    as a test, 32
    of Western civilization, 35
    whether it is sinful, 106
work
    applying for, 95–96
    as blessing, 43, 54, 58, 68
    as curse, 43, 45, 51–53, 57–58,
        69
    disincentives of, 72
    in heaven, 57
    its moral status, 51
    public vs. private, 64
    redeemed, 44
    and rest, 54, 69
    Sabbath rest, 54, 76–77
    switching jobs, 46, 60, 96–97

ALSO FROM JIM NEWHEISER ON MONEY

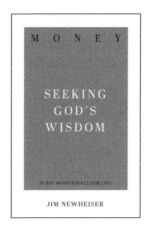

Do you have money trouble? Biblical counselor Jim Newheiser reorients your heart to worship God rather than wealth and presents the wisdom of Scripture on financial and work-related topics.

In the 31-Day Devotionals for Life series, biblical counselors and Bible teachers guide you through Scripture passages that speak to specific situations or struggles, helping you to apply God's Word to your life in practical ways day after day.

Also in the 31-Day Devotionals for Life series:

Anger: Calming Your Heart, by Robert D. Jones
Anxiety: Knowing God's Peace, by Paul Tautges
Chronic Illness: Walking by Faith, by Esther Smith
Contentment: Seeing God's Goodness, by Megan Hill
Fearing Others: Putting God First, by Zach Schlegel
Forgiveness: Reflecting God's Mercy, by Hayley Satrom
Grief: Walking with Jesus, by Bob Kellemen
Marriage Conflict: Talking as Teammates, by Steve Hoppe
A Painful Past: Healing and Moving Forward, by Lauren Whitman
Pornography: Fighting for Purity, by Deepak Reju

MORE QUESTIONS & ANSWERS FROM JIM NEWHEISER

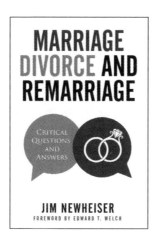

In marriage counseling, the issues can be especially complex. Drawing on decades of marriage counseling experience, Newheiser overviews the key questions counselors face, exploring the answers given in God's Word.

"Over the past forty years, I have counseled hundreds of couples who were struggling with questions that this book answers with clarity. But unlike most books that cover a similar subject, this volume by Jim Newheiser handles these questions with biblical precision and grace. . . . This book will provide a clear direction."
   —John D. Street

"[Newheiser] answers the knotty questions from God's Word, making this volume valuable for a pastor bringing counsel, or a spouse caught up in a difficult marriage. Newheiser's pastoral insight, lucid analysis, and biblical focus make this book a must-read for people with questions about marriage and a valuable resource for a pastor's bookshelf."
   —Tedd Tripp

Did you find this book helpful?
Consider leaving a review online.
The author appreciates your feedback!

Or write to P&R at editorial@prpbooks.com
with your comments. We'd love to hear from you.